Wisdom

LESSONS FOR LIVING

ROBB D. THOMPSON

✦

WISDOM IS GRANTED
ONLY TO THOSE WHO ARE WILLING
TO SEARCH FOR HER.

Get wisdom! Get understanding!
Do not forget, nor turn away from the words of my mouth.
Do not forsake her, and she will preserve you;
Love her, and she will keep you. Wisdom is the principal thing;
Therefore get wisdom. And in all your getting, get understanding.

Proverbs 4:5-7

✦

Living Wisdom Daily Devotional
ISBN 1-889723-76-2
Copyright © 2006 by Robb Thompson
Robb Thompson International
18500 92nd Avenue
Tinley Park, Illinois 60487
www.robbthompson.com

Committed One,

My background is anything but envious. It is one of handouts, hand-me-downs, eviction notices, witchcraft, alcoholism, and drug addiction. It appeared there was no way out, which led me to the door of insanity. This happened primarily because I believed the lie that the image I was experiencing was the gloomy portrait of my future. Even as an unsaved teen, I knew I did not want to be like my ancestors; I despised my origin. But there just had to be a way to take control of my life and change. But how? I didn't have any answers, but I knew I sure wasn't doing a very good job of things on my own.

To reach beyond the agony of my past, I had to find another solution. In 1975, in the dark halls of a mental institution, I found my answer in Jesus Christ. It was all or nothing for me. I did not give Jesus a half-hearted effort. I needed a way out, and I knew this was it. That choice changed my life, and it can change yours as well.

So now, the choice is yours. Why not start today by making the power-packed decision to change your life, directing it toward success? Make the choice right now to create the future you've always wanted. Your old life is dead! No enemy can resurrect your past—only you can do that. Only you can revisit those antiquated, worn-down dwelling places of living and thinking. You have been given the power you need to move in the direction of Heaven's will for your life. Use this devotional as a vehicle to take you to the place where God's voice can be clearly heard.

Humble Servant,

Dr. Robb D. Thompson

TOPICAL INDEX

THE BIBLE IS NOT JUST ANOTHER BOOK; IT IS A MANUAL FOR LIFE

"Your Word is a lamp to my feet and a light to my path."
Psalm 119:105 (NKJV)

Making sure that their lamps were adequately filled with olive oil was a daily ritual for those who lived during the time of Christ, as was collecting water and baking fresh bread. In the Jewish synagogues, lamps burned continuously. And as David so marvelously stated, "God's Word is a lamp to my feet and a light to my path," we do well to remember that every time we go to the Word of God, we must go with Christ's willingness to surrender to His Father's every instruction, seeking to be set ablaze by whatever we read.

Only when we surrender our lives to His Word is Heaven able to guide our footsteps. Many people see God's Word as a textbook or an interesting documentary about religious life. Refuse the temptation to take God's Word to the same level as just another ordinary book.

God's Word was not written to increase our knowledge; it was written to divinely guide our lives. His Word contains the perfect answer to every question, and the exact solution to every problem that could ever arise. As we ponder the Scriptures and open our hearts to the Holy Spirit, He begins to reveal to us the true meaning of what we read. We can go to the Word and expect to hear God speak to us. The words on those pages are God's voice to His people. He desires to speak to us and guide us down the complex paths of life.

His Word is the lamp that we are to shine upon the path we are called to undertake. When we use the Word of God as our roadmap, we experience true and abundant life along the way.

DAILY CONFESSION
Father, I thank You that I use Your Word as a guide for my life.
Your Word is a lamp to my feet and a light to my path. I understand Scripture
was not written to increase my knowledge, but to direct my life.

THE SECRETS OF LIFE
ARE ONLY REVEALED TO THOSE WHO PURSUE THEM

*"Ask, and it will be given to you; seek, and you will find; knock,
and it will be opened to you. For everyone who asks receives, and he
who seeks finds, and to him who knocks it will be opened."*
Matthew 7:7-8 (NKJV)

✦

Asia—home to millions upon millions of inhabitants, countless numbers of them, having found the secret of Jesus Christ, currently risk their lives as they refuse to bow before idols and men. Having found the secret, they must now meet in secret, assembling in house churches all over the continent. Tiny apartments have quickly become covert places where souls are reborn and refreshed. Jesus declared, "I am the way, the truth and the life. No man comes to the Father but by Me." God's Word is powerfully alive. **Real life is a life that is surrendered to the Spirit of God.**

So many individuals go through their time on this earth without experiencing the true life Heaven offers. We must come to grips with the fact that this life on earth has nothing to offer us. Whatever this world presents is nothing in comparison to knowing our Lord and Savior. This true life from Heaven abides in man because Jesus said, "the Kingdom of God is among us."

Is there any real life apart from knowing the Lord? Many search in vain for what they need in all the wrong places. They desire to know the secret of life, but reject the very Person who can grant it to them. Like our Asian brothers and sisters, we possess the secret of life; Christ Jesus is in us, and we dwell wonderfully in Him. Now we are called to help others find the One who is life from Heaven, called to help them move in the direction of His truth. And that's a secret we must tell everyone!

DAILY CONFESSION
*Father, I thank You that I found the secret of life. Christ dwells in me
and I dwell in Him. I ask and it is given to me, I seek and I find,
and I knock and the door is opened to me.*

THE VALUE I PLACE UPON WISDOM
WILL DETERMINE THE LIFE IT WILL PRODUCE IN ME

*"Getting wisdom is the most important thing you can do!
And whatever else you do, get good judgment. If you prize wisdom,
she will exalt you. Embrace her and she will honor you."*
Proverbs 4:7-9 (NLT)

When one of the wisest queens who ever lived was asked by a visiting prince, "What is the secret to your country's success?" Queen Victoria soberly handed the African leader a large Bible. Placing the volume in his hands, she declared, "Here is the secret of England's greatness." As we see in Proverbs 4:7-8, wisdom is the most important thing we can ever hope to obtain. When we place a value upon something, it is able to offer us amazing results. We all have moments when we wish we knew the right answer or were able to discern exactly what to do in a certain situation. **By obtaining wisdom and placing value upon her** (just as we might our most costly gem), **we experience how she can substantially transform our lives.**

To love something is to find it desirable, but to value something is to find it essential. Wisdom is essential to the outcome of our lives. Is wisdom only wanted by us, or do we truly place value upon it? Our level of pursuit proves the answer to that question. Consider the following: *How much time do you spend in God's Word? How much of an effort do you make to heed the wisdom of Godly men? What does your pursuit of Him look like?*

The degree of honesty to which you answer these questions is the degree you will begin to see the value you place upon wisdom. England's Queen Victoria knew that getting wisdom through God's Word was the principal thing. Start today thinking of ways in which you can do the same.

DAILY CONFESSION
*Father, I thank You that I pursue Your Word with all my heart.
I am filled with Your wisdom, which is the principal thing; therefore,
I gain wisdom and understanding.*

PROGRESS IS GUARANTEED THE MOMENT YOU COMMIT YOUR LIFE INTO THE HANDS OF GOD

"Commit your work to the Lord, and then your plans will succeed."
Proverbs 16:3 (NLT)

"And my blessings are for Gentiles, too, when they commit themselves to the Lord."
Isaiah 56:3 (NLT)

No one desires to go through life without making significant progress. God placed within every person a craving to succeed. All of us want to get better, do more, and help others achieve their dreams. Those desires are given to us by God. Nevertheless, **progress is only guaranteed to those who choose to commit their lives to Him, having cut, scraped, and eroded away the very core of their old lives.**

It is only a matter of time before we see those who have yet to commit their lives to God cry out for help. Although they may have all the possessions one could want, their internal lives are in shambles, crumbling away into particles of raw dust. God always begins on the inside before He ever manifests on the outside. **True progress is when one commits his life and plans to the Lord, allowing Him to guide and lead his steps.** As we commit our work to the Lord, our plans succeed.

Why not choose today to give God not part, but your entire life? He deserves it. God desires to make you and I great; all He requests is our compliance! When presented with the possibility of losing everything he had worked for so tirelessly, John the Baptist said, "I must decrease and He must increase." That means that the more we pursue God, the less we desire the pleasurable things this world has to offer, thereby causing great progress to be made.

DAILY CONFESSION
*Father, I thank You that I commit my life and my work to You,
and You cause my plans to succeed. I receive the blessings You have
for me because I commit my life to You.*

TRANSFORMATION IS THE FINISHED PRODUCT OF EMBRACING GOD'S THOUGHTS

*"Don't copy the behavior and customs of this world, but let
God transform you into a new person by changing the way you think.
Then you will know what God wants you to do, and you will know how
good and pleasing and perfect His will really is."*
Romans 12:2 (NLT)

⚜

Someone had an idea—and its concept is transforming the way corporate employees do business. In an effort to achieve the highest standard of health, a number of top U.S. business people voluntarily joined running teams. Instead of stepping foot into gourmet restaurants, adding on unwanted pounds, those same feet are now adorned with trendy athletic shoes. The result is noteworthy; not only are these folks improving their bodies, their bottom lines have benefited as well, since networking among these teams has proven enormously profitable. It all began with one transforming thought.

The practice of mind renewal is one that Christians must never overlook. All of us desire to be successful in life, because God deposited within us a longing for more and an intense passion for growth. We have an inherent desire for improvement. **But we must understand that we do not attract what we want; we attract who we are.** God gave us an avenue through which we can become the person who will attract the very things we desire.

By using God's Word to renew our minds, He gave us the ability to effectively transform our lives. Transformation belongs only to those who pursue it, working diligently to achieve it. We are not transformed over night; it is a process that very few are patient enough to endure. God tells us, "…be transformed by the renewing of your mind…" As we embrace the thoughts of God, transformation is the result.

DAILY CONFESSION
*Father, I thank You that I no longer live or think like the world.
I am transformed because I diligently renew my mind to Your Word.
I embrace Your thoughts as my own.*

A MAN'S PROGRESS IN LIFE IS IN DIRECT PROPORTION TO HIS CONTINUAL PURSUIT OF EXCELLENCE

"I press toward the goal for the prize
of the upward call of God in Christ Jesus."
Philippians 3:14 (NKJV)

✦

Most Biblical scholars agree; the Middle Eastern landscape, particularly the area known as the "Fertile Crescent," is some of the most excellent terrain for agriculture in the world. Useful plants such as wheat, oats, barley, and rye, originated in that habitat, and then spread throughout Africa, Europe, and finally the West. Without that excellent soil, we might not even enjoy our morning toast.

Long ago, someone pursued that excellent soil, tilling, weeding, and harvesting it in order that they might receive the prize of fresh grain. Remember, "good enough" is not acceptable behavior to a man of excellence. We must refuse the temptation to merely settle. Many people have what I like to call the "destination syndrome." People reach a certain goal or point in life, and for some reason, their pursuit stops. They settle contentedly at this one destination that they worked so hard to attain, perched like a weary crow. **But the moment we settle in life is the moment we no longer make any progress.** And nature reveals to us that anything that does not grow (as in those lovely grains) is in the process of dying.

Why not pursue God with everything you have? At all cost, find ways to become more like Christ. Pursue the things of God; you won't be disappointed. Write down this principle where you can see it every day — **"A Man's Progress In Life Is In Direct Proportion To His Continual Pursuit Of Excellence."** Meditate on it, live it, and share it with others.

DAILY CONFESSION
Father, I thank You that I press toward the goal for the prize
of Your upward call in Christ Jesus. I pursue excellence and therefore
I make continual forward progress.

JOY BECOMES MINE
THE MOMENT I PURSUE GOD'S PRESENCE

"You will show me the path of life; in Your presence is fullness of joy;
at Your right hand are pleasures forevermore."
Psalm 16:11 (NKJV)

✦

What can be more satisfying or superbly fulfilling than setting aside time to be alone in God's presence? Satan knows that if he can keep us from spending time with God, he can eventually starve us of spiritual strength. **One of the greatest benefits we receive from continual pursuit of God's presence is joy.** That joy is a result of realizing God's guiding and protecting hand on our lives. The Scripture tells us, "The joy of the Lord is your strength." If Satan can keep us from spending time in God's presence, joy will cease to exist, and our strength is vanquished. Furthermore, it becomes an opportune time for Satan to attack.

In ancient Israel, it was customary to plant a tree at a child's joyous birth. At another moment of great joy (his or her wedding), branches from that very tree planted several years earlier were used to hold up the marriage canopy. JOY—a wondrous gift direct from the right hand of God.

As we broaden our knowledge of the subtle tactics and deceptive schemes of Satan, I believe we will better understand how to combat them. The devil only needs to keep us from God's presence long enough to diminish our strength so that he can take us to our knees in defeat. We must be serious about pursuing the presence of God. In His presence is where we belong; it is where we grow and where God's Word comes alive within us. Similar to the branches used to uphold the canopy at the joyous Hebrew wedding ceremony, allow His presence to uphold you, causing that same joy to swell within, empowering you to relentlessly defeat the enemy.

DAILY CONFESSION
Father, I thank You for showing me the path of life. In Your presence is fullness
of joy and at Your right hand are pleasures forevermore.

STOP TRYING TO APPLY THE WORD TO YOUR LIFE
AND BEGIN TO APPLY YOUR LIFE TO THE WORD

"How shall a young man cleanse his way? By taking heed and keeping watch
[on himself] according to Your Word [conforming his life to it]."
Psalm 119:9 (AMP)

Erroneously thinking that the untimely death of his only son was God's punishment for his sins, America's fourteenth President, Franklin Pierce, refused to use a Bible at his swearing-in ceremony. Little did President Pierce realize that the Word of God was the very thing he needed—if only he had taken the time to conform his life to the very Bible he so bitterly ignored. If we merely apply a scripture to a situation when it arises, we can't expect to see growth, change, or mind prosperity. **Instead, we must cause our lives to fastidiously conform to God's Word, as it is the only constant we will ever have in our lives.**

In Matthew 16:19, Jesus made a fascinating statement. He said, "And I will give you the keys of the Kingdom of Heaven..." Notice the phrase, "the keys of the Kingdom." He did not say "the key of Heaven..." Why is this significant? I could hold the key to your house in my hand, but that doesn't mean I have the keys of your house. It is true that the key to your house would allow me access into the front door, but then I might find that every door inside your house was locked. I want more than the key to your house—I want the keys of your house.

In the same way, Jesus wants you to experience more than just entry into Heaven. He said, "I will give you the keys of the Kingdom." In other words, "I want you to experience, in this life, every treasure and promise hidden inside My Word!" Make the decision to conform your life to His Word.

DAILY CONFESSION
Father, I thank You that I no longer try to apply Your Word to my life,
I now begin to apply my life to Your Word.

REGARDLESS OF WHAT YOU ARE GOING THROUGH, REMEMBER, GOD'S WORD IS ALWAYS TRUE

"Sanctify them by Your truth. Your Word is truth."
John 17:17 (NKJV)

If you study the origin of the English word "worry," you find that it means, "to strangle." It means to harass or treat roughly with, or as with continual biting or tearing with the teeth…to annoy, bother or harass…to cause to feel troubled or uneasy, make anxious…

While wandering in the wilderness, the Jews worried about everything—food, enemies, and how long it would take. Worry is really nothing more than believing in your circumstances more than you do God's Word. Yes, it is true that many don't see worry as something that is amiss. But we all can agree that worry is surefire proof that we do not believe God's Word.

God does not lie. He cannot lie. In fact, it is impossible for God to lie. It took forty long years (and then some) for the Israelites to learn this overlooked truth. So if I am worried over a given situation, it is because I don't truly believe what God said concerning my circumstance.

Jesus said, "Do not worry…" Many people feel that Jesus made a suggestion, but Jesus commanded us never to worry about another thing, no, not ever again. And if He commanded us not to worry, rest assured He gave us the power to do so. I discovered that God's greatest pleasure is to be believed. His greatest disappointment is to be doubted.

DAILY CONFESSION
Father, I thank You that I am sanctified by Your truth.
Your Word is truth!

A MAN'S CHARACTER IS A PROPHECY OF HIS DESTINY

"He who walks with integrity walks securely,
but he who perverts his ways will become known."
Proverbs 10:9 (NKJV)

✦

If you had the opportunity, would you desire to know the outcome of your life? It's easy—just closely examine your character, scrutinizing it, as a farmer would search his fields for weeds. It is impossible to separate yourself from your character. **Character is who a person is.** The great thing is—character can be developed. You are not born a good person; in fact, you are programmed to fail the moment you are born. The Bible says we are all born slaves to sin. But God sent His Son to die and live again so we can walk as He walked. Jesus' destiny was predicted long ago by His unwillingness to compromise. When Jesus was tempted in the wilderness, He refused to negotiate His integrity for momentary pleasure.

Your character is a prophecy of your destiny, just as the status of a farmer's field is a prophecy of the goods he will sell. Choose to break your integrity, and you will alter your destiny for that which is bad. **Choose to live according to divine principles, and you will alter your destiny for that which is good. It is your choice!**

Through God's Word, you can cultivate the character of Christ. Heaven and Hell are literal destinies of a chosen path. Walk according to God's Word and Heaven will be your final destination. Choose to live according to the desires of your flesh, and Hell cruelly awaits you. Today, cross-examine yourself with the precepts of God's Word. Ask God to help you live like Christ and pay whatever price you must to ensure you never lower your standard of living.

DAILY CONFESSION
Father, I thank You that I choose to walk in integrity and therefore I walk securely;
I choose not to pervert my ways and become known.

TO THE OBEDIENT, GOD IS A LOVING FATHER;
TO THE REBELLIOUS, GOD IS A JUST JUDGE

"The day will surely come when God, by Jesus Christ,
will judge everyone's secret life. This is my message."
Romans 2:16 (NLT)

⚓

It is a statement as everlasting as the city of Zion—God has no favorites. He does not arbitrarily choose to bless one person and ignore another. **He gave all men a choice to live as they determine to live, and He preordained consequences to follow their selected path.** God then becomes a loving, gracious, merciful Father to the person who submits to His Word and lives a life of obedience. Conversely, God becomes a righteous, holy, just Judge to every man who seeks his own way of doing things, the individual who wittingly neglects God's principles, and callously tramples on the blood of His Son.

Along with daily hygiene, olive oil was used extensively for lamps, food preparation, anointing kings, priests, and prophets, and for polishing warriors' shields. Knowing this, the Bible declares that precious olive oil would be denied Israel when they disobeyed. Remember, friends, there are no secrets with God!

At this very moment, we have the privilege of choosing which aspect of God's nature we will encounter when this life comes to a close. In the words of Isaiah, "If you are willing and obedient, you will eat the best of the land; but if you resist and rebel, you will be devoured by the sword." Once we become obedient to the commands of God, we must do our duty to communicate God's true nature as we spread the Gospel throughout the world, following Him through every stage along the way.

DAILY CONFESSION
Father, I thank You that the day will surely come when You, by Jesus Christ,
will judge everyone's secret life. I walk according to Your Word in all that I do.

THE DESTINY OF ONE'S LIFE
IS SHAPED AT THE MOMENT OF DECISION

"...'Do you also want to go away?' But Simon Peter answered Him,
'Lord, to whom shall we go? You have the words of eternal life. Also we have
come to believe and know that You are the Christ, the Son of the living God.'"
John 6:67-69 (NKJV)

⚜

If God gave us the inherent freedom to choose our destiny, then how can other people—co-workers, family members, neighbors, or just plain friends—determine whether or not we succeed in life? The truth is, they can't. **The outcome of our lives is based solely on the decisions we make.** We are actually landlords of the apartment building that gives shelter to our own consequences. Therefore, we cannot blame the unhappiness of our present condition on the actions of others.

As diligent landlords, we must realize that the rewards we enjoy in life depend entirely on us. No longer must we think from the perspective of whether or not a decision is right or wrong. Instead, we must thoroughly contemplate future ramifications every time a decision is made. We can ask ourselves, "What are the long-term effects going to be if I choose this?" It's time to learn to make decisions based on long-term consequences, rather than short-term gratification. In other words, we must pay the price today, in order to enjoy the greatest benefits tomorrow.

In the above passage, we catch a glimpse of how our destiny is shaped by "The moment of decision." Many walked hastily away from Jesus that fateful day, never to return, while the twelve disciples made the astute, heartfelt decision to stay and serve the One who would ultimately save them. It was a moment in time that potently determined the rest of their lives. How often do we, in the course of our bustling lives, experience such life-changing moments?

DAILY CONFESSION
Father, I thank You for giving me the ability to choose my destiny.
I know You have a will for my life and I desire to fulfill it.

TO HEAR THE WORD AND NEGLECT TO ACT
IS TO PLOW A FIELD AND FORGET TO PLANT

"But be doers of the Word, and not hearers only, deceiving yourselves.
For if anyone is a hearer of the Word and not a doer, he is like a man
observing his natural face in a mirror; for he observes himself, goes away,
and immediately forgets what kind of man he was."
James 1:22 (NKJV)

✦

"Didn't he just preach the same thing last week?" the perfectly manicured wife whispered agitatedly into her husband's right ear. Having listened half-heartedly, the man shifted in his seat, tipping his head forward, fervently trying to recall. In a few seconds, his wife leaned over again, "Did that ignorant woman at the end of our row step on your foot like she did mine, fumbling around trying to find a seat?" Slowly nodding, the smiling husband finally remembered—it was as clear as a church bell. "Hey, I remember what he talked about last week—love. Last week, like today, he preached about loving one another." Squirming around uneasily the wife bristled, *Why did I even ask?*

Week after week we continually hear the Word of God, but do you realize we are to be doers of the Word, and not hearers only? I find it interesting how two people can hear the same message, but one benefits and the other does not. The prophet Isaiah tells us, "The Word of God does not return void." This means that there is no inherent defect in the seed of the Word of God. Nevertheless, Jesus tells us in Mark 4:17-19 why the Word of God can be void in a person's life—as a result of the condition of the soil.

In Hebrews 4 we see that the Word does not profit us because we do not mix what we hear with faith and action. **God's Word only transforms us in accordance with our commitment to hear and do what He speaks.**

PRIDE IS THE FORERUNNER TO DESTRUCTION, WHILE HUMILITY LEADS THE WAY TO HONOR

"The arrogance of all people will be brought low. Their pride will lie in the dust.
The Lord alone will be exalted! Idols will be utterly abolished and destroyed."
Isaiah 2:17-18 (NLT)

✦

Since Adam and Eve sinned, all of humanity has been infected with pride, contaminated as bleakly as a garden of wilted leaves. However, there is wonderful news: Christ came to cure us of that infection, which even caused Satan to be ousted from the magnificent splendors of Heaven. But how are we to conquer pride in our lives, once and for all? Well, there are two things we must do. **First,** we must humble ourselves, becoming as meek as young children. **Second,** we must willingly accomplish exactly what God called us to complete. As we continually place ourselves under His mighty hand, eventually, we will be exalted.

Prideful people customarily demand respect and admiration, but respect that is demanded is not true respect. You see, just as a doctor must earn his license in order to practice medicine, true respect also must be earned.

Humility—do you realize that is the highest virtue any man can possess? God's Word continually tells us to humble ourselves; Jesus is our prime example. The apostle Paul explains it in Philippians 2:8, "And being found in appearance as a man, He humbled Himself and became obedient to the point of death." The Son of God became a human to save all of humanity. What greater example do we need? Jesus was highly exalted and obtained a name that is above every other name. Likewise, we must humble ourselves as children today, in order to be exalted as praiseworthy men and women in the future.

DAILY CONFESSION
Father, I thank You for teaching me wisdom because I fear You.
I choose humility, doing what You called me to do.
I will be exalted and honored by Heaven.

SUCCESS IS ONLY A DREAM
FOR THOSE WHO TALK ABOUT IT;
SUCCESS IS A REALITY TO THOSE WHO PURSUE IT

"This Book of the Law shall not depart from your mouth, but
you shall meditate in it day and night, that you may observe to do according
to all that is written in it. For then you will make your way prosperous,
and then you will have good success."
Joshua 1:8 (NKJV)

🙏

Intellectual Greeks, proud Romans, ancient Syrians, cultured Egyptians, fiery Arabs, colorful Persians, and worldly Babylonians occupied half of Palestine on the eve of Jesus' birth. The other half was Jewish—a divine culture split into many rival, often hostile sects. But from the beginning, Jesus lived and breathed success. Let me remind you, however, success doesn't come because you're a nice person or because you yearn for it. **Success only comes because you achieve it.** You earn success by being willing to exchange your time and effort for what you desire.

Well known author, James Allen, says, "Achievement is the crown of effort." No significant achievement in all of history ever came without paying a significant price. The marked effort you are willing to exert ultimately determines your success.

Fulfilling your dreams and achieving your goals is your responsibility. God gave you the tools, but you are the one who must build the house, which represents your life. What kind of home would you like to have—large or small? It is your choice. You are the master architect, the chief builder, and the eventual homeowner. Your life is the result of your own construction. God supplied you with everything you need in order to build a great life. The only requirement is that you must build it according to your own standards of success.

DAILY CONFESSION
Father, I thank You that Your Word does not depart out of my mouth,
but I mediate on it day and night, and I do all I am commanded to do.

THE INTAKE OF BIBLE DOCTRINE IS THE MOST IMPORTANT PART OF A BELIEVER'S LIFE

"Thy Words were found, and I did eat them; and Thy Word was unto me the joy and rejoicing of mine heart: for I am called by Thy name, O Lord God of hosts."
Jeremiah 15:16 (KJV)

How many times have you heard the oft-used term, "conveniently located?" Perhaps you've listened as some announcer enthusiastically declared, "Our mall is conveniently located next to three major expressways," or, "Our museum is conveniently located near all the downtown sites," or, "The best Italian restaurant in the county is conveniently located within walking distance of the city's scenic shoreline." Likewise, everything we need to live a Godly life is "conveniently located" within the pages of God's Word.

Every thought from God we could ever need to make right decisions is conveniently stored inside the book that we hold in our hands. While the life of a believer is multifaceted, **the single most important part of any believer's life is the time they devote to the study of God's Word.** Whereas singing about God causes great feelings, and praying connects us with our Father, it is the written Word of God that teaches us how to live a life that is pleasing to God.

We must fervently commit within ourselves that no amount of busyness is going to keep us from our time to study God's Word. Jesus said in Matthew 4:4, "It is written, 'Man shall not live by bread alone, but by every Word that proceeds from the mouth of God." You must take that verse and make it your heart's deepest desire; allow His Word, "conveniently located," to utterly consume your mind and heart.

DAILY CONFESSION
Father, I thank You that I don't find the source of my life in my daily duties but rather in Your Word. Your Word is the desire of my heart, and I thank Heaven for opening my eyes to the wonderful truths it contains.

GREATNESS IS DEFINED NOT IN A MOMENT
BUT IN A LIFETIME

"Patient endurance is what you need now, so you will continue to do
God's will. Then you will receive all that He has promised."
Hebrews 10:36 (NLT)

"And a righteous person will live by faith.
But I will have no pleasure in anyone who turns away."
Hebrews 10:38 (NLT)

⚜

**God destined every man and woman for greatness, but few finish
life stronger than they began.** Many people started off admirably, but
hit rock bottom towards the conclusion of their lives. They throw
overboard their vision and purpose at the first sign of waves of oppo-
sition or squalls of misfortune. There are a few, however, who carry on
in spite of all resistance.

Greatness is not defined in a meager moment. Romans considered
their empire and rulers as great. But were these coldhearted leaders
and egoistical empire indeed great? Their eventual destruction proves
otherwise.

Although an athlete may experience a great game, it does not qualify him to be labeled as great. Only those who have a great career are
inducted into the Hall of Fame. We must, therefore, pace ourselves
throughout life. Life is about maintaining, not merely achieving. The
individual who finishes strong is the one who ultimately succeeds.
God said in Hebrews 10:38, "…I have no pleasure in anyone who
turns away." We must ardently persist and finish the race we began if
we desire to fulfill the will of God for our lives.

DAILY CONFESSION
Father, I thank You that I do not quit, but I finish strong.
I continue to do Your will, knowing I will receive what You promised.

YOUR MIND IS THE KEY THAT UNLOCKS
THE DOOR TO YOUR FUTURE

"This book of the law shall not depart from your mouth, but you shall meditate in it day and night, that you may observe to do according to all that is written in it. For then you will make your way prosperous, and then you will have good success."
Joshua 1:8 (NKJV)

We often embrace the faulty impression that the men and women of God we read about in the Bible were not human like us, and that they didn't go through the same experiences and emotions we do. How would you like to be the one who replaced Moses, the great prophet and national deliverer, like Joshua did? It is guaranteed that Satan came immediately to notify Joshua how he was going to miserably fail. What Satan did yesterday, he does today. He lies!

Joshua was petrified. Satan armed himself with brutally negative thoughts the moment God gave Joshua the assignment. He probably told Joshua how he could not do what God asked, and questioned why God chose him. These are the same things he tells you and me. God said to Joshua (and He says to us), "My thoughts must be continually in your mouth. You must meditate upon them day and night in order to overcome the lies and the fears that the evil one brings your way." If we follow this formula of success, we overcome insurmountable odds.

Our mind is actually the power plant of our future, capable of generating blessings and success. Even as a youngster, Jesus' mind was continuously upon progress, growing in favor with God and man. The thoughts we think today progress into a distinct reality tomorrow. But we must stay long enough under God's Word to be transformed into the man or woman God called us to be.

DAILY CONFESSION
Father, I thank You that I meditate upon Your Word and speak it aloud continually. Because I am a doer of Your Word, I am blessed in my deeds.

THE ROAD OF AVERAGE IS PAVED BY GOOD INTENTIONS; THE ROAD OF GREATNESS IS PAVED WITH ACTIONS

"And remember, it is a message to obey, not just to listen to.
If you don't obey, you are only fooling yourself."
James 1:22 (NLT)

⋏

While the buttons on her cell phone were nearly worn off, the college girl's new Bible (received at last year's birthday party) lay beautifully untouched. She intended to read it every morning, just as she was encouraged by her church, but with those calls—so many friends from the neighborhood and school—there just was never enough time. Intentions never move anyone anywhere. I wonder just how many people intend to be wealthy, healthy, fulfilled, and happy—the majority I would imagine. Over the years, I have discovered only a few who turn their intention into action. Their reward is achievement. **Achievers don't talk about what they are going to do, because they are too busy doing it.**

If you find yourself living by intention, I encourage you to take immediate action:

- *What have you been putting off?*
- *Is it cleaning the house, spending time with your spouse, finishing a project?*
- *And what is one thing you can do immediately to move you closer toward your intended destination?*

Whatever it is, do it without delay after reading and meditating upon this success key. Many people will read this with the intention of taking action but never will. I don't believe that about you. I believe you will make the decision to put your life on the right course and take immediate action. Don't wait another minute. Take action, and your life will never be the same again!

DAILY CONFESSION
Father, I thank You that I am a doer of Your Word,
not just a hearer.

THE OUTCOME OF YOUR LIFE IS COMPLETELY DEPENDENT UPON THOSE WHOM YOU CALL FRIEND

"He who walks with wise men will be wise,
but the companion of fools will be destroyed."
Proverbs 13:20 (NKJV)

♣

There are essentially two kinds of people in our lives–those who seek comfort, and those have an insatiable passion to change. Individuals who make us comfortable don't have the ability to spur us on.

- *They don't cause us to change.*
- *They don't urge us to become better.*
- *They are content with mediocrity, stuck in their comfort zone, and truly never break free.*

On the other hand, there are those who are assigned to our lives to help us change.

- *They are usually the authorities God places over us.*
- *They exist in various arenas of life, including our employers, parents, and pastor.*
- *They are vital to our growth.*

Although we may feel pressure from those assigned to our lives to help us change, we must stay connected to these people since this type of pressure is for our growth and development. It is a necessity for you to become what God desires. If we turn our backs on our authorities and become a companion of those who are disrespectful, the Word of God tells us we will suffer severe consequences. We must acknowledge the significance and importance of relationships! **Those we call "friend" determine the outcome of our life.** May your friends only be those who draw you closer to the will of God for your life, and may you do the same in their lives.

DAILY CONFESSION
Father, I thank You that I walk with wise men and I am wise.
I am a companion of those who cause me to grow and mature.

YOUR VALUE TO OTHERS IS IN DIRECT PROPORTION TO THE PROBLEMS YOU ARE WILLING TO SOLVE FOR THEM

*"Therefore, as we have opportunity, let us do good to all,
especially to those who are of the household of faith."*
Galatians 6:10 (NKJV)

Do you realize that by 1995 the most dynamic and rapidly growing economies in the world were right there on the Asian Continent, particularly the nations along the Pacific Rim? By practicing free enterprise, capitalism, and encouraging small businesses, backed by their legendary lifestyle of discipline, nations like Taiwan, South Korea, and Singapore grew to solve problems for people all over the world.

This principle can become easily misinterpreted if you don't understand it—I don't choose to become what other people need because I'm afraid of what may happen if I don't. In other words, I do not passively allow myself to be molded by another person. **I become what is necessary to others, because I realize that doing so gives me a real reason to be in relationship with a person.** I am in relationship to add value, not just to hang around. Similar to the way in which the Asian nations have filled in the gap, I add value the moment I begin to solve problems for other people. I am the one they seek, because I possess concrete answers and specific solutions to their problems.

Many people grow very frustrated in life because they don't see a purpose in what they do. They feel valueless and unappreciated. Do you know the cure for this? Become what another needs. Answer questions that no one else can answer. Keep promises that others break. Be willing to go where no one else will go. Be willing to do what no one else will do, and do it well. Take a moment and think about the relationships you are currently in—*How do you add value to their life? What problems do you solve? What answers do you bring?*

DAILY CONFESSION
*Father, I thank You that I have opportunity I do good to all,
but especially to those who are of the household of faith.*

YOU MUST CHOOSE TODAY
HOW YOU WILL RESPOND TOMORROW

"...choose today whom you will serve."
Joshua 24:15 (NLT)

Perhaps the most documented missionary of the 19th century was David Livingstone, born into a poor, yet devout, Scottish family. Though he deeply yearned for an education, David was sent to work in a cotton mill at age 10. Instead of self-pity, with his first wages, David made the right choice to purchase a book of Latin grammar, thereby beginning his sought-after schooling on his own. Eventually able to study theology and medicine, he subsequently served God in Africa for 30 years.

If you haven't noticed already, life doesn't always deal us the hand we want. I have three important questions to ask:

- *How will you respond to tomorrow's setbacks?*
- *How will you respond to an adverse situation on the job?*
- *How will you respond to your spouse's poor attitude?*

You're bound to make a bad decision if you wait until the situation arises. Poor decisions are made as a result of inordinate pressure in our lives. For example, you must make a decision tonight to pray tomorrow morning. If you wait until you feel like it, you may never get around to actually doing it. Why allow your flesh to keep you from making the right decisions? Choose today how you will respond tomorrow.

Follow the example of Dr. Livingstone by never permitting the pressures of life to dictate how you respond. Commit yourself to God's Word and make the choice to obey it, regardless of the cost or situation.

DAILY CONFESSION
Father, I thank You that today is the day I choose life and blessings.
I thank You for giving me the wisdom and discipline in my decision making process.
I make the right choices today that guarantee a great future.

WORDS ARE THE CATALYSTS
THAT IGNITE THE FIRES OF TOMORROW

"Likewise, look at the ships: though they are so great and are driven by
rough winds, they are steered by a very small rudder wherever
the impulse of the helmsman determines."
James 3:4 (AMP)

In the 1850's, no European had ever set foot in the heart of Africa. Though mauled by a lion, separated from his family, and deserted by native helpers, Dr. David Livingstone faithfully spoke these words: "I shall open up a path into the interior or perish." As a result of his resolute words and corresponding actions, Africa was fully opened to the gospel of Christ.

These Scriptures in James clearly reveal the invincible power of the tongue. Although the tongue may appear minuscule, it ultimately controls the actions of the entire body. James compares the tongue to a horse's bit (James 3:3); the one who controls that small bit has complete jurisdiction over the whole horse. James also uses a ship's rudder as an example; a rudder is usually very small in comparison to the ship, but when the captain turns that rudder, the huge ship turns along with it.

Just as the rudder controls the destination of a ship, the tongue is the rudder of our lives. No matter how big life's problems appear, we must use our mouths to guide and steer us in the direction God desires. It takes time to direct a huge ship; it also takes time for our transformation. Circumstances don't change instantaneously. **By continuing to confess His Word and keep the rudder turned, in due time our lives line up with what we say.** As did the great Dr. Livingstone, let's confess what we want to happen in the future instead of moaning about what we see today.

DAILY CONFESSION
Father, I thank You that I speak Your Word and I believe in my heart without doubting. I know the things I speak and believe will come to pass in my life.

PROGRESS IS HALTED THE MOMENT
YOU OPEN THE DOOR TO WRONG ASSOCIATIONS

"He who walks with wise men will be wise,
but the companion of fools will be destroyed."
Proverbs 13:20 (NKJV)

Have you ever stopped to consider how lightning is made? The neg-atively charged water of a thundercloud fatefully meets positively charged atoms in the air, forming a path between the cloud and the ground. Billions of negative charges rush down this path, meeting positive upward charges that potently heat the air, resulting in the superheated glow called lightning. When lightning occurs, it may be fascinating, but unfortunately, it is often fatal.

In the same way, we are exactly like those with whom we associate. **There are no greater limitations placed upon an individual than those brought about by negative relationships.** When God wants to bless you, He sends a person into your life. When Satan wants to destroy you, he too sends a person into your life. Therefore, it is vital to have guidelines to enter into relationship with others. Not everyone is called to be our friend. If there are specific qualifications to enter into relationship with Jesus, shouldn't we hold the same requirements for our relationships with people?

To have positive relations with others, we must become the person we want to attract. If we attract the disrespectful and those who neg-atively walk in sin, we must take a closer look at ourselves and see what we need to change. Become principally based; stand mightily for principle and keep yourself safe from those the enemy sends. The moment others begin to walk by the same principles is when they walk with us. Two are better than one (two positives that is), for two have a greater reward for their labor than just one.

DAILY CONFESSION
Father, I thank You that I walk with wise men, and so I will be wise.
I progress in life because I choose to spend my time with those who pursue You.

OBEDIENCE IS THE KEY
THAT OPENS THE DOOR FOR HEAVEN'S DIRECTION

"Now the Lord had said to Abram: 'Get out of your country,
from your family and from your father's house, to a land that I will show you'
...so Abram departed as the Lord had spoken to him, and Lot went with him."
Genesis 12:1, 4 (NKJV)

✦

Psalm 37:23 tells us, "The steps of the Godly are directed by the Lord, for He delights in every detail of their lives." When a young child takes his first steps, unexpected things happen—misshapen movements, irregular strides, and hard falls. But as this same child listens to tender, reassuring parental instruction, he gets back up. Almost every parent loves to cheer on their child as they take those initial steps.

God does not and cannot direct the steps of everyone; only those who choose to comply, those who listen with ready ears to His instructions. We see a man in Genesis who chose to comply with the voice of God. God commanded Abram to travel to a place about which he knew nothing. Abram's response was immediate, unparalleled obedience. Because of Abram's readiness to act, God was able to direct his steps.

Not every path the Lord leads you on is freshly paved, bordered with colorful flowers, and totally detour free—actually, quite the opposite is true. Nevertheless, God's paths consistently lead you to an abundant harvest.

Remember, Heaven can only direct the steps of the individual who is willing to act upon God's Word, but we must choose to immediately obey His promptings. As we quickly comply to Heaven's orders by taking those first steps of obedience with the innocence of a young child, we experience God's mighty hand of precise direction, abundant provision, and steadfast protection.

DAILY CONFESSION

Father, I thank You for directing my steps so that no sin comes upon my life.
Thank You that You delight in every detail of my life. I act upon Your Word,
knowing that Your mighty hand directs me.

THE MOTIVES OF YOUR HEART ARE REVEALED THE MOMENT YOUR INTENTIONS AND ACTIONS CONVERGE

"Why are you so polite with Me, always saying 'Yes, Sir,' and 'That's right, Sir,'
but never doing a thing I tell you? These words I speak to you are not mere
additions to your life, homeowner improvements to your standard of
living. They are foundation works, words to build a life on."
Luke 6:46-47 (Message)

William Pryor Letchworth was a New York conservationist, historian, and philanthropist. Upon observing the way orphans and the mentally ill were treated in our nation's facilities, Letchworth traveled to Europe to study the ways in which the mentally ill could be humanely treated, transforming antiquated practices throughout the entire region. Mr. Letchworth devotedly took under his wing scores of orphaned young men, taking them to his country estate to escape the crime and soot of the big city. Called the "man who always did right," the pure motives of Letchworth's heart were blatantly revealed.

Jesus does not look for those who merely talk about obedience; He looks for those who truly obey. The moment we have an opportunity to do what God has tells us is when we either find a heart that longs after God or one still enslaved to the desires of the flesh.

God called us to produce and bear fruit. Jesus told us, "By this My Father is glorified, that you bear much fruit; so you will be My disciples." The moment we have an opportunity to do what God told us to do, is the moment we either find a heart longing after God, or one still enslaved to the desires of the flesh. Wouldn't you, like Mr. Letchworth, also like to be called a man or woman who "always did right?" If so, then choose today to become a person who not only intends to do what is written, but who actually completes it.

DAILY CONFESSION
Father, I thank You that I glorify You by bearing fruit doing what You ask
of me. My faith and good works will be a witness to many.

WHENEVER YOU SOLVE GREATER PROBLEMS, YOU WILL RECEIVE GREATER REWARDS

"The master said, 'Well done, my good and faithful servant.
You have been faithful in handling this small amount, so now
I will give you many more responsibilities.'"
Matthew 25:23 (NLT)

It is nine a.m. on Monday morning and the telephones are already buzzing. Clients file in and out of this bustling partnership as if it were the local supermarket, and more communicate through written correspondence and email. On the second floor of this lucrative law firm, a secretary earns $12.00 an hour processing all sorts of legal documents, setting them up by using a certain brand of computer machinery. An attorney in the same office earns $300.00 an hour, arguing in court over a new patent, a rapacious improvement of that same series of high-tech office equipment. Why this seemingly unfair discrepancy? It's not that the attorney is nicer, better looking, or even smarter than the secretary, or that he is somehow a superior person. It is just that the attorney chooses to solve a greater problem. There's no doubt about it—the type of problem a person solves for others determines the manner of reward they receive.

In our culture, it is common to expect a raise each year, just like we anticipate Thanksgiving in November, Christmas in December, and New Year's Day in January. But if an employee truly desires a raise, an employer has the right to ask, "What new kinds of problems are you going to solve for me that warrant more money than you make right now?" As a believer, you must have a ready answer, showing that you are willing to become tangibly more valuable to your employer before you expect a promotion.

DAILY CONFESSION
Father, I thank You that I am faithful over little, and You cause me to be faithful
over much, and I thank You that You open my eyes to see the great problems
I can solve for those above me.

UNTIL THERE IS HEARTFELT RESTITUTION, THERE IS NO TRUE REPENTANCE

"For Godly sorrow produces repentance leading to salvation, not to be regretted; but the sorrow of the world produces death."
2 Corinthians 7:10 (NKJV)

⚜

The horrific plight of African-American slaves, the disaster of Native American land treaties, and the degrading internment of Japanese American families all have one thing in common—the valid need of restitution. Whenever we do wrong, guilt remains until there is a wholehearted attempt at restitution. Guilt doesn't depart when the people we have wronged leave; it stays until we humble ourselves to make restitution.

Repentance without restitution is nothing more than a futile exercise in smooth talk, words with no backbone. We may try to squirm our way out of the responsibility of restitution by saying, "But I repented for what I did. That person just has not forgiven me." Nevertheless, there must be some type of restorative process to prove to the person we wronged that Godly sorrow for our sin struck us so deeply that we now are willing to make those changes stick forever.

If we truly repent for what we did, there should be no problem whatsoever going to the person we wronged (every day if necessary), letting them know how much we need their love and acceptance. If we do this, God guarantees our release from guilt and shame.

DAILY CONFESSION
Father, I thank You for creating in me a clean heart and renewing a steadfast spirit within me. I choose to bring restitution to every area of my life where I have been wrong.

DISRESPECT IS THE THIEF
WHO HAS BEEN STEALING YOUR PROMOTIONS

*"... 'So if it please the king, we suggest that you issue a written decree,
a law of the Persians and Medes that cannot be revoked. It should order
that Queen Vashti be forever banished from your presence and that
you choose another queen more worthy than she."*
Esther 1:19 (NLT)

The topaz is stunning, one of the most precious of earthly gems. Extremely hard, topaz is also very brittle, splitting and cracking away in seconds. Though stunningly beautiful, Vashti must have been quite a lady! After refusing an instruction from her husband, the king, the most powerful man in all of Babylon, her flagrant disrespect caused her to become as topaz: hard and brittle. There was no way the king could overlook her disrespect and successfully continue his rule.

Think of it—for the rest of Vashti's life, she would be known as the queen who refused to honor the King. Her life was ruined, having split and cracked away within seconds. Now she could never step into the promotion that was once so easily within her grasp.

We may do everything right on our jobs, in our marriages, and in our homes, but one moment of disrespect can set us back for years. Mistakes can be overlooked. Poor performance can be improved. But disrespect leaves a sour taste in the mouth, making it exceptionally difficult to forget.

Have you grown too familiar with someone? Have you crossed boundaries? Think about these questions and determine to never let disrespect become a thief, getting the best of you, as it did Queen Vashti.

DAILY CONFESSION
*Father, I thank You that I see others as better than myself, and I am able
to respect them. I choose to put others first and I always do unto
others what I want them to do to me.*

AN ABUSED LIFE
IS SIMPLY A LIFE WITHOUT PURPOSE

"Don't store up treasures here on earth, where they can be eaten by moths and get rusty, and where thieves break in and steal. Store your treasures in Heaven, where they will never become moth-eaten or rusty and where they will be safe from thieves. Wherever your treasure is, there your heart and thoughts will also be."
Matthew 6:19-21 (NLT)

Did your mother ever fragrance the family's closets with handfuls of those slippery, tiny white spheres called mothballs? If she did, that unforgettable odor will probably stay with you for the rest of your life, an aromatic reminder that things down here can be easily "eaten up." Moths and rust are simple facts of life – telltale hazards of placing all our valuables within this dying world.

The person to whom Jesus refers in Matthew 6 is the one who lives without a purpose. Perhaps their life is filled with a great number of temporary things, but they accomplish zilch when it comes to an eternal return. Since everything around us is one day going to vanish, how foolish it is to live just for the here-and-now. We could call that "life abuse."

We have a choice to make the very second our eyes converge upon the next sunrise. Either we can use the day to make something out of the life God has so graciously given us, or we can squander our hours on fleeting pleasures and self-centered aimlessness, our time rusting away like the body of an old, discarded automobile. God's grace is available to all who come to Him, offering themselves as living sacrifices. That needs to be our initial step. And as God has the final authority in our life, we do whatever we must to make sure that our life is used to the fullest, for our good, and for the good of the people around us. We will live our life, on purpose.

DAILY CONFESSION
Father, I thank You for giving me the gift of life. I thank You for giving me the grace I need to make each day worthwhile and full of purpose.

PROMOTION IS NEVER AWARDED BY PERFORMING THE TASKS YOU ARE ALREADY PAID TO DO

"And whoever compels you to go one mile, go with him two."
Matthew 5:41 (NKJV)

Having been so infuriated by his people being forever pushed around by foreign thugs, a Hebrew priest named Mattathias finally decided to go beyond limitations. Walking up to the city's Greek altar, Mattathias smashed it into pieces, starting a twenty-four year conflict. After winning Jerusalem, the first thing they did was toss away every object of Greek idolatry from the temple, and gave back the holy site to God's people. This victory is known today as the Feast of Hanukkah.

You must do more than what is expected of you. You may think you are busy, but you must realize that everyone is busy, not just you. There are never-ending opportunities available to a person who is willing to go beyond the confines of their Positions Results Description. Taking on extra work by your own initiative shows your superiors that you are determined to succeed. **Chances are your company aspires to expand. If you can add fuel to that fire, in time, you will be rewarded.**

We all have things that are required of us: work duties, domestic chores, legal obligations, social expectations, and spiritual requirements. Many people stop and never discover what it means to be pleasing. You cannot please your employer by doing only what he pays to you do. You only bring pleasure by doing more than your salary requires. Our promotion in life cannot come by simply fulfilling our current requirements. The pure, refreshing water of promotion only flows when we discover what is desired of us. Mattathias went above and beyond his priestly duties. It takes concentrated effort, but the reward is well worth going the "extra mile."

DAILY CONFESSION
Father, I thank You that I go above and beyond what is required of me.
I chose to do everything as if I were doing it for You.

LIVE EVERY DAY AS THOUGH
YOU HAVE SOMETHING GOOD TO GIVE

*"Now He who supplies seed to the sower and bread for food will also supply and
increase your store of seed and will enlarge the harvest of your righteousness."*
2 Corinthians 9:10 (NIV)

Yesterday we talked about promotion, and how the priest
Mattathias began the Feast of Hanukkah, which is still celebrated
in Jewish homes today. But do you know the story behind the
"Menorah," the nine-candled stand that sits in many Jewish homes
during this celebratory time? While the Jews celebrated the return of
their temple, they encountered a lamp with only a one-day supply of
oil. Miraculously, God gave enough illumination to the candelabrum,
allowing it to burn for eight extra days and nights.

During Hanukkah, one candle in the menorah is lit each day to
remember this miracle that God so wondrously gave. The Scriptures
promise us that God gives seed to the person who desires to sow.
Some may say that they having nothing to give, but that is never the
case as far as God is concerned. Take a look around and think:

- *What do I have that can become a blessing for another?*
- *Do I have something material like money, clothes, books, etc.?*
- *What about intangible things like a great attitude, a thankful
  heart, or a helping hand?*

**You always have something you can sow. God would be a liar if
you truly had nothing.** Change your mind about how you see your
life. Rather than looking for people to solve your problems, find out
what you can do to solve theirs. As always, God is faithful to His
Word, giving illumination, providing seed as you "enlarge the harvest
of your righteousness."

DAILY CONFESSION
*Father, I thank You for providing me with seed to sow and
for making me a blessing wherever I go.*

EVERY THOUGHT THAT RUNS
THROUGH YOUR MIND IS SIMPLY NOT YOURS

"The thoughts of the righteous are right,
but the counsels of the wicked are deceitful."
Proverbs 12:5 (NKJV)

Centuries preceding the lives of Mattathias and his sons existed a culture, a people of stimulating thoughts. The ancient Egyptians are considered to be one of the most enlightened, advanced inhabitants of the antiquated world. But most of their thoughts were wrong. They erroneously formed a disturbing template for their lives. One of their most zealous beliefs was that they needed natural items (clothing, tools, weapons, and dishware) in the next life. This was the whole reason behind mummification—preserving worldly things for the afterlife. How deceiving and contrary to God's Word!

If you have received Jesus Christ as the Lord of your life, any thoughts in your mind that are contrary to God's Word are not your thoughts. How do I know this? Proverbs 12:5 says, "The thoughts of the righteous are right, but the counsels of the wicked are deceitful."

God declared you righteous—not based upon what you do, but upon what Jesus did. Therefore, if your thoughts are not right thoughts, they are not your thoughts. You may even argue, "Yes, but I'm the one thinking those thoughts!" No, those lying thoughts are just passing through. You don't have to feel condemned about thinking them, but you do have to sharply reject them, as fervently as you would the erroneous beliefs of the ancient Egyptians. From there, you must replace lying thoughts with correct ones. Doing so prevents wrong thinking from taking hold of your subconscious thoughts, and with enough effort, you can make right thoughts your template for life!

DAILY CONFESSION
Father, I thank You that I think Your thoughts, and they form the template for my life. I understand that not every thought that runs through my mind is mine, and so I take captive the thoughts that do not align with Your Word.

YOU CAN NEVER DISCOVER YOUR NEW IDENTITY WHILE GAZING AT THE OLD ONE

*"I have been crucified with Christ; it is no longer I who live,
but Christ lives in me; and the life which I now live in the flesh I live by faith
in the Son of God, who loved me and gave Himself for me."*
Galatians 2:20 (NKJV)

⚜

Ah, the unmatched excitement of moving into a new house—the feel of new carpeting beneath your feet, the scent of fresh oak lingering in the air, and the sight of unmarred walls, just waiting to be decorated – by you. No matter what memories your old environment holds, your full concentration now lies upon this wonderful new dwelling. Knowing that your old self no longer exists is the foundational truth that gives you not only the understanding, but also the confidence that your future is going to marvelously exceed your past. Understanding who you are in Christ is the foundation of your Christian life, helping you better identify which thoughts are God's, and which thoughts are not. Understanding and embracing this new identity protects you from past issues that often hinder your current progress.

People constantly say to me, "You know, I read the Bible, I pray, I go to church, and I witness to people about the Lord. So why does it seem like whenever the pressure is on, I resort to my old ways?"

The answer to that question is simple: you haven't yet come to understand who Jesus created you to be and what He did for you through His death and resurrection. In order to successfully withstand the pressures of this world and renovate your mind according to the new life that is yours in Christ, you must understand righteousness — the ability to live continually in right standing with God. You are the righteousness of Christ. You have a bright future in store. Embrace your new identity, just as you would that new house, and you'll soon enjoy the promise land that God is building especially for you.

DAILY CONFESSION
*Father, I thank You that I have been crucified with Christ.
It is no longer I who live but Christ lives in me; and now I live by faith
in the Son of God who gave His life for me.*

OBEDIENCE IS THE CONDUIT THROUGH
WHICH GOD'S BLESSINGS FLOW TO YOUR LIFE

"But it shall come to pass, if you do not obey the voice of the Lord your God,
to observe carefully all His commandments and His statutes which I command
you today, that all these curses will come upon you and overtake you…"
Deuteronomy 28:15 (NKJV)

Although God desires to reward us all, He says in Deuteronomy 28:15, "If you do not obey the voice of the Lord your God…these curses will come upon you and overtake you." If you and I disobey, we are severed like a weed from God's hand of blessing. You can alter your future by applying Godly principles to your life. You cannot expect any future contrary to the principles you live. **The principles you enjoy today crucially determine the future you experience tomorrow.**

If you want financial security, there are specific principles to which you must adhere. If you desire to walk in divine health, there are also principles you must follow. **Whatever future you desire, you must apply the principles that bring those desires to pass.**

In order to continue any future progress, you must have a system by which you evaluate your progress, and that is what obedience to God's Word does for you.

DAILY CONFESSION
Father, I thank You that I am obedient to Your Word
and I am careful to observe Your ways. I thank You that I walk
in Your blessings all the days of my life.

WHAT YOU LEARN ON SUNDAY WILL BE STOPPED BY YOUR WORRY ON MONDAY

"The thorny ground represents those who hear and accept the good news,
but all too quickly the message is crowded out by the cares of this life
and the lure of wealth, so no crop is produced."
Matthew 13:22 (NLT)

⚜

"Gas prices skyrocket! Shocking new terrorist plots! Illegal drugs cause an upsurge in crime! Supermarket produce tainted with deadly bacteria!" Today's global headlines could make even the tiniest sparrows stop flying and start worrying. But the Bible tells us that worry chokes the Word of God, congesting our lives like strangling traffic jams, making it of no effect. Can you imagine that? Worry actually stops God's Word from working inside your life. We must understand that worry is not something with which to toy or take lightly. Our every worry is the proof that God-honoring faith is sorely absent!

You cannot worry and walk in faith at the same time. The moment faith boldly enters the room is the moment worry must fearfully exit. Whenever we worry, we factually document that we don't truly believe what God said. **Remember — God's greatest pleasure is to be believed, and His greatest disappointment is to be doubted.** So what does our worry say about our faith in God?

Although we may get excited about the principles taught to us on Sunday, we must refuse worry on Monday to see God's Word manifest in our lives. Never forget: **when worry fretfully and nervously knocks at your door, you must allow the Word of God to valiantly answer!** Then, worry will flee in stark terror like an enemy exposed.

DAILY CONFESSION
Father, I thank You that I walk by faith and not by sight. I refuse to look
at my circumstances knowing that whatever I focus on will multiply.
I will have Jesus answer the door when worry comes knocking. I stand
on Your Word and I refuse to allow worry to enter my life.

THE TRANSFORMATION OF ONE'S LIFE
IS IN DIRECT PROPORTION
TO THE ALTERATION OF ONE'S MIND

"Do not copy the behavior and customs of this world,
but let God transform you into a new person by changing the way you think."
Romans 12:2 (NLT)

✦

One of my passions in life is to see others on a continual upward swing of transformation. It hurts me to see people in church hear the Word for many years on end and be no different from the day they stepped foot through the church doors. God did not design life for stagnation. Nothing living stagnates; it continually transforms from season to season or ultimately dies.

Shouldn't we be the same? If you cannot look back on your life six months ago, or even one year ago, and see any growth, you should examine yourself as to why there hasn't been any progress. We are to go from glory to glory.

One of the reasons God birthed the message of excellence into my heart is because excellence causes a person to pursue change. Jesus does not allow an individual to stay the same, just as He doesn't allow the landscape to languish. I have heard it said like this, "God loves you just the way you are, but He wants you to be like Jesus."

Isn't it interesting that when God welcomed you into His family, He said, "Now you must die and Christ must live through you." It is not that God doesn't love us. Remember, **transformation of your life is in direct proportion to the alteration of your mind.**

DAILY CONFESSION
Father, I thank You that my mind is continually renewed by Your Word. I desire transformation, and I understand that transformation only comes through mind alteration. I choose to alter my mind in accordance with Your Word.

THE ONLY TIME IT IS RIGHT
TO LOOK DOWN UPON ANOTHER IS
WHEN YOU ARE BENDING OVER TO PICK THEM UP

"Be kindly affectionate to one another
with brotherly love, in honor giving preference to one another…"
Romans 12:10 (NKJV)

✦

As the capital of Hitler's Third Reich from 1933 to 1945, Berlin was a boastful, gregarious city, singing praises of its famous museums, institutes, and theaters. During the last two years of World War II, however, 75,000 tons of explosives were dropped on Berlin, virtually destroying the largest city in Germany. Their boasting was harshly and brutally stopped. Now quietly settled among the great cities in Europe, Berlin sits in tranquil humility.

There is no need to boast or brag of your advancement because true greatness never boasts. You shouldn't have to. Whenever you find one who sings his own praise, you can be sure insecurity and doubt are in his heart. **By allowing your attitude to convey that you are a man or woman of excellence, you continue to excel in everything you do.**

Right now, why not begin to cultivate this attitude of increase, stalwartly refusing to look down upon another? Always seek to see yourself as lesser than those you are around. Take the posture of a servant. Samuel Milton Jones said, "What I want for myself I want for everybody." With that humble intent, promotion has no choice but to track us down! Be kindly affectionate to one another, in honor giving preference to one another by terminating the brutality of boastful living.

DAILY CONFESSION
Father, I thank You that I am kindly affectionate toward others
with brotherly love. In honor I give preference to others.

GOD'S TIMING IS DESTROYED
BY THE DEADLY ENEMY OF DOUBT

"That you may not be sluggish, but imitators of those
who through faith and patience inherit the promises."
Hebrews 6:12 (NAS)

⚜

Why would anyone doubt God? Since the beginning of time, Satan has attempted to convince us that God is not going to come through for us. God told us what was going to happen, He just never told us when. God's timing is right no matter when. We live in a world run by the economy of evil, but God gave us the power and authority to live above the world's system. He gave us His Word so we can walk by faith, and not by sight.

Matthew 11:12 fervently states, "And from the days of John the Baptist until now the kingdom of Heaven suffers violence and the violent take it by force." That is exactly what we must do. The reason we are called to take God's kingdom is because Satan is attempting to steal it away from us. The enemy tries to stop anyone from taking the kingdom. He erects roadblocks and sends every demon and lie to you daily about how God is not going to come through by keeping His own promises. At that point, many lose heart and never receive what God faithfully guaranteed.

We must stand strong and continue to press in and believe God, knowing that He is not a man that would lie, but what He said, He will do. Through faith and patience, we will receive what is promised.

DAILY CONFESSION
Father, I thank You that I am full of faith and I am patient.
I receive what is promised, for You are not slack concerning Your promise.

THE FULFILLMENT OF THE GREAT COMMISSION
DEPENDS UPON THE HARMONY OF GOD'S PEOPLE

"'Look!' he said. 'If they can accomplish this when they have
just begun to take advantage of their common language and political unity,
just think of what they will do later. Nothing will be impossible for them!'"
Genesis 11:6 (NLT)

"Go therefore and make disciples of all the nations, baptizing them
in the name of the Father and of the Son and of the Holy Spirit."
Matthew 28:19 (NKJV)

⚹

It's time for to the Body of Christ to unite. We must eagerly join forces to accomplish the great mission that has been given us. Although every doctrinal issue may not be settled, harmony is necessary for the spreading of the Gospel. And the Gospel is the foremost reason why we are here on earth. Satan's aim is to bring division. He understands if he can cause us to be divided, our strength is sorely limited. Seemingly, we no longer fight against him; we now fight one another. This discord must end! And it begins with you and me.

As bees mold tightly within the hive under the command of the queen, we must also unite under the direction of Heaven. **The strength of the church is non-existent if we refuse to come together.** The mission is the same for every believer; nothing is impossible to those who walk in harmony. Satan deceived us into using our spiritual weapons to fight against one another for too long—we must unite our strengths and influence to render the gates of hell powerless, once and for all. When we walk in cohesive accord, there is no devil able to stop what we set out to do. May God help us come together and preach this Gospel to a lost and dying world!

DAILY CONFESSION
Father, I thank You that I unite under the instruction and direction
of Heaven with my brothers and my sisters in Christ. I thank You that
I am mature and full grown in You, fitted together with the
body of Christ and doing my part.

YOUR MOOD IS DETERMINED
BY WHAT HAS CAPTURED YOUR FOCUS

*"We do this by keeping our eyes on Jesus, on whom our faith depends
from start to finish. He was willing to die a shameful death on the cross
because of the joy He knew would be His afterward. Now He is seated
in the place of highest honor beside God's throne in heaven."*
Hebrews 12:2 (NLT)

Have you realized that if something can quantitatively capture your
focus, it eventually alters your entire life? Many stories and charming
little poems have been written about a tiny, yet intriguing insect.
Known to scientists as the "ladybird beetle," these colorful insects do
not just arbitrarily flit through the air, landing on any old site—they
possess a focus, an expressed concentration.

The emotions you feel, whether good or bad, reveal what has avidly
captured your attention. Choose your focus! Don't live discouraged,
sad, or habitually depressed. **Happiness, joy, and peace can become
permanent fruit, skillfully gleaned from your spiritual garden.**

Why harbor negativity? It only thwarts comprehensive, satisfying
achievement. Negative thoughts restrain you from pursuing what you
desire. If you think you can't, you won't, and you will never walk
in the destiny God has for your life. Without paying strict attention
to their landing strips, the ladybug will never attain continual sustenance. Anything you want requires you to passionately pursue it;
otherwise, you will fall short every time. While focusing on the
sustenance of God's Word, go after everything He promised you.

DAILY CONFESSION
*Father, I thank You that I fix my eyes on Jesus, the Author and the Finisher of
my faith, who for the joy set before Him, endured the cross, despising the shame,
and sat down at the right hand of Your throne.*

THE FRAGRANCE THAT PLEASES GOD IS THE AROMA OF YOUR HOURLY OBEDIENCE

"Samuel replied, 'Has the Lord as much pleasure in your burnt offerings
and sacrifices as in your obedience? Obedience is far better than sacrifice.
He is much more interested in your listening to Him than
in your offering the fat of rams to Him.'"
1 Samuel 15:22 (TLB)

Obedience is the only thing God ever explicitly requires. Although a faithful and loving God, precious few are quick to obey His instructions. On occasion, what God tells us may seem utterly illogical, or brutally disappointing. It may also, at diverse times, keep us from getting something we desire. Yet, it is not until we obey Him without restraint that our obedience infiltrates Heaven with its pleasant aroma.

The apostle Paul instructs us to "present our bodies a living sacrifice, holy, acceptable to God, which is our reasonable service." **We must give up claim to our childish wants, individual desires, and selfish reasoning so we can stalwartly obey our Lord.**

God delights in our obedience, and requires us to conform to His construction. The obedience we offer Him far exceeds our daily sacrifice, since God does not ask us to make a grand sacrifice; He simply requests daily obedience in the little things. That is the only sacrifice He is pleased to accept; it is the way He crafted us.

DAILY CONFESSION
Father, I thank You that I am willing and obedient and I eat the best of the land.
I understand that You delight in obedience far more than any sacrifice I can offer.
I choose to obey Your instruction, for my desire is to please You.

THE MEASURE OF THE SEED YOU SCATTER
WILL DETERMINE THE SIZE OF THE HARVEST YOU REAP

"He who sows sparingly will also reap sparingly and he who sows
generously will also reap generously."
2 Corinthians 9:6 (NIV)

⚰

The forefathers of the United States of America sowed an abundant seed, going far beyond anyone else's visions and dreams. Following years of late-night wrangling with the Continental Congress, along with the agony of the vicious Revolutionary War, the new government (one designed to honor man's right to worship God) was underway. Its top executive, however, needed a place for him and his family to dwell. By the year 1800, the "President's House" was completed and occupied. But fourteen short years later, British troops brazenly set ablaze the grand edifice. By the next morning (what many call a "sign" from God), a hurricane with tremendous winds doused the raging flames, saving the great house's shell; the charred skeleton was amazingly harvested, reaped as a symbol of freedom for all.

As you study this principle, you may find yourself in a season of lack in your finances. **If we desire any type of increase in our life, we must be willing to sow further in the financial arena than ever before.** But remember—without sowing a seed, there can be no harvest to reap.

Everyone can give while things are going well. But those who give during the times of struggle, as did America's forefathers, really impress the heart of God. We must establish a plan of giving more to God so He can sequentially begin to release more finances in our lives. Let me encourage you—continue the flow of giving during times of lack. Do you recall the widow woman who gave two pennies when she had barely anything to give? Jesus favored the widow woman because she gave out of her lack, not her abundance. I encourage you to do the same.

DAILY CONFESSION
Father, I thank You that I am a generous giver.
I sow abundantly knowing I will reap abundantly.

FAILURE COMES ALIVE
THE MOMENT YOU LOSE FOCUS

*"What I always feared has happened to me. What I dreaded has come to be.
I have no peace, no quietness. I have no rest; instead, only trouble comes."*
Job 3:25-26 (NLT)

Born with the rare defect of fused legs, sometimes known as the "mermaid syndrome," the Peruvian parents of this otherwise vivacious little girl did not fear. Instead, they allowed doctors to perform the risky surgery of separating her tiny legs, the outcome a great success. And it's no wonder – they had named the child Milagros, focusing upon the "miracle" that they believed would ultimately come to pass.

But rather than dwelling upon the good things of life, Job began to focus on loss. His broken focus invited fear to show its menacing face, which is why he candidly declared, "What I have always feared has happened to me." Though Job was a righteous man in every aspect, when he decided to focus on the expressed possibility of losing his splendor, he opened the shabby door of fear to overtake him.

Do you live in fear? Do you focus on the possibility of negative things coming to your life? If you choose to focus on the "what-ifs" of life, you'll persistently exist as a hostage to fear, incarcerated within the solitary prison of pessimistic dread. Conversely, Jesus did something quite different. The "what-ifs" were of no concern to Him. He trusted in the faithfulness of God—confidently recognizing that He himself was able to determine the outcome of His life.

Remember, God is the one who calls into existence what never existed before. You can do the same. So change your focus today, and believe with the fervor of little Milagros' parents, directing your sights completely upon the God who will never, ever fail.

DAILY CONFESSION
*Father, I thank You that You are my God and that You care for me.
I choose to focus on Your promises of eternal life even while I live in this world.*

You Must Sacrifice What You Already Have In Order To Possess What You Desire

"The kingdom of Heaven is like a treasure that a man discovered hidden in a field.
In his excitement, he hid it again and sold everything he owned to get enough
money to buy the field—and to get the treasure, too!"
Matthew 13:44 (NLT)

⚔

While Union and Confederate troops were bleeding and dying in the battlefield and the war effort was in serious need of supplies, the President's wife, Mary Todd, was resolute. She purchased 400 pairs of gloves during her first year in the White House, and her most famous acquisition was an ornate rosewood bed that was never slept in by the President. Though challenged to sacrifice, she refused even during a gory, treasury-depleting civil war. Quite prosperous in her own right, Mary Todd Lincoln had no inclination of setting an example of sacrifice.

One of the main reasons so many Christians stray from the faith is because they were never challenged to pay a price to follow Christ. The only proof that you value something is your willingness to sacrifice something you already have in order to possess it. Did not God value us so much that He was willing to sacrifice His only Son? But the Gospel message has been so watered down that we don't even mention the sacrifice people are required to make to live for Jesus.

What have you given up to follow Christ? I have never seen a Christian enjoy life who was unwilling to sacrifice his own life and the desires that typically come. To be honest, I believe there is more joy for an unbeliever living in sin than a Christian who stubbornly withholds his life from Christ Jesus. May God help you give up your life to serve and live for Him. Then you will possess the abundant life Jesus offers.

DAILY CONFESSION
Father, I esteem and value my relationship with Christ more than life itself.
It is my treasure. I lay down my life for Christ that I may gain and
possess all You have for me.

PAIN IS THE SIGNAL DIRECTING TRAFFIC
ON THE ROAD OF PROGRESS

"So then, since Christ suffered physical pain, you must arm yourselves
with the same attitude He had, and be ready to suffer, too. For if you are
willing to suffer for Christ, you have decided to stop sinning."
1 Peter 4:1 (NLT)

"The lazy man does not roast his game, but the diligent man prizes his possessions."
Proverbs 12:27 (NIV)

⚜

The saying, "No pain, no gain," has proved true throughout time. In health, wealth, knowledge, and personal development, many attempt success without paying a price. God never promised us an easy road to attain His will for our lives; in fact, His presence creates (and actually stimulates) the pain of pronounced growth. Remember, the Father prunes those who bear fruit so they might bear more.

The apostle Paul tells us, "I harden my body with blows and bring it under complete control…" That doesn't sound pain-free to me. If there was anyone who knew about pain, Paul did. Although he served the Lord and walked a life of obedience, pain was not absent from his life.

Are you aware that pain and peace often securely join hands? The peace surpassing all understanding flows from our spirit, though we may have physical or emotional pain. **When everything seems to go wrong, God's peace causes us to see our situation through the omniscient eyes of Heaven.** Growing pains are inevitable. But we must choose to embrace pain, arming ourselves with the refining effect it has on us. Our reward is worth any pain we must presently endure.

DAILY CONFESSION
Father, I thank You that I arm myself with the same attitude Christ had,
and I am ready to suffer. I work diligently to attain what You desire for me.

RIGHT MUST NEVER BE PENALIZED
AND WRONG MUST NEVER BE REWARDED

*"Even while we were with you, we gave you this rule:
'whoever does not work should not eat.'" 2 Thessalonians 3:10 (NLT)*

Some Americans may have forgotten, but the United States Constitution did not consign the nation to be ruled by judges. Established with the divinely inspired system of "checks and balances," America's unique government is separated into three branches—legislative, executive, and judicial—one continually serving the other. That is exactly how "liberty and justice for all" was created. Recently, however, it seems there has been a disproportionate shift in standards, accentuating an imperial judiciary instead of this branch being the least powerful of the three, consigning the nation to be ruled by judges.

Paralleling this unjust trend, the standards once held by the early Christian church have also declined. Additionally, a shift within the body of Christ from exclusivity to all-inclusive has begun to take place. We have communicated an errant message that everyone can be rewarded in Heaven without doing what is right. This plainly is not just. The shift is evident throughout the entire world, and has infiltrated the church, causing it to be filled with so-called "Christians" who don't produce Godly fruit. Repeatedly, God's Word reveals that rewards are extended only to those who obey.

There must be a balance between seeking the lost and allowing people to determine their own course. Did Jesus ever chase after those who wanted to abandon Him? Absolutely not! Once people knew who He was, Jesus allowed them to decide who they would follow. He did not force Himself upon anyone. If He would have, there would be no reward because God only rewards those whose faith causes pursuit. We must commit to the Word of God and stand our ground to receive what is rightfully ours. Now that is truly "liberty and justice for all."

DAILY CONFESSION
*Father, I thank You that I am a doer of the Word and not a hearer only.
I produce much fruit that brings You glory.*

THE ACTIONS YOU EMBRACE ARE A DOCUMENTATION OF WHAT YOU BELIEVE

"Yea, a man may say, thou hast faith, and I have works: shew me thy faith without thy works, and I will shew thee my faith by my works."
James 2:18 (KJV)

⚜

For a substantial number of sessions, we are going to enter God's dwelling place of Palestine, exploring its vibrant culture, its Biblical symbolism, and its majestic pageantry. Did you know that Old Testament Hebrew boys typically followed their father's vocations such as shepherding, weaving, or fishing? Their distinct actions became a documentation of what they believed about their distinct trades. Shepherds were recognized by their expertise for gathering flocks and extensive knowledge of the elements, while weavers were acclaimed for their technological operation of intricate looms and shuttles, and fishermen were esteemed for the physical challenges produced by the ever-changing sea.

What you believe is always revealed by your actions. As believers, there are times when we think we believe the Word of God when in fact, our actions prove otherwise. James states that the "proof is in the pudding." If someone says they believe God's Word, but doesn't support it with their actions, their faith is as dead as the nearly extinct occupation of "town crier." **True faith is continually followed by actions.** The apostle John confirmed this when he wrote these words, "Now by this we know that we know Him, if we keep His commandments" (1 John 2:3).

Jesus asked His disciples, "Why do you call Me Lord, Lord, and do not what I say?" Like the shepherd, weaver, and fisherman, allow God to help you prove your actions by trusting daily through unwavering obedience.

DAILY CONFESSION

Father, I thank You that I am a doer of the Word, not a hearer only. My faith is alive and working, and I prove my faith in Your Word through my actions.

HAPPINESS IS DETERMINED BY WHO YOU ARE, NOT BY WHAT YOU POSSESS

"So when Jesus heard these things, He said to him, 'You still lack one thing.
Sell all that you have and distribute to the poor, and you will have treasure
in Heaven; and come, follow Me.' But when he heard this,
he became very sorrowful, for he was very rich."
Luke 18:22-23 (NKJV)

✦

Once you hear the soul-pounding reverberation of the shofar (or ram's horn), by far the oldest of all Jewish musical instruments, you will never be the same. Professional musicians, as well as minstrels, regularly played in the palaces and temples of Israel, creating happiness and elation for their adoring listeners. But it was not the harp, lyre, trimbrel, or kinnor that generated this happiness. It was the gift and enthusiastic flair of the musician, the heavenly melodies and sacred rhythms that dwelt within, exuding those delightful songs. Society would have us believe happiness is what we have, not who we are. No doubt you have heard people say, "I would be happy if I had a million dollars," "...lived in a mansion," or "...drove an expensive car." **Sure, it is possible to have these things and still be happy, but these material possessions do not, and will not, produce happiness.**

Ask the wife who has all the jewelry and clothes she could ever imagine, yet discovers her husband is cheating on her. Is she happy? Although someone may have all the money, cars, and houses one could ever want, that does not mean they are happy. Life is more than just achieving your personal goals and acquiring material possessions. True happiness is the direct result of knowing God and living out your purpose. It is about who you are inside, not the things you possess. Without purpose, life is meaningless and ultimately very dissatisfying. Start today living life to the fullest and pursuing God with everything you have.

DAILY CONFESSION

Father, I thank You that my true happiness is determined by who I am,
not by what I possess.

PERCEIVE YOURSELF AT THE LEVEL WHICH YOU DESIRE
LONG BEFORE YOU EVER ATTEMPT TO GO THERE

"Then the Lord brought Abram outside beneath the night sky and told him,
'Look up into the Heavens and count the stars if you can. Your
descendants will be like that—too many to count!"
Genesis 15:5-6 (NLT)

Although most Hebrew young men agreeably followed the footsteps of their fathers, occasionally some rebelled, seeking alternative careers. In these cases, Jewish boys were apprenticed, either by Samaritans or a pagan master called a rav. So great was the boy's determination to be a stonemason or sculptor that he would observe his rav for hours on end, scrutinizing his master's fingers, analyzing the proper usage of the tools, seeing himself one day performing those very same tasks. He envisioned himself as his master—completely. God gave Abram an unforgettable portrait of what his future would hold. From that night on, every time Abram beheld the stars, he was reminded of the promise.

You and I must do the same. Though God may not give you such a tangible picture of your future, He endowed you with a divine imagination. **In the solitude of your mind, you can create any picture you like; you can see yourself being, doing, and having virtually anything.**

Once you define that reality in your mind, move toward it as steadfastly as the Jewish boy toward his rav and the occupation they shared. Your indomitable heart will begin to search out the best path towards its attainment. What you must do is see yourself having already accomplished it. Proverbs 23:7 tell us, "As a man thinketh in his heart, so is he." This is true whether or not we like it. If we are wise, we'll learn to use this divine concept for our benefit. God lives on the inside of us, therefore, our responsibility is to allow Him to express Himself through us.

DAILY CONFESSION
Father, I thank You that I have the mind of Christ.
I think upon Your Word because I am what I think in my heart.

PROMOTION IS THE REWARD FOR STANDING HEAD AND SHOULDERS ABOVE THE REST IN THE EYES OF THOSE WHO MATTER

"Work hard and cheerfully at whatever you do, as though you were working for the Lord rather than for people. Remember that the Lord will give you an inheritance as your reward, and the Master you are serving is Christ."
Colossians 3:23-24 (NLT)

God's holy name is thrown around quite carelessly these days. But did you know the ancient scribe was required to recite a prayer before ever placing ink upon the papyrus whenever using the Holy One's name? And if three or more errors were found on a single page, the entire scroll became unusable, the entire transcription needing to be written anew. But scribes who proved exact and cautiously exceeded all others were rewarded by promotion. Senior scribes were often assigned to their own quarters in the palace or temple, adorned in fine garments, and sought out with high regard. This is a principle about being everything you can be—not about competing with those around you. Nevertheless, you are evaluated by your superiors relative to the performance of your co-workers.

You must exceed the requirements of those around you—not because you want to look better, but because you represent the King of kings who lives and abides in you. Our King demands the highest quality work so others may see your example and give glory to God.

We must stand head and shoulders above the rest. We can't merely stop our efforts when we reach a position that exceeds our current surroundings; we must rise to the absolute highest level possible then stand in faith that God will bring promotion to us. Consistently striving for excellence (as did those senior scribes), coupled with patience and a great attitude, can only bring increase to our life.

DAILY CONFESSION
Father, I thank You that I have the privilege of being called by Your name. I work hard and cheerfully at whatever I do as though working for You rather than people.

NO ONE CAN SURVIVE
THE VICES OF WRONG FRIENDSHIPS

"But Eliezer…prophesied against Jehoshaphat, saying, 'Because you have allied your-self with Ahaziah, the Lord has destroyed your works.' Then the ships were wrecked, so that they were not able to go to Tarshish."
2 Chronicles 20:36-37 (NLT)

✦

If the Bible tells us that King Jehoshaphat did what was pleasing in the sight of the Lord, why then did the Lord destroy his works? It would seem that God would bless Jehoshaphat for his sake, even though the man with whom he went into business was wicked. But no, the opposite actually occurred. The Lord destroyed the work of that good man because he partnered himself with a wicked man. The Mosaic Law taught the Jews and the rest of the world how to live. Cautioning them not to partner with their pagan neighbors, the high-level sanitary code under which the Hebrews dwelled spared them from many a plague. The law additionally employed an elevated standard of integrity, wisely forbidding partnerships, marriages, and worship with iniquitous associations of the foolish, heathen societies surrounding Israel. Whenever they faltered and sought wrong associations, destruction was never far behind.

This challenges much of what has been taught in Christendom over the past several decades. We have believed that God accepts us no matter who we choose as our friends and partners.

Unfortunately, that way of thinking is erroneous, and that very mindset was held by some of our ancient Hebrew ancestors. **In reality, there truly are people God does not want to bless—those who stubbornly reject the principles of His written Word.** No matter who we are, we cannot, and will not, survive the partnership of a wrong relationship when we willfully choose to do so.

DAILY CONFESSION
Father, I thank You that as I walk closely with wise people I myself become wise. I therefore refuse to associate with fools knowing destruction is near.

GODLINESS IS PROOF OF REPENTANCE

"Prove by the way you live that you have really turned
from your sins and turned to God."
Matthew 3:8 (NLT)

There was great proof that the Jewish soldiers who fought during the Hasmonaean uprising were vastly different—transformed by an unknown Force. What was that proof? Refusing to carry arms and engage in combat on the Sabbath, even during a war! After a great number of Jews were ruthlessly slaughtered, however, the rabbis finally decreed that fighting would be permitted during sieges and wars. But this, my friends, frankly proved that these Jewish soldiers gave their lives by honoring God. The apostle James stated, "You show me your faith without your works, I will show you my faith by my works." God is interested in proof. Jesus confirms this by saying: "You will know them by their fruit."

Let us not kid ourselves any longer. **Our daily actions mightily prove whether or not we repented of the wrong we did.** Although many people say, "God knows my heart," that statement doesn't hold up in the courtroom of Heaven. If we truly repent, it is evidenced through our corresponding actions.

Repentance does not exist in the words one speaks, but in the actions of one's life, as it did with the actions of those devout, Jewish soldiers. God requires us to prove what we say to be true with our actions. Jesus tells us, "A good person produces good works from a good heart, and an evil person produces evil works from an evil heart." We must ask ourselves: "Who do my actions prove I am?" The answer may not feel or sound good, but only the truth sets us free.

DAILY CONFESSION
Father, I thank You for forgiving me of the wrong I have done.
I will prove to You by the way I live that I have really turned
from my sins and turned toward Your ways.

CONSISTENT SOWING
IS THE PRECURSOR OF CONSISTENT REAPING

"Don't get tired of doing what is good. Don't get discouraged and give up,
for we will reap a harvest of blessing at the appropriate time."
Galatians 6:9 (NLT)

✦

Thirty-one wonderful years of being a Christian! And what is the greatest negligence I have witnessed in the body of Christ? **Consistency**. So very few are prepared to consistently do something until they attain the desired harvest they are promised. After the early October rains, the Palestinian farmer rose at dawn to sow seeds, either by hand or from a box attached to his plow. Farm owners, slaves, young men and women, children, just about everyone labored from sunrise to sunset, consistently planting seeds in the ground. Even as darkness enveloped the land, many farmers stayed in the fields, relentlessly protecting their crops. It is quite intriguing that God promised all of us the same blessings, but why do some walk in more blessing than others?

I don't ever want to come to a point in my life and discover I could have had something if I would have only stuck with it. In America, it is easy to move from one way of doing things to another. We have a very difficult time being patient because we begin to believe the rest of the world is getting what belongs to us. We then undertake and institute the world's philosophy instead of God's, mistakenly looking to the world to show us how to get what we desire.

The Bible says, "The blessing of the Lord makes one rich and He adds no sorrow to it." **God's way may seem to take a little longer than we would like, but if we continue to consistently do what He commands, we will see our desired harvest.** The key is unfailing consistency!

DAILY CONFESSION
Father, I thank You that I do not give up and grow weary in doing good.
I am unfailing in my life, and I undertake tasks according to
Your standards and not the world's.

BLAMING OTHERS IS PROOF
YOU HAVE NOT YET ACCEPTED RESPONSIBILITY

"'Yes,' Adam admitted, 'but it was the woman You gave me who brought me the fruit, and I ate it.' Then the Lord God asked the woman, 'How could you do such a thing?' 'The serpent tricked me,' she replied. 'That's why I ate it.'"
Genesis 3:12-13 (NLT)

Enclosed in glass, the illustrious sign stated, "The Buck Stops Here." Many of you are no doubt aware that plaque sat humbly on President Harry S. Truman's desk in the White House. The motto boldly implies that I alone take sole responsibility for my life, refusing to blame anyone, or anything, for my present state of being.

The Israelite kings held several crucial responsibilities: commander of the army, supreme judge, absolute master, and imposer of taxes. Some kings blamed others for their rebellion, as in the case of Israel's first king, Saul. King David accepted complete responsibility for his sin, becoming one of the greatest kings ever.

Nevertheless, it all began in the garden; a victim mentality ruthlessly befell humanity. To this day, that mentality afflicts mankind. People believe they are not accountable for their own failure. They blame dysfunctional parents, overwhelming circumstances, insensitive teachers, and anyone else who had a particular role in their life. This conveniently removes the guilt of unfulfilled responsibilities from them.

Winning in life is not hard. Doing it God's way may take longer than we prefer, but it is the safest route. God gave men the power to choose their thoughts. Therefore, we cannot fail without our consent, and we cannot succeed without our participation. We must use the seed in our own hand. Success is not an accident, but neither is failure. Follow the example of King David and stop blaming others. Make the decision today by saying, "The Buck Stops Here."

DAILY CONFESSION
Father, I thank You that You cannot be mocked. Whatever I sow is what I reap.
I thank You for giving me the power to create my future with my seed.

Giving Up What You Want Is The Beginning Of Giving God What He Wants

"For whoever desires to save his life will lose it, but whoever loses his life for My sake and the Gospel's will save it." Mark 8:35 (NKJV)

⚔

Here are two extraordinary questions for you to carefully consider:

- *Why do I want what I want?*
- *How could I even suppose my own desires could compare with the desires God divinely prepared for me?*

Now, here are some possibilities:

Pride—Individuals with a proud heart won't admit they still cling to their own desires. They convince themselves that their own way of doing things is correct, superior, and even Godly.

Comfort—Whatever God leads us to will be great, but it will not be comfortable. People stop surrendering their will to God when the next step requires sacrificing more comfort than they are willing to accept.

Misunderstanding—It is impossible for people to surrender their desires when they don't believe in God's goodness. Those who view God as a traditional dictator (as opposed to a benevolent king) never understand that the scope of God's plan is infinitely more wonderful than a personal dream.

God firmly prohibited the Jews from charging interest on loans of silver, chattel, or produce. Nonetheless, selfish moneychangers often consented to this desire for greed, in direct disregard of the law. Do you currently have a difficult time trying to let go of your own selfish desires? Have you dealt with pride, comfort, or misunderstanding in your life? Deal with it today. Make sure you ask God to search your heart and divest you of any desires that are contrary to Him.

Daily Confession
Father, I realize my life is worth nothing unless I use it to do the work assigned me by You—the work of telling others the Good News about Your wonderful kindness and love.

THE PLANNING OF TODAY
DETERMINES YOUR PERFORMANCE OF TOMORROW

"Good planning and hard work lead to prosperity,
but hasty shortcuts lead to poverty."
Proverbs 21:5 (NLT)

⚓

Following sluggish PC sales and stiff rival competition, one computer corporation was forced to formulate a sweeping plan to tactically overhaul its complete method of operations. "We will restructure, resize, and repurpose," humbly proposed the company's CEO. Thankfully, this executive had a plan, one that would rescue the company's future, and thousands of jobs along with it. Understanding this principle of good planning is vital to the future progress of our lives.

There are countless numbers of individuals who exist discontentedly because they're not where they wish to be. There are others, however, who experience great joy because they reap the rewards of the life they planned. Additionally, far too many believers foolishly reject the interval of time when God attempts to lay the groundwork in order to decisively develop their character. This crucial season of planning is necessary to qualify them for what God desires them to accomplish.

Like the computer company executive who skillfully devised a stratagem, we cannot afford to neglect to plan for our future. What type of builder would attempt to build a skyscraper without first having a blueprint? Why is it any different when building a life? **God wants to bring all of us a great future, but only those who plan will ever experience it.** Although opportunity may come to all, only those who ready themselves can recognize that opportunity when it lands upon their own threshold. Take time now to develop a plan to attain the future you desire. Now is a great time to formulate a sweeping plan.

DAILY CONFESSION
Father, I thank You that good planning and hard work lead to my prosperity,
but hasty shortcuts lead to poverty.

FOCUSING ON WHAT YOU'VE GOT
WILL CAUSE YOU TO FORGET WHAT YOU'VE NOT

"And the Lord said to Abram, after Lot had separated from him: 'Lift your eyes now and look from the place where you are—northward, southward, eastward, and westward; for all the land which you see I give to you and your descendants forever.'" Genesis 13:9, 14-15 (NKJV)

The world's oldest lock is said to be an Egyptian pin tumbler lock found in the ancient ruins of Nineveh. It is fascinating to note that modern cylindrical door locks still operate on this same tumbler principle, discovered thousands of years earlier. The call to follow Jesus requires us to give up, to lock up, and lock away, many things of our past. Whether it is a destructive relationship, a harmful thought pattern, an injurious addiction, or some other negative endeavor, God summons us to sacrifice what we already have in order to possess what we truly value. We, as believers, are required to focus on who we are, and what has been given to us in Christ Jesus. As we focus on what we possess, we will begin to overlook what we have lost. Many of us reading this have lost a job, a home, money, or even a loved one. If we begin to focus on what we've lost in the past, we will become bitter towards others, as well as towards Heaven. So, **we must continually focus on what we have right in front of us.**

God has given to us and done so many things for us—we are blessed. There is no one who can say they have nothing. All possess something for which they can be truly thankful. Society influences many to dwell on what they have lost, and then to devise a plan to retrieve it. We must choose to direct our focus upon what we have in an attempt to forget the things we don't. We must maintain our focus and give thanks for everything we have in our possession, locking up and locking away those things that are behind, throwing away the proverbial key, reaching forward to the upward call of God.

DAILY CONFESSION
Father, I thank You that I do not count myself as having apprehended, but I forget those things which are behind and reach forward to those things which are ahead.

MAN IS GOD'S INSTRUMENT
CREATED TO HEAL HIS PEOPLE

"The Spirit of the Lord is upon Me, for He has appointed Me to preach
Good News to the poor. He has sent Me to proclaim that captives will be released,
that the blind will see, that the downtrodden will be freed from their oppressors."
Luke 4:18 (NLT)

Ah, the translucent warmth of the Caribbean's sunshine. Or perhaps it's the captivating lure of the television set, a new plasma screen beckoning us to watch just "one more movie." While leisure is necessary, how often have we pondered the fact that God called us to fervently continue and lovingly complete the mission of Jesus? **We are ambassadors of God's Kingdom, commissioned on earth to rescue humanity. We are not here simply to relax and enjoy vacations in the sun. We are God's instruments to transmit His will to the nations.**

Whereas Israel relied on the Lord God as their Chief Physician, medical doctors were so highly esteemed in Egypt that they were frequently deified. About 3000 B.C., Egyptian temples were erected to these early doctors of physical healing, many of whom possessed some surgical skill, maintaining a surprising familiarity with the human body. We must never forget what God said in His Word, "Love never fails." People are hurting; people are crying out for someone to come and help them. People want to be free, but they don't know where to turn.

We, as children of the "Great Physician," must help those who are wounded and hurt. Jesus gave us the necessary tools to bring liberty to those in bondage: authority, instruction, love, anointing, and His Holy Spirit. Isn't it time we take our place as instruments of God and begin to allow Him to love and heal His people through us?

DAILY CONFESSION
Father, I thank You that You give me Your love that I may love others as You love me. Your Spirit is upon me and anoints me to preach the Gospel to those who haven't heard.

YOUR FUTURE IS ONLY AS BRIGHT
AS THE PRINCIPLES YOU EMBRACE

*"Now it shall come to pass, if you diligently obey the voice of the Lord
your God, to observe carefully all His commandments which I command you
today, that the Lord your God will set you high above all nations of the earth.
And all these blessings shall come upon you and overtake you, because
you obey the voice of the Lord your God."*
Deuteronomy 28:1-2 (NKJV)

They all qualified—but only a handful served. All males were deemed competent to serve as judges in civil matters, but only priests, Levites, and Israelites of principle—those with spotless character and ancestry—were eligible to judge a criminal case. Christianity eagerly embraces the person of Christ, but ruefully neglects His principles. The person of Jesus creates your peace; His principles create your productivity. Both are as necessary as soil and seed!

People greatly aspire to prosper, but why are so few willing to accurately apply God's principles to their lives? **Our willingness to do what God says is the key to experiencing what God promises.**

God never promised you something without first giving you an instruction. Always rewarding the obedient, He never hands out random promises and rewards like candy at a parade. God is selective in whom He blesses. And you and I determine whether or not God blesses us.

The qualifications of Israel's judges were simple yet distinctive— thorough knowledge of the Law and an ethical lifestyle. Therefore, this principle stands historically correct: Your future is only as bright as the principles you embrace. Apply His principles today and watch God move on your behalf.

DAILY CONFESSION
*Father, I thank You that I diligently obey Your Word and observe
Your commandments. Your blessings come upon me and overtake me
because I choose to obey You.*

FREEDOM IS AN INTERNAL JOURNEY, NOT THE ABSENCE OF EXTERNAL TURMOIL

*"So Christ has really set us free. Now make sure that you stay free,
and don't get tied up again in slavery to the law."*
Galatians 5:1 (NLT)

⚜

Tacky blood dribbled down his stolid face, dotting his muscular forearm with tiny scarlet points. Nonetheless, the strapping middle-aged man did not flinch. His ear was now pierced, proof positive that he rejected the freedom that was dutifully offered him. Biblical law uniquely required that his ear be pierced with an awl if, after six years of servitude, a slave refused to be liberated and decided to remain permanently with his master. He made the decision inwardly, therefore, an outward sign was needed to demonstrate that decision to the world—he chose not to become free.

This principle must be totally understood in order for us to be freed spiritually, financially, emotionally, and physically. **Freedom does not happen from the outside in, but from the inside out.** God clearly called us to walk in this divine freedom. However, we cannot obtain true freedom unless we focus on changing what lies on the inside, before ever attempting to change what's on the outside. Solomon wisely exhorts, "Above all else guard your heart, for from it spring the issues of life." Then the apostle Paul states, "Be ye transformed by the renewing of your mind."

God gave us His Word, the divine handbook of life. We are to fill our hearts and renew our minds with its substance. As we sow the seed of God's Word into our minds, we experience the freedom Jesus purchased for us on the cross. Jesus said, "Continue in My Word, and you shall know the truth and the truth shall make you free." I desire to walk freely, and I believe you do too. Freedom begins with His Word.

DAILY CONFESSION
Father, I thank You that I am free to live as Christ lived. I walk in freedom because I am changed from the inside. I have the truth, and the truth makes me free.

OBEDIENCE IS THE MOST VITAL INGREDIENT
TO INTIMACY WITH GOD

"When you obey Me, you remain in My love,
just as I obey My Father and remain in His love."
John 15:10 (NLT)

By omitting the essential ingredient of obedience, we cannot exhibit the confidence, boldness, and liberty needed to maintain an intimate relationship with God. **Our obedience is vital to the maintenance of daily fellowship with God because He cannot continue a relationship with anyone who is unwilling to comply with His instructions.**

Unfortunately, people continually attempt to have a relationship with God while they live in sin. God does not "incline His ear" nor does He open His mouth to any individual who omits obedience to His Word from his daily spiritual faire. Hasn't God called us to live overcoming and supernatural lives? Indeed. Therefore, He intensely desires to have an intimate relationship with all His children, but only by way of the compelling ingredient of obedience is that made possible.

The more we obey God, the closer we begin to walk with Him. What a privilege it is to have fellowship with God as we intimately hear and willingly carry out what He instructs. Let us never take for granted the grace that has been shown to us. Obedience—never fellowship with God without it!

DAILY CONFESSION
Father, I thank You that as I obey Your Word, I have the confidence,
boldness, and liberty to maintain an intimate relationship with Jesus.
I remain in Your love because I obey Your Word.

ACTION IS THE MISSING LINK
BETWEEN ZEAL AND REWARD

"For I bear them witness that they have a zeal for God,
but not according to knowledge."
Romans 10:2 (NKJV)

✦

The unexpected richness of sweet figs, the soothing texture of apricot sourdough bread, the hearty flavor of stewed barley, and the delicate symbolism of roasted lamb joyously sing a harmony of delight for those who relish the Palestinian cuisine. Trapped in a complex web of unwholesome, prepared foods, more and more people around the world are gaining knowledge concerning the healthy benefits of a Biblical, Mediterranean diet. But how many people are alert enough to seek this information with great zeal? It is the same with Christians, many of whom never truly experience the rewards of Heaven because of their own lack of knowledge. **If Satan keeps us out of the Word of God, he keeps us where we are—feeble, undernourished, and ignorant of our rights and rewards.** We see a great example of this in the parable Jesus illustrates in Luke 15:31, "Son, you are always with me, and all that I have is yours." The son didn't realize that he could partake of his father's goods any time he wanted. God says the same to us today.

In the book of Hosea, we see that God's people perish for lack of knowledge. And isn't it the same in regard to proper food? Remember, Jesus came to give us abundant life. But we will never partake of that life until we know what it includes. We can go no further than the knowledge we possess. We must commit ourselves to careful study and examination of God's Word to discover what is rightfully ours. Passion concerning good health requires great knowledge. Our zeal, combined with our knowledge of Him, propels us like a fighter jet, straight into our Heavenly inheritance.

DAILY CONFESSION
Father, I understand that zeal without knowledge is not good.
Therefore I study Your Word, and search out the information
I need to possess the reward You have for me.

WE ARE CALLED TO FINISH THE RACE,
NOT JUST KEEP THE FAITH

"I have fought the good fight, I have finished the race, I have kept the faith."
2 Timothy 4:7 (NKJV)

⚓

Bread is so recognizable that Jesus even equated Himself to it—"the Bread of Life." But did you know that one of the oldest breads in the world is the "Desert Flat Bread," initially prepared by Moses and his family in the wilderness? Utilizing only four main ingredients, flat bread could be made in a hurry, completed before any number of situations might occur. Our lives are full of starters, but how many actually finish? Everyone has their hair combed, their muscles flexed, and their clothes pressed at the start of a race, but it is how a person finishes the race that really matters. Diplomas are not handed out on registration day; they are handed out on the day of graduation.

All of us start this spiritual race with the intention of finishing, but few actually walk away from the race with a trophy. The apostle Paul victoriously made it to the end of the race God set before him. It did not matter that he got a late start in the race; all that mattered was that he finished it.

We must determine from the very outset that we are going to finish our course better and stronger than when we began. Although we may encounter trials and difficulties, we can overcome them by using them as steppingstones to completion in no time. At the finish line of this race, the King Himself will bestow upon us the victor's crown of life; at that moment, we'll know that all of our striving was worthwhile. May we each finish stronger than we began.

DAILY CONFESSION
Father, I thank You that I fight the good fight. I keep my faith,
and I will finish the race You set before me.

FOCUS IS THE LENS
THROUGH WHICH THE DETERMINED EXPLORE LIFE

"Let your eyes look straight ahead, and your eyelids look right before you.
Ponder the path of your feet, and let all your ways be established.
Do not turn to the right or the left; remove your foot from evil."
Proverbs 4:25-27 (NKJV)

Because of the scent and sight of savory stew, Esau's focus was broken, ripping away his inheritance, his birthright, and his entire life. One of our greatest enemies in life is broken focus. The Bible tells us, "Where there is no vision, the people perish." **People of excellence refuse to break focus because they realize that doing so results in their demise.** The mediocre always focus on what they go through; the excellent focus on what they go to.

How many times have we decided to rise earlier in the morning to pray more? Then, without realizing it, the distractions begin. Perhaps an untidy area catches your attention and you want to straighten it; your child calls and you tend to them; and then a phone call saps your time. All the while, in your mind, you tell God, "I'll be back in a minute." One thing leads to another, and before you know it, the day is half gone. This situation is not uncommon. Days lead to weeks, which lead to months, until one day we look back at our lives and ask, "How did I get here?"

We must continue to look straight ahead and not allow ourselves to be distracted. Esau was sorely distracted and he lost everything! Our ability to maintain focus causes us to rise above the circumstances that come our way, and excel above the expectation of those God called to promote us.

DAILY CONFESSION
I attend to my Father's Words and incline my ears to His sayings. I keep
His principles before my eyes and keep them in the midst of my heart,
for they bring life and health to all my flesh.

ALL FAILURE IS LINKED
TO A DISREGARDED INSTRUCTION

"My child, listen to me and do as I say, and you will have a long, good life.
I will teach you wisdom's ways and lead you in straight paths. If you live a life guided
by wisdom, you won't limp or stumble as you run. Carry out my instructions;
don't forsake them. Guard them, for they will lead you to a fulfilled life."
Proverbs 4:10-13 (NLT)

⚜

The Word of God constantly points us in the direction of success in all areas of life. We have the blueprint of success achieved by the men and women of God who ran this race before us. This blueprint shows us the reward of a life filled with wisdom.

The only times we have breakdowns in our lives is simply because we missed, disobeyed, or disregarded an instruction. We basically missed an ingredient in the recipe of life. However, when we follow the instructions of the Master and do what He says, we can expect a life of fulfillment and peace with others.

Remember, failure comes only to those who do not choose the narrow pathway that leads to success. Today, why not strive for the application of the wisdom of God and watch how your life is transformed and blessed!

DAILY CONFESSION
Father, I listen to Your Word and I do what You say. I live a life guided by wisdom; I won't limp or stumble as I run. I carry out Your instructions and guard them for they lead me to a fulfilled life.

OBEDIENCE BEGINS IN THE HEART
LONG BEFORE IT EVER REACHES YOUR FEET

"And I will give you a new heart with new and right desires,
and I will put a new spirit in you. I will take out your stony
heart of sin and give you a new, obedient heart."
Ezekiel 36:26 (NLT)

Obeying the dietary needs given in God's Word, the Jews served a number of beans and peas, necessary for protein and nourishment. Petrified beans have even been discovered in recent excavations. Without proper obedience, those ancient Jews would have walked around undernourished and frail.

Jesus told the story of two boys who were given an instruction. One said he would do it, but he never did. The other said he wouldn't do what he was asked, but shortly afterward, he felt conviction in his heart and completed the instruction. Even though this boy denied the instruction with his lips, his sense of obedience permeated all the way to his heart. From there, he went to work, and no doubt afterward returned to his father to tell him he obeyed.

I believe very strongly in voicing our desire to obey, but I believe even more strongly in putting our obedience into action. If you are a believer, you have a new heart that really desires to obey. But sometimes, heartfelt obedience is imprisoned by pride, bitterness, and offense. **We must go to battle to rescue the obedient heart God gave us.** Then, we can get to work with our instructions, both from men and from Heaven. And last, we can declare, "I obeyed."

DAILY CONFESSION
Father, I thank You that You took out my old, stony heart of sin and gave me a new, obedient heart in its place. I follow through with every instruction I'm given, both from You and from delegated authority.

ALL PROMOTION MUST BE EARNED; IT IS NEVER A RESULT OF YOUR EXISTENCE

"Good planning and hard work lead to prosperity,
but hasty shortcuts lead to poverty."
Proverbs 21:5 (NLT)

In my own life, I had to come to grips with the fact that I must earn any promotion I desire. In America, it is easy to believe we should be rewarded for simply showing up. Many believe you should receive a bonus for being employed through the end of December. God shows us throughout His Word that He desires for us to be promoted. God is our employer, and that is why the apostle Paul encourages us to "work hard and cheerfully at whatever you do, as though you were working for the Lord rather than for people."

The modern state of Israel was born in 1948, but it is based upon four thousand years of history and tradition. When Jews around the world learned of their nation's birth, each one was spiritually promoted. God finally brought them back to their ancient land, and it is the same God who promotes us.

Any promotion that we receive unethically or through cutting corners will be taken away from us. However, if we earn a promotion through hard work and faithfulness, there is no level we will not attain, either at our workplace or in our spiritual walk. Begin today to earn the promotion you desire. **A promotion is not a miracle God grants us apart from our earning it. God promotes anybody who is productive and happy.** Heaven watches just waiting, as it did over the Jews, for a reason to promote those who willingly apply God's Word.

DAILY CONFESSION
Father, I thank You that I am diligent all the days of my life.
I refuse to expect promotion for which I do not work.
I choose to work hard and cheerfully at whatever I do.

OBEDIENCE IS THE ONLY EVIDENCE THAT STANDS UP IN THE COURT OF HEAVEN

"He who has My commandments and keeps them, it is he who loves Me.
And he who loves Me will be loved by My Father, and
I will love him and manifest Myself to him."
John 14:21 (NKJV)

The Passover Seder is an ancient holiday meal symbolizing the Jews' escape from Egypt. Because of their love for God, Jewish communities even today still celebrate this festive meal. The apostle James said, "You have faith and I have works, show me your faith without your works and I will show you my faith by my works." Only when you obey what is written do Heaven and earth know your love for God. Jesus confirmed it saying, "So that the world may know that I love the Father, I do as He commanded."

True love can be plainly seen; false love only wants to be obnoxiously heard. God rarely verbally declared His love—He simply showed it. You will notice that the Bible says, "For God so loved the world that He gave…" (John 3:16). "For God commendeth His love towards us in that while we were yet sinners Christ died for us" (Romans 5:8). It doesn't say that God verbally declared His love to His people. No, He demonstrated His love by sending a gift. Not just any gift might I add; a very costly gift—the best He had to offer.

God proved His love through His Son. And we must prove our love, loving God as passionately as the Jews celebrate the Passover Seder, through our faithful obedience to His commands.

DAILY CONFESSION
Father, I thank You that I have Your commandments and I choose to keep them.
I love You and continually prove my love to You by obeying Your commands.

FORGIVENESS IS THE PERFUME
THAT THE BROKEN HEART CASTS BACK
UPON THE FOOT THAT CRUSHED IT

"You must make allowance for each other's faults and forgive the person who offends you. Remember, the Lord forgave you, so you must forgive others."
Colossians 3:13 (NLT)

✦

The bitter herb found on the Seder plate, usually foul-smelling horseradish, helps Jews around the world deal with the remembrance of the bitter things that happened before and during their flight from Egypt. One of the most effective weapons hell possesses is bitterness. God gave us the mighty weapon of forgiveness to combat bitterness. Bitterness wipes the smile from the heart and siphons passion from someone who desires to serve God and love His people. It paralyzes the gifts and abilities God placed within us.

In order to experience true happiness, we must overcome any offense that Satan brings our way. People will utter unkind words concerning us, hurt us, and even betray us. Yet, we must respond in faith and forgive anyone who wrongs us. **Through forgiveness, we defeat the spirit of bitterness, conquering it once and for all.**

Understanding how much Jesus forgave us is crucial when it comes to us forgiving others. We cannot afford to harbor offense within our hearts. Unforgiveness leads to sickness and disease within our bodies. We must be quick to follow the words of the apostle Paul, "Let all bitterness, and wrath, and anger, and clamor, and evil speaking, be put away from you, with all malice: and be kind one to another, tenderhearted, forgiving one another, even as God for Christ's sake hath forgiven you" (Ephesians 4:31-32). By following this instruction to forgive, we can walk free from bitterness (and its foul smell) and live tenderhearted, peaceable lives.

DAILY CONFESSION
Father, I thank You that I make allowance for the faults of others and I forgive those who offend me.

THE ENVIRONMENT YOU EMBRACE
WILL DETERMINE THE PERSON YOU BECOME

"But they delight in doing everything the Lord wants; day and night they think about His law. They are like trees planted along the riverbank, bearing fruit each season without fail. Their leaves never wither, and in all they do, they prosper."
Psalm 1:2-3 (NLT)

✦

By embracing this principle, we understand the importance of maintaining God's presence. I personally consider the morning hour as the gauge for the rest of my day. I always begin my day by pursuing God's presence. I then carefully maintain His presence throughout the day. The progress and success of my day is methodically linked to the time I spend with God in the morning.

A bowl of salt water sits upon every Passover table. What does it represent? The salty water represents the tears that were shed by those who made the trek to the Promised Land, the environment that would determine that the Jews were truly the people of God.

We must surround ourselves with God's presence, either by listening to the Word of God or playing worship music. Our environment determines our progress, just as getting to the Promised Land determined the progress of the Jews.

As Christians, our desire should be to intimately know God and to possess the character of Christ. To do so, we need to create the proper environment. While a farmer must cultivate the soil before planting seed, we must create an atmosphere in which our life can be shaped into the likeness of our Lord. We must make a commitment to create the environment that assures us of future progress.

DAILY CONFESSION
Father, I thank You that I do not follow the advice of the wicked, or stand in the way of sinners, or join in with scoffers. My delight and desire is in Your Word, and I habitually meditate and orally recite Your Word day and night.

PEACE IS NOT THE ABSENCE OF TURMOIL;
IT IS KNOWING THE PRESENCE OF GOD

"These things I have spoken to you, that in Me you may have peace. In the world
you will have tribulation; but be of good cheer, I have overcome the world."
John 16:33 (NKJV)

Not only was there a bitter herb set upon the Passover table, but there was also a sweet, delicate herb. Parsley is that customary herb, used to remind Jews of the sweet, peaceful incidents that no doubt occurred during their long journey to the land God prepared for them. **But God cares far more about your faith than He does about your comfort.** We read in 1 Peter 1:7 that trials are only tests of our faith, to show that it is strong and pure.

In Job 23:8-9, Job records his search for God, "I go east, but He is not there. I go west, but I cannot find Him. I do not see Him in the north, for He is hidden. I turn to the south, but I cannot find Him." It could have appeared to Job that God had entirely abandoned him. All of his efforts to find God's presence in his turmoil led to nothing until we come to verse 10, which says, "But He knows..." Job acknowledges that God knows his state, and if God knows, then He must be near!

He continues, "But He knows where I am going, and when He has tested me like gold in a fire, He will pronounce me innocent." Do those sound like the words of an anxious, fretful man? No! His words come from a heart that is assured of God's faithfulness even in his trouble, and because of that, great peace, as celebrated with the sweet herb, guards his heart and fixates his mind.

Let me ask you, has God ever failed you before? Even once? Then why would He fail you now? Remember His faithfulness in times past, and rest in the peace He so generously provides.

DAILY CONFESSION
Father, I thank You that I walk in Your righteousness, and that You never
allow me to be moved, made to fall, slip, or fail.

YOUR REWARDS IN LIFE
ARE IN DIRECT PROPORTION TO THE PROBLEMS
YOU ARE WILLING TO SOLVE FOR OTHERS

*"Work hard and cheerfully at whatever you do, as though
you were working for the Lord rather than for people."*
Colossians 3:23 (NLT)

Salt water, parsley, horseradish, and now a hard boiled egg curiously rest upon the Jewish table. Why a hard boiled egg? Rolled or roasted over a fire or stove, the egg represents the many sacrifices offered to God upon the Hebrew altar. And sacrifice comes in many ways. It is easy to understand why so many people go unrewarded in life—they rarely seem to understand the correlation between the sacrifice of solving problems that eventually leads to the sure road of promotion. Most people stop progressing upwardly the moment their present environment no longer pleases them. **Our value is linked to our willingness to solve problems for those God placed over us…in our lives…at our jobs…and even in our marriage.** When we begin to passionately solve problems, we receive the favor necessary to bring us the promotion we desire.

Many simply exist at their jobs and in their daily routines, sailing roughly through life's meandering seas, unwilling to serve those around them. We can never grumble about life and expect the blessings of Heaven. Although productivity plays a great role within our lives, it is our attitude that causes our productivity to become pleasing. Everyone loves to be around an individual with a great attitude. Therefore, we must cheerfully and sacrificially solve the problems of those we serve. Let us ask: What problems can we solve for our authorities? What can we do to make their lives more productive?

The sacrificial fulfillment of these answers brings you ever-increasing promotion. Choose to be a problem solver today.

DAILY CONFESSION
*Father, I thank You that I do everything cheerfully as unto You.
I possess a great attitude. I am a problem solver and
continue to walk in ever-increasing favor.*

YOUR PRESENT PERSPECTIVE IS NO MORE
THAN AN EXPRESSION OF YOUR SELF–IMAGE

"There we saw the giants (the descendants of Anak came from the giants);
and we were like grasshoppers in our own sight, and so we were in their sight."
Numbers 13:33 (NKJV)

✦

Now, please allow me to ask which of the following questions is the most important in regard to the way you see yourself:

- *How others see you?*
- *How you see yourself?*
- *Or how God sees you?*

At first guess you may say, how God sees me, of course! Although it is important how God views us, it doesn't override the inner image we have of ourselves. Let me clarify. While you were living in sin, distant from God, did God view you any different than He does right now? No, He certainly didn't. His Word is the same yesterday, today, and forever. Psalm 139:17 says, "How precious also are Your thoughts to me, O God! How great is the sum of them." God has always thought only positive things about you.

In His eyes, you are righteous. You are pure, holy, and just. But how do you see yourself? Do you see yourself as righteous, holy, pure, and just? Or do you see yourself worthless even in Christ? Do you like yourself? Do you see yourself victorious? The Israelites saw themselves as grasshoppers, but Solomon said it like this, "As he thinks in his heart, so is he." **How God thinks about you is not the issue; it is how you think about you.** Begin today to implant God's thoughts into your internal hard drive and cultivate the self-image of Christ Himself. Only then, can you walk as Christ did.

DAILY CONFESSION
Father, I thank You that my present perspective is an expression of my inner
self-image. Therefore I choose to embrace Your thoughts and take captive
every thought that is contrary to what You say about me.

YOUR HEART IS THE SOIL WHERE THOUGHTS
BECOME THE SEEDS THAT CREATE THE FUTURE

"Keep your heart with all diligence, for out of it spring the issues of life."
Proverbs 4:23 (NKJV)

⚜

The final item on the Passover table is something called charoses. Charoses is made from ground apples, red wine, cinnamon, and sugar. This paste looks very much like mortar and represents the mortar the Israelites heaped upon the bricks when they were slaves. Charoses is the very heart of the Passover table, the seed that created Israel's future.

The voices and thoughts that enter your mind are also seeds. You have a choice over which seeds get planted and which get rejected. Your heart becomes the fertile soil where those seeds are planted, become mature, and produce fruit. There is no way to avoid this process of "heart germination," for the Bible tells us in Proverbs 4:23 that this is how God designed the human heart to function. "Keep [manage, tend, protect, safeguard, watch over, preserve, chaperon, care for, be a good steward over] your heart with all diligence, for out of it spring the issues of life." The only way to assure good outcomes in your life is to plant good seeds inside your heart.

When I went through a difficult period in my life, it primarily occurred because early in my childhood, bad seeds were planted inside my heart, and those seeds matured, producing bad fruit. Destructive thought-seeds take root and begin to grow because you choose to believe what they say is the truth. Additionally, you even begin to believe evil concerning yourself. It is important to realize that any thought left unchallenged is established as fact. Therefore, take the abundance of seeds of God's Word and sprinkle them onto the soil of your heart (the charoses, the mortar), give it some time, and watch it grow a bountiful and life-changing harvest.

DAILY CONFESSION
Father, I thank You that I keep my heart with all diligence for out of it spring the issues of life.

GOD'S WILL FOR YOUR LIFE IS HIDDEN
WITHIN THE PAGES OF HIS HOLY WORD

"Friendship with the Lord is reserved for those who fear Him.
With them He shares the secrets of His covenant."
Psalm 25:14 (NLT)

✦

I hear it far too often, "Pastor, I just want to know God's will for my life." My simple response to them is, "What does His Word tell you to do?" Have you stopped to realize that God rarely speaks to those who are unwilling to do His Word? His will for our lives is simple—obey His Word! When Israel obeyed, eagerly and respectfully following God's desires, things went great. But when they stubbornly ignored Him, their enemies were waiting at the front gate!

Obedience to His Word is His will for our lives. Some may say, "Well, Pastor, who am I supposed to marry… What am I supposed to do for a career…?" Obey! Obey! Obey! There is no way around it.

Obedience is the path that leads you down God's hidden will for your life. He does not, and will not, reveal His hidden will until we first do His known will. As you journey down the path of obedience, a divine peace will capture your soul concerning the unknown will of God for your life. Refuse to follow the example of the ancient Israelites when they ignored God. Choose now to obey!

DAILY CONFESSION
Father, I thank You that I am a doer of Your Word and I am continually transformed. I choose to obey having complete confidence that Your unknown will for my life will be manifest.

Obedience Is The Key That Unlocks The Door To God's Purpose For Your Life

"If you keep yourself pure, you will be a utensil God can use for His purpose.
Your life will be clean, and you will be ready for the Master
to use you for every good work."
2 Timothy 2:21 (NLT)

How would you react if you were in dire need of an operation, but every surgeon in town refused to take time to sterilize his equipment? Would you take the chance of being slashed open with dirty, bacteria-laden instruments?

Cleanliness possesses an immeasurable worth in almost every area in of life. And since God has a specific purpose and plan for each of our lives, this unique plan can only be discovered through daily obedience – keeping ourselves pure, clean, and ready. The moment we begin to obey is the precise moment that destiny's door begins to swing adventurously open. **The dreams and desires God has for our futures are contained within the seed of diligent obedience.** It is a sad thing, but many individuals never discover what they were meant to do here on earth simply because they refuse to obey.

Satan attempts to keep the door shut tight to the room of our assignment; but God promises that our obedience is the strategic key to unlock that closed door. Heaven always uses the obedient to do great and mighty things in the earth. But before Heaven can use us, we must change our thinking from "Obedience is all God requires of me," to, "I have an assignment and a divine purpose, and obedience will take me to it." I believe we are of those who will do great and mighty things for our King in the earth, don't you?

Daily Confession
Father, I thank You that I am a pure utensil You can use for Your purpose.
My life is clean, and I am ready for You to use me for every good work.
I hear Your voice, and I am obedient to Your Word.

OFFENSE IS NEVER ALLOWED TO ENTER
THE ATMOSPHERE OF A SERVANT

"Then David stood at the mouth of the cave and called to Saul, 'My master!
My king!' Saul looked back. David fell to his knees and bowed in reverence.
He called out, 'Why do you listen to those who say 'David is out to get you'?
This very day with your very own eyes you have seen that just now in the cave
God put you in my hands. My men wanted me to kill you, but I wouldn't do it.
I told them that I won't lift a finger against my master—he's God's anointed.'"
1 Samuel 24:8-10 (MESSAGE)

What could possibly be a greater reason to get offended than being hunted by the one you are trying to serve? David gave his life for the king's service—he served faithfully in the army and loyally in the palace. In everything he did, his heart was toward Saul, and for Saul's prosperous reign. Never did he see himself as the one who should be king in Saul's place, though he knew very well that such would be the case one day. **He entrusted himself to the hand of God, who always judges justly, and who sets kings on thrones or removes them from power.**

While in the wilderness, the Jews were in constant offense. Sometimes it was Moses. Sometimes it was their environment. And most often it was God. They literally breathed an atmosphere of wretched offense.

Do you or I have any reason to get offended in light of what David endured? Have we left our family and all our desires for another's sake? And have we, in turn, been hunted for our death? Of course not! What kept David from being offended with Saul? It was his purity of heart—he wanted what was best for the king, not what he could get from the king. If we develop that heart toward the people around us, especially our superiors, we won't have further bouts with offense.

DAILY CONFESSION
Father, I thank You that I love Your Word and I do not get offended.
I develop a servant's heart so that I am always free from the offense of others.

THE GENUINE SERVANT WELCOMES
THE OPPORTUNITY TO PROVE HIS AUTHENTICITY

*"Investigate my life, O God, find out everything about me; cross-examine and
test me, get a clear picture of what I'm about; see for Yourself whether I've
done anything wrong—then guide me on the road to eternal life."*
Psalm 139:23-24 (MESSAGE)

✦

Genuine servants have nothing to hide. They are not interested in
any selfish gain, nor do they wear their feelings on their sleeves.
Rather, they set aside their personal agenda to become whatever is
necessary for the one they serve. At first, this way of thinking is very
difficult to conceive. Thoughts like: "But what about me?" and "I'm
not a slave!" wrestle with a person's decision to become a servant. In
time, though, **a genuine servant develops a heart that really desires
the best for the one being served, regardless of the personal sacrifice involved.**

If we truly are servants, then no task requires more than we can
bestow. Whatever it takes, that's what we will do. In Psalm 139, the
Psalmist makes himself entirely vulnerable to God. This request
comes from a confident and humble heart. Confidence because he did
everything he knew to do, humility because he was willing to learn
what he didn't know about himself. A genuine servant must develop
these virtues as he searches for an authentic seal of approval.

DAILY CONFESSION
*Father, I thank You that You search me and know me through and through.
Create inside of me all that is pleasing to You.*

INTEGRITY IS THE FOUNDATION
UPON WHICH YOUR LIFE IS BUILT

"He who walks with integrity walks securely,
but he who perverts his ways will become known."
Proverbs 10:9 (NKJV)

A number of years ago, my father, Peter Daniels, and I traveled to California to meet with Dr. Robert Schuller. Dr. Schuller proceeded to tell us how the "Golden State" was experiencing an influx of new homebuyers. He also mentioned that when most of the people buy homes, they place great emphasis on the state's beautiful scenery and gorgeous weather, forgetting to think about the ground upon which the house rests. (If you are not aware, most of California sits on the dreaded San Andreas Fault.)

These people failed to realize how important the foundation is to the very future of the home they so greatly desired. In the same way, character is the only sure foundation to any successful business, healthy marriage, or fulfilling life.

It is your daily decisions, constructive thoughts, and encouraging associations that firmly shape your character. Neglect a stable foundation, and whatever you build in life will soon come tumbling down as if destroyed by an earthquake. Don't set yourself up for disappointment. Why not stand upon God's Word in all that you do?

DAILY CONFESSION
Father, I thank You that I walk in integrity therefore I walk securely.
I refuse to pervert my way, for he who perverts his way becomes known.

POVERTY IS NOT THE LACK OF MONEY; POVERTY IS THE PROOF OF MISGUIDED MONEY

"It is possible to give freely and become more wealthy,
but those who are stingy will lose everything."
Proverbs 11:24 (NLT)

⚜

For some time, the body of Christ has identified poverty with lack of money. Just because you don't have money doesn't mean you are impoverished. Many times, the lack of money or what is known as poverty is the result of years of someone misguiding their money. Those who are obedient to sow their money always tend to have more. God is a God of abundance, and He has insight as to where we should sow.

I remember years ago, when I was a young boy, hearing a conversation between my mother and father. My father inquired of my mother, "What should we buy—beer or bread?" At that time, we didn't have enough money for both, so they had to choose between beer and bread. My mother responded, "Let's buy beer." It wasn't that my parents didn't have money. They just used their money in the wrong way.

God calls us to give a tenth to our church. He calls us to feed the poor and help those less fortunate, and to sow into the lives of others for the good they did in our lives. The moment we begin to follow these instructions is when our days of lack are over. **When we focus our money in the right direction, money increases. We reap only what we sow.** If we don't sow anything, we have no right to expect a harvest. How do you spend your money? Do you see it as a seed, or simply money? Do you generously give it, or do you hoard it? Does it go toward the things of God, or toward fulfilling the lusts of your flesh? Where your money goes determines whether you walk in abundance or in poverty. Poverty is not the lack of money; poverty is the proof of misguided money. The choice is yours.

DAILY CONFESSION
Father, I thank You that I am a giver. I generously scatter abroad,
and I increase more. I refuse to withhold knowing it will lead to lack.

GOD'S PROTECTION IS ACTIVATED
THE MOMENT YOU WALK IN INTEGRITY

"He grants a treasure of good sense to the Godly.
He is their shield, protecting those who walk with integrity."
Proverbs 2:7 (NLT)

⚜

No matter what problem or challenge we may face in our lives, we must, at all costs, conduct ourselves as people of integrity. Our integrity unmistakably defines who we are. We must fervently keep our word and conduct ourselves with a resolute adherence to God's standards in order to represent Christ effectively. By doing so, we are kept securely beneath the covenant promise of God's protection. He is unable to protect us when we step out of the perimeter of His principles, which are clearly defined in Scripture.

Solomon speaks of this when he declares, "He is their shield, protecting those who walk in integrity." We are to be absolutely committed to keep, not only the Word of God, but our word as well.

We can never afford to allow our integrity to be questioned. We must live above the expectations and standards set by others, over performing in all of our assignments. Remember, Satan comes to steal, kill, and destroy; he prowls around like a lion, seeking whom he may devour.

Only our integrity delivers us from the brutal attacks of the enemy. But **we must choose integrity, knowing that our future success depends upon it.**

DAILY CONFESSION
Father, I thank You for granting a treasure of good sense to me because
I walk in Your ways. You are my shield protecting me in all of my dealings,
for I walk with integrity.

ACTION IS THE MISSING INGREDIENT
TO A LIFETIME FILLED WITH PRODUCTIVITY

"…but the message they heard did not benefit them,
because it was not mixed with faith…"
Hebrews 4:2 (AMP)

⋏

Strategically placed against the serenity of the emerald blue Mediterranean Sea, like a sapphire adhered to its setting, the tiny area of Palestine is even today desired for the robustly productive territory it contains. Known as the land of "milk and honey" in Old Testament times, distinctive crops and indigenous plants such as black cumin, coriander, anise, cassia, and pomegranate make their home in the rich soil of modern Israel. When this soil is actively cultivated, delicious goods are produced.

All of us know how important it is to make our works count, and to make certain that what we say actually happens. If we relentlessly hear about God's Word and never act upon it, then nothing will happen for us. But we must stir the Word of God into our daily habits, as if combining tender Palestinian seasonings into a fantastic dish. Blending it into our home life as well, it will wonderfully produce. As we daily act on God's Word, we experience productivity.

Develop an ability to act; you don't need to rush, but neither should your time be squandered. Act when the instruction is fresh. There are many who intend to take action, but wait too long and the passion to produce dwindles away like seeds in the wind.

Take action today on whatever you have procrastinated. Remember, faith is acting on the Word of God.

DAILY CONFESSION
Father, I thank You that I am a person of faith. I mix action with what I hear from Your Word. I walk by what You say, and not by what I believe.

FAILURES FOCUS ON THE PAIN
OF THEIR PRESENT WHILE WINNERS FOCUS
ON THE PLEASURE OF THE FUTURE

"While we do not look at the things which are seen, but at the things
which are not seen. For the things which are seen are temporary,
but the things which are not seen are eternal."
2 Corinthians 4:18 (NKJV)

It happens every year, doesn't it? Whether it's the winter's first few inches of slushy snow, the tiniest threat of a brewing hurricane, or the slightest possibility of any perceived shortage; just as soon as the rumor hits the airwaves, what usually happens? You guessed it—the supermarkets are flooded with people, anxiety-driven folks who must charge out for milk and eggs, even though many of them have two refrigerators completely filled with food. Friends, we have to stop panicking! If we are going to believe God, then let's act like it! Care, anxiety, and heart-stopping fear indicate that we lost sight of God's promises. But how do we become fully persuaded, once and for all? Romans 10:17 says tells us that "faith comes by hearing, and hearing by the Word of God."

To find a place of peace and overcome the worries in life, we must realize that everything externally functions precisely according to what we believe internally. Unless we are meditating on God's Word, the outcome of our lives won't be very appealing. Neither prayer nor any other activity can override the turmoil created by neglecting the meditation of God's Word. **We must install God's Word into our conscious and subconscious minds** (with as much desire as when loading our favorite DVD), **before we can walk in the peace that passes all understanding, creating an unwavering scarcity of anxiety and fear for the remainder of our lives.**

DAILY CONFESSION
Father, I thank You that Your Word is eternal and unchanging.
I am a champion, and I focus on the dream of my future.

IT IS NOT WHAT HAS BEEN DONE TO YOU THAT DETERMINES THE OUTCOME OF YOUR LIFE BUT HOW YOU RESPOND TO INJUSTICE THAT DECIDES YOUR DESTINY

"And David was greatly distressed; for the people spake of stoning him, because the soul of all the people was grieved, every man for his sons and for his daughters: but David encouraged himself in the Lord his God."
1 Samuel 30:6 (KJV)

✦

The Hebrew farmer's preparations did not always go according to plan. Wind, hail, mildew, hot desert winds, or invasion by locusts, cankerworms, and caterpillars may have devastated his crops. When this happened, did that farmer give up and curse God? When life doesn't go the way you planned, step back. How can you righteously respond to the situation?

Remember, you are in charge of your attitude, so you cannot blame your response on anyone or anything but yourself. Understanding why you feel the way you do can relieve a lot of your frustration. Filter your emotions through God's Word. Find out how Jesus would respond. What would He do in your situation?

Attitude is not based on circumstances or people. It's all about how we choose to respond! A wife cannot blame her depression on the way her husband treats her. An employee can't blame his bad attitude on the boss. When his crops failed, the Hebrew farmer always had another season in which to plant, a divine opportunity to start all over again. **There's always something positive to focus upon—discover it, and you are on your way to a great future!**

DAILY CONFESSION
Father, I thank You that as David encouraged himself in You, so I encourage myself in You. I understand what is done to me does not seal the fate of my life, but how I respond to injustice determines my destiny.

YOUR VALUE AS A PERSON DOES NOT COME FROM YOUR RACE, COLOR, OR CREED BUT BY THE TYPES OF PROBLEMS YOU SOLVE IN LIFE

"In this new life, it doesn't matter if you are a Jew or a Gentile,
circumcised or uncircumcised, barbaric, uncivilized, slave, or free.
Christ is all that matters, and He lives in all of us."
Colossians 3:11 (NLT)

⚜

"Red and yellow, black and white…" brown, green, purple, or plaid, it doesn't matter! All that matters in the world in which we live is the problems you choose to solve for others. Now, I understand that certain socio-economic backgrounds or cultural characteristics may present you with more obstacles than another person, but you both have the same bulldozer with which to knock down those obstacles—problem solving is the key!

Israel's farmers are blessed with two major seasons: the rainy season from October to April, and the dry season from approximately mid-May to mid-October. No matter what occurs with the weather, these skillful planters are well prepared with irrigation systems arranged to water the fields. They have a huge problem to solve—feeding the people of their nation.

Unfortunately, many people nurse their own wounds, claiming that because of this or that, life isn't fair to them. That's certainly not true, and it rarely does any good. Instead, stand up tall, declare who you are in Christ, and set out to be the answer to the problems in the world today. **Life is no respecter of persons.** God does not deny a person whose heart is set on solving problems. He is always faithful to you when you choose to be a problem solver.

DAILY CONFESSION
Father, I thank You that I am in Christ and
all that matters is that Christ is in me.

EVERY RELATIONSHIP HAS BOTH RULES TO ENTER AND TO REMAIN WITHIN IT

"You are My friends if you do whatever I command you."
John 15:14 (NKJV)

God says that those whom He placed within our lives to lead us do not bear the sword in vain. If our superiors have to use the "sword" on us, we know that we did not qualify for God's rewards.

God has scheduled the benefits I will enjoy if I love my wife as Christ loves the church. He has also scheduled negative consequences if I choose not to love my wife. That is why I don't concern myself with her role as a wife; that is her responsibility. My job is to make certain that I fulfill my role as husband so I can enjoy the benefits of my obedience to God!

God cannot change the consequences of our choices, for consequences are dictated by the universal law of sowing and reaping, experienced by farmers of every race, color, and creed. If we choose to be disobedient, our rebellion initiates a time bomb that will eventually explode into a thousand pieces, bringing destruction into our lives, and shattering the lives of those around us

I realize that I strongly influence the lives of those who are close to me. If that influence is not positive, then I don't qualify for that relationship. Knowing this to be true, my prayer is that my friends and my superiors will confront me with what must be changed. This is the humble attitude God requires all of us to consistently maintain in our relationships. Only then can we experience the reward of positive relationships.

DAILY CONFESSION
Father, I thank You that I am a friend of Jesus, not because He died for me, but because I obey the instructions He gives to me.

ALL MEN WANT TO EXCEL,
BUT FEW ARE WILLING TO PAY THE PRICE

*"Do you not know that those who run in a race all run,
but one receives the prize? Run in such a way that you may obtain it."*
1 Corinthians 9:24 (NKJV)

⬥

Often working in conjunction with the Hebrew farmer was the shepherd. Few Bible students realize, however, the tremendous sacrifice true shepherds faced. Often exposed to frigid, inclement weather, he dressed in rough animal skins, carrying a thick club for protection against thieves and wild animals. When the flocks remained outdoors at night, the shepherd slept attentively beside his flock, waking several times to ensure their safety. Sacrifice—this principle stands true in any area of life—diets, stronger relationship with God, finances, intimacy between spouses, etc. **I have discovered that life doesn't usually give us what we want. Life usually gives to us what we deserve.** Or perhaps I can state it this way: life gives us what we work for, not what we think we should have. The Bible says, "Go to the ant you sluggard! Consider her way and be wise, which, having no captain, overseer or ruler, provides her supplies in the summer, and gathers her food in the harvest."

Excellence doesn't just happen by chance. You have to passionately and diligently pursue it. Excellence comes with a price tag, but I guarantee it is cheaper than compromise. Compromise costs your life, whereas excellence asks from you to give 100% every day. Make every day count. Live as though today was your last day on earth. Learn sacrifice, and obtain the prize by:

- *Paying any price to change.*
- *Paying the price to have a deeper relationship with God.*

You'll never be the same once you make the dedicated decision to pursue excellence in every area of your life.

DAILY CONFESSION
*Father, I thank You that I run the race of life in such a way as to win the prize.
I compete against myself and I always look to help others obtain the prize as well.*

THE SEED YOU CAST UPON THE WAVES OF ETERNITY
WILL RETURN UPON THE SHORES OF THIS LIFE

"Cast your bread upon the waters, for you will find it after many days."
Ecclesiastes 11:1 (NKJV)

Faith and patience are key factors in the process of sowing seed. Anyone who has been a giver for any length of time understands there is a vital season of waiting between every seed sown and every harvest grown. Notice the scripture above states, "…it will come back to you after many days." There is a season of time between when we sow our seed, and when we reap a harvest.

One's unwillingness to wait patiently has aborted the harvest of countless seeds. You must be willing to trust God through the seasons of waiting. Israel's shepherds had a choice—they could either sow superior seeds with their neighbors by being careful where their flocks grazed, or they could sow unfavorable seeds by allowing their animals to roam freely upon other people's properties, instead of waiting for suitable lands. Their peers viewed those who were impatient as dishonest.

Impatience weakens our faith to the point where we begin to entertain thoughts that sowing doesn't work. We must keep up our faith, remain patient, and decisively obey the laws of God concerning sowing and reaping…then our harvest is assured. Friends, never grow weary, for in due time, you shall receive your overflowing harvest.

DAILY CONFESSION
Father, I thank You that I am a giver. I know that with the measure I give,
my harvest will be given back to me; good measure, pressed down,
shaken together, and overflowing shall men give unto my bosom.

YOU'LL NEVER HEAR WHAT JESUS IS SAYING UNTIL YOU FIRST HAVE DONE WHAT JESUS SAID

"So why do you call Me 'Lord,' when you won't obey Me?"
Luke 6:46 (NLT)

Isn't it interesting to note how many believers tell people, "This is what Jesus told me," when there is no evidence that they ever intended to obey the Word of God in the first place? Let me encourage you—remove the phrase, "God told me" from your vocabulary today. I am not saying that God will not speak to you, but people who place God's name upon a specific thought or a certain action cause great confusion in the body of Christ. Just imagine if you tell somebody that God told you to do this or that, and you made a mistake and it wasn't really God at all. What is going to happen on the inside of that other individual?

In my opinion, too many believers seek to hear the voice of Jesus before they are ever willing to meditate and submit to His Word. **God will not instruct anyone who does not take the time to meditate upon and consistently obey His Word.** God only speaks in accordance to what His Word already declares.

And isn't it also amazing that believers attempt to say Jesus told them something that goes contrary to what the scriptures declare? Friends, we must be faithful to filter our thoughts through His Word in order to make sure they line up. If our thoughts do not line up with His Word, then we must dismiss the thought, "God told me." You will never truly hear what Jesus *says* until you do what Jesus *said*.

DAILY CONFESSION
Father, I thank You that You gave me Your Word.
I refuse to believe anything that contradicts what is written.
I am a doer of Your Word.

GRATITUDE IS THE FRAGRANCE OF A CONTENTED HEART

"So when He saw them, He said to them, 'Go, show yourselves to the priests.'
And so it was that as they went, they were cleansed. And one of them, when
he saw that he was healed, returned, and with a loud voice glorified God,
and fell down on his face at His feet, giving Him thanks."
Luke 17:14-16 (NKJV)

✦

Olive oil—considered an engaging gift from God to His people, was one of the most neglected oils until recently. In the past few years, doctors around the world have begun promoting the usage of one of Palestine's main agricultural crops, grateful for the olive and its priceless oil, which serves a variety of purposes. **One of the most neglected virtues in all of humanity is that of sincere gratitude.** Throughout the ages, individuals have become increasingly ungrateful for their present condition—the people they have and the things they share together.

God is a good God; He is faithful to meet every one of our needs. Let us practice being thankful for what we have. **The more we focus on appreciating what we have, the more we cultivate a true and sincere heart of gratitude.** As we focus upon that which is good, joy rises within our hearts. God does not need our thanksgiving; but we are in need of being thankful to Him. God understands the unrivaled benefits thanksgiving achieves inside a person's life.

In the passage above, Jesus showed mercy to ten lepers by healing them of leprosy. Only one returned to offer Jesus gratitude for what He did. That one man possessed the proper response mercy required. He was rewarded for his gratitude by being made completely whole, free from any scars or any trace of the limb-deforming disease called leprosy. Heaven continuously responds favorably to those who regularly respond with heartfelt gratitude.

DAILY CONFESSION
Father, I thank You for all You do.
I shout with joy; I worship You with gladness;
I come before You with singing and joy.

ROUTINE AND HABIT ARE THE ROADS
WHICH LEAD TO UNDENIABLE EXCELLENCE

"Where there is no revelation, the people cast off restraint;
but happy is he who keeps the law."
Proverbs 29:18 (NKJV)

Habits determine our ultimate success or eventual failure in life. Our daily routines are critical to our success. There was a set routine put into place by growers to obtain olives for oil production. Just before the olives were ripe, they were either firmly shaken from the tree or nimbly beaten down from its branches with a light pole, tumbling to the ground like hollow rocks. This habit of harvesting is still a familiar Mediterranean sight in September and October when the olives are ready to be crushed for their oil.

If we create and maintain the right habits, we are propelled toward our dream every step of the way. On the other hand, if we put the wrong things into our lives, we actually are carried into the wilderness of life, headed toward failure and frustration.

Our daily habits are the avenue by which we accomplish our vision. If you don't have a clear vision of what you want your life to become, how will you know which habits to create? It is impossible. Vision keeps us moving forward, driving us to obtain the reward of accomplishment. Without a clear vision, we become a wandering generality, aimlessly looking for a purpose in life. Let's allow the vision of our lives to prompt us to establish routine responsibilities that are scriptural in nature, in addition to daily habits that are Kingdom-building in purpose.

DAILY CONFESSION
Father, I thank You that I have a vision for my life and I do not perish.
I establish habits that cause me to be a success in everything I set my hand to.

INTEGRITY WITHOUT PURPOSE IS WORTHLESS;
PURPOSE WITHOUT INTEGRITY IS USELESS

"Happy are people of integrity, who follow the law of the Lord."
Psalm 119:1 (NLT)

✦

As believers, our purpose in life is to seek and satisfy our Lord and Savior. Our lives must hinge on that one pursuit – to please God. Within our purpose, God places upon each individual an assignment that He calls us to fulfill. Yet far too many believers zealously seek to fulfill their assignment while leaving behind a trail of wounded people and broken hearts.

Due to the vast amount of time, labor, and patience it took for the cultivation of the olive, the integrity of the Israelite soldier (even in something as seemingly replaceable as a tree) was indeed very crucial to the nation, as well as to God. Because of their love for country and God, even in time of war, soldiers were trusted not to damage an olive grove. The deliberate destruction of one individual tree was strictly forbidden.

We, too, are called to walk in love and live with integrity. God is not pleased with the man who did what was instructed but lacked integrity. God does not separate our character from our purpose. We cannot cheerfully fulfill one while harshly neglecting the other. **Always be diligent and serious about living a life of integrity, a life in which you keep your word and do what you know to be right.** The moment our integrity lines up with our purpose, no devil can stop us from changing lives.

The abundant life full of joy and satisfaction only belongs to those who choose to apply integrity with their purposed life. Today we must make the choice to do the same.

DAILY CONFESSION
Father, I thank You that I am a person of integrity, therefore I am happy.
I live by Your Word and I build my life upon the sure foundation of Your character.

ALL OF US HAVE TWENTY-FOUR HOURS IN A DAY. THE ONLY DIFFERENCE BETWEEN ANY TWO OF US IS HOW WE SPEND THEM

"His parents didn't miss Him at first, because they assumed He was with friends among the other travelers. But when He didn't show up that evening, they started to look for Him among their relatives and friends. When they couldn't find Him, they went back to Jerusalem to search for Him there. Three days later they finally discovered Him. He was in the Temple, sitting among the religious teachers, discussing deep questions with them." Luke 2:42-46 (NLT)

When one fast-food restaurant chain began offering toasted sandwich buns, it wasn't long before the rest of them quickly followed suit. Famous chains like "Subway" and "McDonald's" wasted little time before arming themselves with new, high-tech ovens, realizing that if they didn't wisely utilize the time their customers spent in their establishments, these same customers would eat somewhere else. Isn't it interesting that while all the other boys were off playing, Jesus made His way to the Temple of God, utilizing His time in a place where He could discuss the Scriptures in great depth? He made the wise choice to devote Himself to studying the Word of God, even as a young boy. That decision was subsequently critical to His future, since even though He was the Word made flesh, He still had to learn the Scriptures in His human life, just like everyone else.

Jesus had twenty-four hours a day, and so do we. We can be like Him and use our time to learn, grow, study, and prepare, or we can squander our moments in fleeting pleasures which will literally be "burnt away," toasted into tiny, unusable crumbs. Certainly, there is a time for relaxation. Nevertheless, if we are going to step into our future, we must be willing to make the necessary sacrifices to use our time today in order to be ready for tomorrow. You and I have twenty-four hours— so spend those hours doing the things that will bring the greatest return in the powerful days to come.

DAILY CONFESSION
Father, I thank You for giving me the gift of life. I pray that You help me to direct my hours into the activities that glorify You and prepare me for the assignment You have for me.

NEVER ATTEMPT TO PURSUE ANY RELATIONSHIP
FOR WHICH YOU HAVE NOT QUALIFIED FOR

"Zeal without knowledge is not good; a person who moves
too quickly may go the wrong way."
Proverbs 19:2 (NLT)

"There is a time for everything, a season for every activity under Heaven."
Ecclesiastes 3:1 (NLT)

⚹

**Like nothing else on earth, relationships determine the outcome
of your life.** All other factors of your being—the extent of your
intelligence, the graciousness of your appearance, the scope of your
background—can modify that outcome, but none are as significant as
the richness of your relationships. For this reason, each of us must
strive to build the relationships that will launch us into the future we
desire. There are people in our life who distract us from our focus and
drain us of our energy, but there are also those who invigorate us as
readily as a crisp, autumn day. Nevertheless, there is still a time for
everything, and stepping into relationships before you are ready to
make the required investment can be hazardous. It is like attempting
to swim before you take lessons.

Once you discover the people with whom you can build a life,
consider what it takes to make the most of those relationships:

- *How will you add value to their life?*
- *What can you do for them that no one else can or will?*
- *And finally, is now the time to build these relationships?*

If it is time, then pull out all the stops and go after it. If it isn't yet
time, learn to wait and prepare, because your time is coming soon.

DAILY CONFESSION
*Father, I thank You that I acquire knowledge to accompany my zeal.
I refuse to be a person who moves too quickly.*

MAKE NO MISTAKE, THOSE CLOSEST TO YOU
WILL DETERMINE THE OUTCOME OF YOUR LIFE

"As iron sharpens iron, so a man sharpens the countenance of his friend."
Proverbs 27:17 (NKJV)

⚜

As noted yesterday, the single most important factor defining your future is the relationships you embrace. Your life is built by relationships. **Relationships are like those red, illuminated buttons on an elevator: some take you up, but many take you straight down. Some take you up fast, while others take you down even faster.** Whether or not you recognize it, every relationship you have takes you somewhere. In fact, these influential relationships make you the person you are today.

A good olive tree could yield from ten to fifteen gallons of oil per year. An entire grove, therefore, had the potential to influence an entire village, caring for their daily needs. And several groves influenced nations—the oil having been shipped to nearby countries, as well as distant lands. So a good relationship with olive growers was vital for everyone concerned.

Be protective of the time you give to others. Don't allow just anyone to be your friend. Those closest to you determine the outcome of your life. Associate with those who are going somewhere in life—those who are farther along than you are today. As you do this, you will soon walk into your divine destiny!

OBEDIENCE IS THE ONLY WEAPON THAT IS STRONG ENOUGH TO OVERCOME YOUR FLESH

"…but let the Lord Jesus Christ take control of you,
and don't think of ways to indulge your evil desires."
Romans 13:14 (NLT)

✦

During Israel's grand epoch as a world empire, washing the body daily was done as a matter of course, as well as scrupulous washing before and after meals. Many will be surprised to learn that in addition to gentle olive oil, lye gleaned from Israel's plants and minerals, myrrh from the Commiphora Myrrha tree, fragrant balsam, and aloe were provided to smooth and calm the flesh, putting to death the stench and agitation of the long, Middle-Eastern day. Just as Christ's body was scourged and crucified on the cross, so we must do the same to our flesh. We are called to put to death the stench-filled desires and agitated passions of our old nature.

The apostle Paul encourages us to be led by the Spirit so we do not fulfill the desires of our flesh. The Spirit of God always leads us to a place of obedience. There we must put to death the very desires that lurk around our lives, fitfully lingering like wolves around a rabbit's den. Obedience is the tactical weapon we must use if we ever expect to emerge victorious.

Each measured act of obedience is another strike against the back of our tainted flesh. Every time our flesh tells us to cuddle within the cozy blankets and crinkly laundered sheets of our bed just a few more minutes, eat just one more piece of grandma's warm apple pie, or refuse to love our neighbor who kept us up all night with raucous ethnic rhythms, we must crucify our flesh by choosing the narrow route of obedience. As we continue to stand up against the pressure placed upon us, our flesh bows its knee once and for all.

DAILY CONFESSION
Father, I thank You that I boast in the cross of Jesus Christ
by whom the world has been crucified to me and I to the world.

THE PRIZE OF CHARACTER IS ALWAYS GREATER THAN THE PRICE OF ADVERSITY

"These trials are only to test your faith, to show that it is strong and pure. It is being tested as fire tests and purifies gold—and your faith is far more precious to God than mere gold. So if your faith remains strong after being tried by fiery trials, it will bring you much praise and glory and honor on the day when Jesus Christ is revealed to the whole world." 1 Peter 1:7 (NLT)

After hearing of the massacres of two Central African missionaries, British-born gentleman, James Hannington fought the criticism and objection of his peers, forsaking a comfortable lifestyle in preparation to take their place. Before being martyred in 1885, Mr. Hannington first lifted his hand to his captors, requesting that the Ugandan king be told that he had purchased the road to their country with his death—a perilous path, yet one highly worthwhile. I admit, in this world, you could suffer for choosing Godly character. The Scriptures warn us that this might happen as we follow Christ. One thing is very sure, however; when this life is over and we step into eternity, all injustice will cease. Whatever price you pay to have Godly character (even if with your life) will pale in comparison to the rewards that await you. **You will have difficulty here on earth, but if you choose God's righteousness, you'll never regret the adversity it may include.**

Have you yet realized that God is very interested in rewarding you? Yes, He is gracious and loving beyond comprehension, but we must step up to the plate of service in order to receive what is ours. God's goodness can only be released through our commitment to walk in His ways, as He expertly uses our times of adversity to refine us—making us even stronger than we are already are. We may never suffer martyrdom as did James Hannington, but we do have a mandate to help people in any way that God directs. And the only way we'll accomplish our task and be rewarded for it is if we choose the prize of character, despite the price of adversity.

DAILY CONFESSION
Father, I thank You for Your grace that enables me to represent You. Help me to always do what is just in Your sight.

LIFE IS BUILT BY A SERIES OF CHOICES, NOT BY A SERIES OF CHANCES

"I call Heaven and earth as witnesses today against you,
that I have set before you life and death, blessing and cursing; therefore
choose life, that both you and your descendants may live."
Deuteronomy 30:19 (NKJV)

So you probably thought that life in ancient Israel was drab and colorless, without the flash of contemporary fabrics? Well...nothing could be farther from the truth! God's children only needed to stretch out their hands into nature, pleasantly encountering diverse choices for their garments and homes. Faces, clothing, walls—each were blank canvases of distinctive choice.

Different choices take you down different paths. Wrong choices take you down rock-ridden, destructive paths; right choices take you down delightful, melodious paths. You can wait for life to make your choices for you (most of which will be wrong), or you can intentionally choose to become who you were destined to become. Yes, that choice involves a great deal of change, which isn't always as fun as the ancient Israeli color chart. Nevertheless, through it all, there is a pervading delight because of the promised outcome of such changes.

Once you become willing to do whatever it takes to win in life, nothing can hold you back—not overwhelming pressures, not spiteful criticisms, nor adverse circumstances, all of which are assigned to trap you in the sticky mire of mediocrity. The fulfillment of your destiny rests as a blank canvas of choice awaiting the decision of your selective hands.

DAILY CONFESSION
Father, I thank You that You set before me life and death, blessing and cursing.
I choose life that I and those I love may experience life as You desire it.

CHARACTER IS REFINED
THE MOMENT YOU LEARN HOW TO
USE PRINCIPLE WHILE REFUSING TO USE PEOPLE

"Just as the Son of Man did not come to be served, but to serve,
and to give His life a ransom for many."
Matthew 20:28 (NLT)

Over the years, I have seen far too many people exploit other people in the name of God. We must never misuse other people for our own self-seeking benefit. When two individuals enter a relationship with the sole thought of giving, they both end up as receivers. What I personally plan to bring to any relationship is give/give, not give/take. When the other person enters the relationship sharing an equivalent duty and responsibility to give/give, the benefits for both of us are as abundant as stars in the sky!

This reciprocity, this interdependence and complementary exchange, becomes impossible if you enter relationship with someone who regularly uses others.

Regretfully, our society is filled with depraved individuals who make it their exclusive aim to merely use their relationships to feed their own greed and perverted lusts. Israel's prophets consistently warned the nation's women of the excessive usage of cosmetics, recognizing the moral perils of exaggerated looks through imitation of their heathen counterparts. Manipulation of such immodest usage could have negatively flawed their character in a moment's time. But **your character is refined when you learn to use principle, and not people.**

DAILY CONFESSION
Father, I thank You that as the Son of Man came to serve,
I posture as a servant in all my relationships. I not only look out for
my own interest but the interest of others as well.

YOUR MENTOR IS THE ONE WHOSE VOICE YOU OBEY, NOT JUST LISTEN TO

"My children, listen to me. Listen to your father's instruction."
Proverbs 4:1 (NLT)

Beware of the novice spirit that eventually tries to viciously attack each person as they increase in knowledge. Who is this novice spirit? It is the one who thinks they know so much that they rise as high as a New York skyscraper, towering disdainfully above their leader, seeing him or her as stuck in their ways; this person now possesses spotted learning.

Please understand—everyone knows unique things that no one else knows; hence, I may know a few things my authority doesn't, but the servant is never above the master. I have seen many talented protégés commit financial, emotional, and spiritual suicide. **We must understand that we don't learn much of what our mentor taught us until we are pressed to do it ourselves; only then do we realize how little we knew without them.**

You may possess knowledge, but your mentor has experience. Even though a student may know plenty about their chosen field, their mentor has a vast knowledge of types of people, dangerous pitfalls, and real-life situations. A mentor has priceless information and a treasure chest of wisdom. Since history does repeat itself, we don't have time to make the same mistakes as those above us, so we must learn from them. Are you living as the attentive protégé, or the studied mentor? The Queen of Sheba, though powerful and wealthy, postured herself in the position of an attentive protégé, sitting at the table of King Solomon, becoming teachable and submitted to the wise concepts he learned from the Holy God. **Carefully choose your posture—it affects the rest of your life.**

DAILY CONFESSION
Father, I thank You that I am submitted and obedient to those You place over me.
I am teachable without strife and rebellion.

YOU LEARN MORE ABOUT A MAN BY WHAT HE DOESN'T SAY THAN BY WHAT HE DOES

"But someone will say, 'You have faith, and I have works.' Show me
your faith without your works, and I will show you my faith by my works."
James 2:18 (NKJV)

✦

You can almost see her vivid, sparkling caravan muddle through the sand encased desert hills, camels and men adorned in foreign costumes, the beloved Queen of Sheba and her belongings weighty upon their backs. Retaining in her mind the list of questions she had for the great King Solomon, following the tour of his court, she would be awestruck. There would be no words to express the king's grandeur. If there is one principle that could save you from experiencing great disappointment in relationship it is this: "You learn more about a man by what he doesn't say than by what he does say." In order for me to fulfill God's will for my life, I had to stop listening to a man's words and instead, intently follow his daily actions.

Whatever a person does or does not do eventually reveals exactly who they are. Jesus said, "Many will call Me Lord on that day, but I will tell them, 'Away from Me, for I did not know you.'" Jesus also said that we would know people by their fruit.

We all want to believe what other people readily verbalize, so I do not imply that you question their promises. Nevertheless, when their actions contradict their words, you must believe their actions. Otherwise, you will get hurt. The devil is out to hurt you, but you can protect yourself by surrounding yourself with people of integrity and truthfulness. Listen to what a person says, and then closely watch their actions. If they strictly align, like tires to the road, then you know for certain that they belong in your life.

DAILY CONFESSION
Father, I thank You that I am not just a hearer of Your Word
but I am a doer thereof. I show my faith by my works.

EVERY MISTAKE IN LIFE IS A STEPPINGSTONE
LAID DOWN UPON THE PATHWAY OF PROGRESS

*"They may trip seven times, but each time they will rise again.
But one calamity is enough to lay the wicked low."*
Proverbs 24:16 (NLT)

✦

The moment we make a mistake, Satan shows up, cheering our inevitable self-destruction. Ridicule, heart-pounding fear, nerve-shattering doubt, worry, and depression blare as loudly as police sirens inside our ears, but those of us who persevere ultimately win out. Our refusal to concede defeat separates us from the crowd of the mediocre.

Every time we make a mistake, we must respond with a tranquil spirit of gratitude for the lessons we learned and the impending opportunity to try again. Why not begin to see failure and mistakes from a different perspective? **Those who never stop progressing view problems and mistakes as teachers; sometimes they may seem harsh and cause us pain, but their lessons are invaluable.** Those who fear making mistakes never choose the hard road—the challenging road of excellence.

So we must continue responding with courage and tenacity when obstacles arise and mistakes abound. Sheba's queen did not believe all she had heard concerning Israel's King Solomon—the wisdom of his words, the house he built, the meat on his table, or the apparel of his servants. She made a grave error in thought and judgment. But the Bible eloquently states that after she saw and experienced everything in Solomon's kingdom, she praised his prosperity, and his God, then rose again to her caravan, heading toward home. How she grew by that one fantastic visit! We were created to grow, so let's not give up, shut up, or let up until He takes us up.

DAILY CONFESSION
*Father, I thank You that although I may fall seven times,
I will rise again to serve You. I focus on this one thing: forgetting the past
and looking forward to what lies ahead.*

WISDOM IS GRANTED ONLY TO THOSE
WHO ARE WILLING TO SEARCH FOR HER

"Happy is the man who finds wisdom, and the man who gains understanding."
Proverbs 3:13 (NKJV)

Like parents who wisely set aside a reserve for college tuition, God lovingly stores up unsurpassed wisdom for His children. Although God's wisdom dwells within the pages of His Word, not everyone can simply read the Bible and receive the wisdom of God. No, wisdom is something for which we must search, and it doesn't come easily, so many never find it.

There is a razor-sharp difference between simply knowing the Scriptures, and truly possessing the wisdom of God. Wisdom is the ability to accurately apply the Word to any given situation. Many know the Scriptures on health and financial prosperity, but very few actually experience the fruit of them. Why is that? Because wisdom is lacking within the heart of the believer.

There is no problem other than a wisdom problem. And wisdom was the principal thing for the Jews, as the Hebrew culture viewed education as a lifelong process; therefore, they treasured teachers since the days of antiquity.

Only as we continue to press into the Word of God will we go beyond the realm of knowledge and venture into the realm of wisdom. However, we must consider the wisdom of God as more precious than silver and gold. The more value we place upon wisdom, the more Heaven leads us by it.

DAILY CONFESSION
Father, I thank You that I possess Your wisdom. I do not forsake her, but love her and embrace wisdom as the most precious asset I have.

UNDERSTANDING IS THE REWARD AWAITING THOSE WHO MEDITATE UPON GOD'S WORD

"I have more understanding than all my teachers,
for Your testimonies are my meditation."
Psalm 119:99 (NKJV)

Just as the correct numbers release the combination to the bank vault's safe, understanding unlocks the very life of God. Understanding is the ability to see life as God sees it. Very few people ever draw close to walking in the fullness of what God has for them because they lack understanding. Without it, one cannot fully embrace the truth of God's Word. We see throughout all of Scripture the worthy emphasis placed on meditation of the words of God.

During the era of great prophets such as Ezra and Nehemiah, Hebrew teachers were advised to not only teach their given subjects, but to closely ponder (or meditate upon) the temperaments of the various students they instructed. These teachers were further exhorted to not just read words to their pupils, but to have an understanding, a thorough insight into the spirits and souls of what was happening inside each boy and girl. It is the same with many individuals who routinely read and study the Bible, yet they are not changed by the information they read.

Although the Bible contains the words of God, it only becomes real when we choose to meditate upon it. This does not refer to a type of eastern religious practice; this refers to one's daily hearing, pondering, and confession of the Scripture. If we take just one Scripture, run it through our minds, and put it in our mouths, it will come alive inside, producing more change than reading the entire New Testament would. And just as the ancient Hebrew teachers were instructed to meditate upon their students for success in the classroom, scripture meditation is vital to your success as a believer.

DAILY CONFESSION
Father, I thank You that as I meditate upon Your Word,
understanding rises within me.

THE LIFE YOU LIVE WILL BE DETERMINED BY THE TRUTH YOU EMBRACE

"And ye shall know the truth, and the truth shall make you free."
John 8:32 (KJV)

⚜

"That's it...a little harder now. I know your hands are getting scratched but...just pull a little harder, a little more, and up you go... hey, you made it!" Truth is like that long, dangling rope. All you need to do is take both hands and firmly grip your fingers around the bottom end of it and you can make your way to every other truth up the line. And each of us has that rope dangling within our easy grasp. The only disparity is our willingness to grab on tightly, and to climb up boldly to higher truths. But:

- *Will you exert the effort it takes to climb?*
- *Will you endure the inevitable burns of the rough rope?*
- *Will you cling to truth and keep climbing once you go far higher than you ever thought possible?*

There is a common misconception that if I know something, then that means I do it. For example, think of a few Scriptures you have memorized. Now, ask yourself (be honest!): How well do I actually walk in the truths of those verses?

We all have places where we can grow in our understanding of truth, and most of us can start right where we are, putting into action the Word we already know. In doing so, we'll discover what real freedom is. Don't think it necessary to run and find the latest, biggest, most exciting truth. Just start where you are right this moment, doing exactly what you know to do.

DAILY CONFESSION
Father, I thank You for giving me Your Word. I continue in Your Word and I know the truth and the truth makes me free.

THE VALUE YOU PLACE UPON ANY RELATIONSHIP IS IMMEDIATELY REVEALED BY THE PRICE YOU ARE WILLING TO PAY FOR IT

"Again, the kingdom of Heaven is like treasure hidden in a field,
which a man found and hid; and for joy over it he goes
and sells all that he has and buys that field."
Matthew 13:44 (NKJV)

I came to the realization that I greatly value my relationships because I am willing to give up my own pursuit of greatness in order to bring greatness to another. And, to this day, when I recognize that greatness is coming out of an individual, I tell him, "Your best years are ahead of you! And I'm here to multiply who you are and never bring you a day of grief."

I also discovered that if I actually bring out the best in others, they no longer have to work, strive, and push so hard for themselves. They can begin to sow in confidence instead of guardedly protecting themselves, stringently holding on to what they have. Interestingly enough, now they look to see what they can do in my life. And because they now sow, they actually begin to truly reap. This is the greatest value that I could ever bring to a person's life.

Taught to reverence parents, the aged, the handicapped, and strangers far above their own selves, each Jewish parent often reminded and taught his children that by giving value to others (no matter who they were) they would be blessed. Teaching these types of attitudes brought out the best in the children, and the entire community would ultimately reap—a small price to pay.

DAILY CONFESSION
Father, I thank You that the Kingdom of Heaven is like a treasure in a field,
which I find and hide and for my joy over it, I go and sell all I have
and buy that field.

WHEN COMPROMISE ENTERS THE ROOM
DISAPPOINTMENT IS SOON TO FOLLOW

"If the Godly compromise with the wicked, it is like polluting a
fountain or muddying a spring." Proverbs 25:26 (NLT)

Let's take a quick look at an incredible illustration from nature — the penguin. Traveling many miles from their natural habitat (the ocean), the emperor penguin breeds at specific, often desolate, dangerously icy sites, laying and caring for their eggs in the world's most inhospitable region. Not even 80° below zero temperatures cause these birds to quit. No, they never turn back; they have decided to give no place to compromise.

We must become people of principle. No matter what situation arises, we must never compromise our integrity for anyone, ever. Why is that? Because we have to live with our actions every night when we go home, gazing at ourselves before the mirror every day. We cannot afford to commit ourselves partially to anything. For the most part, principled people do not always feel like doing the things that they must do. Even so, they act by examining the long-term results of every one of their decisions.

If we compromise our principles, we abandon our fortified base and find ourselves behind enemy lines—without weapons, armor, or communication. It is a task that the Commander-in-Chief of Heaven's Armed Forces never appointed to us. Compromise is strictly forbidden in His army. Those who do so are captured by the enemy and forced to defect. Divine rescue missions are rarely successful, and those who compromise are often gone for good. Keep a close watch on yourself and on your service to the King. Although you may find yourself in the most inhospitable region, like the penguin, never allow yourself to compromise your principles for anyone, anywhere, for any reason. It would be a terrible day to be tried for treason by the King of kings.

DAILY CONFESSION
Father, I refuse to compromise. I live by Your Word and am guided by Your
statutes and commands. I understand failure waits for those who
compromise, but I win because I choose a principled life.

THE MOST VALUABLE PERSON YOU WILL EVER ENCOUNTER IN LIFE IS AN AUTHENTIC PROBLEM SOLVER

*"This man Daniel, whom the king named Belteshazzar,
has a sharp mind and is filled with divine knowledge and understanding.
He can interpret dreams, explain riddles, and solve difficult problems.
Call for Daniel, and he will tell you what the writing means."*
Daniel 5:12 (NLT)

Mind-baffling dreams, unexplained prophecies, futuristic visions. Daniel was known as a man who could solve difficult problems. His devotion to excellence and growth was unprecedented, and those traits brought him before greatness. His rewards were no laughing matter—high positions of governmental authority in one of the greatest empires of all time, an array of lavish riches, fine clothing, and honor. At times, like the one mentioned in this verse, Daniel was the sole individual who could solve the problem at hand. That made him the most valuable person around.

So, how about you?

- *Can the same be said of you, that you have a daily commitment to excellence and growth?*
- *Do you prepare to solve greater problems?*
- *Do you make yourself available for those who can bring promotion to your life?*

As we've seen with Daniel, **there is a hefty price to pay for these noble ideals, but as we've also seen, the reward is well worth it.** May God help you to recognize and solve the problems that will bring the greatest return to your life!

DAILY CONFESSION
*Father, I thank You that like Daniel, a spirit of excellence lives inside of me.
I thank You for helping me recognize the problems around me and for giving me
the grace I need to solve them.*

WHO YOU ARE IS REVEALED BY WHAT YOU DO

"You will know them by their fruits…"
Matthew 7:16 (NKJV)

Jesus tells us we shall know another by their fruits. I find it interesting how people judge another by what they do, but refuse to acknowledge their own actions. There are many who tell people, "God knows my heart," yet they live in the depths of sin. Remember, God cannot be mocked. Although we can fool others, we cannot fool God. David prayed, "Search me, O God, and know my heart; try me, and know my anxieties; and see if there is any wicked way in me, and lead me in the way everlasting."

Teachers of the ancient Hebrews did not hesitate to take action if their students misbehaved. Employing a strap of reeds, persistently inattentive or habitually absent children would be strictly chastised. These teachers' actions were a blanket reflection of what they believed —discipline works! **Likewise, our actions are a reflection of what lies hidden deep within our hearts…we cannot believe otherwise.**

Remember, our actions are a documentation of what we believe; and every time we act, we declare to all of Heaven and earth who we truly are. If we ever seek change in our lives, we must begin to understand that our actions are the proof of who we are. May God help us to examine ourselves, revealing who we really are, going deep within.

DAILY CONFESSION
Lord, search me and know me, and rid me of any wicked desire lying within my heart. I am a doer of Your Word. I am known by my fruit and I choose to act upon Your Word. As I act, I bear the fruit of the Spirit in my life.

EXCELLENCE IS THE KEY THAT SWINGS OPEN THE DOOR OF FAVOR

"Do you see a man who excels in his work? He will stand before kings;
he will not stand before unknown men."
Proverbs 22:29 (NKJV)

⚓

Rerouting our exploration of Palestine for a time, we leave the ancient Hebrew culture to enter the dramatic door of modern-day Israel. A notable dignitary in recent Middle-East history, Moshe Dayan (the colorful figure often remembered for his conspicuous black eye patch) was born in 1915 in the first kibbutz (or Jewish cooperative farm) located just south of the Sea of Galilee. An instructor in the underground Jewish militia, Dayan led commando raids against the Vichy French in Syria, assisting in Israel's 1948 War of Independence. And in 1953, due to his excellence on the battlefield, the door of favor opened to Mr. Dayan when he was promoted to Major General and Chief of Staff.

Promotion is something we all desire. But why are very few ever elevated to a higher level in life? Why do so many individuals remain the exact same as the day we first meet them? **Promotion does not come just because we desire it—it resolutely requires us to soar above and beyond that which is asked of us.** Whether in marriage, at work, or serving in God's church, walking in excellence is the key to favor and promotion.

The Bible tells us, "Jesus grew in wisdom and favor with both God and man." As we grow in favor with both God and man, it causes us to rise to the level of promotion God has for us. Maintaining a great attitude and respecting and honoring those to whom we are assigned also are vital to attract the favor of God and man. By doing whatever is required of us, we can become the tool used to solve any problem in life.

DAILY CONFESSION
Father, I thank You that I excel in what You called me to do; I will stand before
kings. I do all things in excellence and continue to grow in wisdom and favor.

FUTURE SUCCESS IS DESTROYED BY GIVING IN TO THE PRESSURE OF INSTANT GRATIFICATION

"He went a little farther and fell on His face, and prayed,
saying, 'O My Father, if it is possible, let this cup pass from Me;
nevertheless, not as I will, but as You will.'"
Matthew 26:39 (NKJV)

⚜

The refreshing sight of the robin...the invigorating scent of newly burgeoning trees...the friendly honking of white-necked Canadian geese—these are some of the luscious wonders of spring. What would happen if the world's farmers decided to relax during this season of growth, taking walks in the woods instead of planting seeds? No doubt, disaster in the fields would ultimately occur! **Everything in God's realm is methodically performed in seasons.** There is an expressed season of sowing seed, and a subsequent season of reaping the harvest. However, because the harvest may take some time to manifest, we don't always notice the cause and effect connection between the seed we sowed years ago, and the negative consequences we currently reap.

We must take the present and sow it as a seed expecting to receive a great future. But why do so many squander their time today, while idealistically expecting a great future tomorrow? It is because their belief system is self-deceiving. The truth is: we reap only what we sow.

At age 12, Moshe Dayan stood sentry duty in his struggling village of Nahalal, where marauding bands of Bedouins routinely attacked. In less than two years time, he became a member of Haganah, a Jewish defense militia. Young Dayan sowed the seeds for one of the most illustrious military careers in modern history.

Please consider: What are you sowing today? Where does your time go? Where is your focus directed? The answers to these questions give you a clear idea of your future.

DAILY CONFESSION
Father, I thank You that I refuse to worry about tomorrow,
for tomorrow takes care of itself. I look at my today as seed
I sow to create the future I desire.

THERE IS NO SUCH THING AS A SHORTCUT
TO THE HIGHER LEVELS OF SUCCESS

"But I keep under my body, and bring it into subjection: lest that by any means, when I have preached to others, I myself should be a castaway."
1 Corinthians 9:27 (KJV)

Moshe boldly attended lectures at the Hannah Meister School. What was so comical, courageous, and sacrificial about attending school you might ask? Well, the Hannah Meister School wasn't just any old school. The Hannah Meister School was an agricultural training center in Dayan's hometown—an all-girl training center for farming. Nonetheless, a dedicated cultivator of the land as well as a soldier, Dayan never chose the easy path.

There is a tendency in all of humanity to proceed down the painless path——the one most often traveled. Let's face it, **we all want to eliminate pain from our lives, but in the attempt to take the easy road, we don't possess the ability to maintain what we desire.** It is like a high school student who does whatever he can to barely eek out a passing grade to get his diploma. He cheats, lies, and allows others to do his work. In his attempt to bypass the pain of studying and working hard to achieve a good grade, he foolishly overrides the preparation necessary for college.

Many believers live the same way. The Bible tells us God has great things in store for us, and that He has an exciting plan for our lives. But unless we embrace the season of preparation and pain, we are not ready to handle the heroic things God has for us to accomplish.

Never gaze dreamily upon the comforts of the easy road. And don't look to override the crucial season of preparation. Enjoy the journey. Remember, life is not a race to be won, but an electrifying journey to be enjoyed!

DAILY CONFESSION
Father, I thank You that I discipline my body and I bring it into subjection lest after I minister to others, I myself become disqualified.

YOU CHANGE YOUR LIFE BY CHANGING YOUR CHOICES

"Do not be deceived, God is not mocked;
for whatever a man sows, that he will also reap."
Galatians 6:7 (NKJV)

⚶

How does one ever begin to change their choices? Well, it is largely determined by one's outlook or perspective on life. **The way you think about yourself and the world in which you live is key to your success.** One of the greatest truths ever written was penned by King Solomon. He stated, "For as he thinks in his heart, so is he...."

Because of one man, an eccentric Englishman, Captain Orde C. Wingate, Moshe Dayan's perspective would be forever altered. An intelligence officer sent to Palestine to suppress skirmishes between the Arabs and Jews, Captain Wingate began training the Haganah, teaching them fundamental night tactics and sharing his expertise on military strategy—the unrivaled value of surprise and speed. Volunteering for Captain Wingate's "Special Night Squads" (the SNS), Moshe Dayan was made second in command at age 22. By changing his outlook via the guidance of Captain Wingate, Dayan's actions automatically followed, initiating a plan for future success as he began envisioning victory at every turn.

It doesn't matter if other people see you as a success. How do you see yourself? You will never obtain God's will in your life until you see yourself as God sees you. As you change the way you think, your actions automatically follow. Case in point: The reason so few people explored the New World was because they erroneously believed the earth was flat. Why would you take the time to explore if you believed the earth was flat? You see, their beliefs governed their actions. But there was a man who believed otherwise, and his actions followed suit. That man gallantly discovered the New World because he believed beyond all doubt the earth indeed was round.

DAILY CONFESSION
Father, I thank You that I am not deceived. You cannot be mocked.
Whatever I sow I certainly reap.

EVERY FAILURE IN LIFE CAN BE TRACED
BACK TO A COMPROMISE OF CHARACTER

"The integrity of the upright will guide them,
but the perversity of the unfaithful will destroy them."
Proverbs 11:3 (NKJV)

If you ever failed in life, would you like to know the main reason why? Most likely, you were willing to compromise your integrity. I like to say it like this: "Integrity is the foundation upon which your life's work is built." If you desire to build a great life and achieve great things, the foundation must be strong as hardened concrete. David said: "If the foundations are destroyed, what can the righteous do?" Every failure you see in the Word of God can be traced back to a compromise of character—from Sampson to David, from Solomon to Judas.

But why do people compromise? I will not attempt to list for you all the reasons, but **one core reason why many people compromise is because they are yet to be persuaded that what God said is true.** Take a look at the Scripture above; if people truly believed they would be destroyed if they compromised, they wouldn't compromise.

After the British (who ruled Palestine during Dayan's youth) signed an agreement with the Arab nations, they outlawed Haganah, instantly recalling Captain Wingate from the field. Thrusting the militia into secret training in 1939, Moshe Dayan (along with other militia members who refused to compromise their activities), were arrested, tried, and sentenced to prison. In spite of that, they would not negotiate what they believed—they inwardly recognized that the future of their people depended on it! The willingness to negotiate their principles is positive proof that people truly don't believe God. If you see any faint beginnings of compromise, deal with them immediately, and firmly embrace God's Word. Your future depends upon it!

DAILY CONFESSION
Father, I thank You that my integrity guides me,
but the perversity of the unfaithful destroys them.

IN ORDER TO ENJOY THE LAND OF INSTRUCTION YOU MUST LEAVE THE SHORES OF CORRECTION

"And you groan and mourn when your end comes, when your flesh and body are consumed, and you say, how I hated instruction and discipline, and my heart despised reproof! I have not obeyed the voice of my teachers nor submitted and consented to those who instructed me."
Proverbs 5:11-13 (AMP)

⚓

With the fervor of the Israeli army, we must purposefully refuse the temptation to take up offense or casually reject the correction of an authority in our lives. Additionally, we must always posture ourselves (like young Moshe beneath the training of Captain Wingate) to eagerly and respectfully receive instruction. I have met very few individuals who are willing, and able, to openly accept correction. We cannot make that same grave mistake. **Our lives go no further than the commitment we make to receive constructive correction from our superiors.** The response we have toward the correction hinges on our positive attitude toward that correction.

When we view correction as an instruction and ask ourselves a few basic questions, we experience true progress in life. These questions include:

- *How do I handle this correctly?*
- *How can I be instructed regarding what this person is saying?*
- *How can I improve in the area that has been requested of me?*

These questions cause us to learn from mistakes we make. They fortify us enough to endure the correction. If Moshe Dayan and the rest of the militia would have refused Captain Wingate's strategic instruction, Israel might have never become what it is today! Never forget, in time, our welcome pursuit of correction leads to the progress we desire.

DAILY CONFESSION
Father, I thank You for sending authority to my life to lead and guide me in the way I should go.

THE CULTIVATION OF ONE'S CHARACTER IS DETERMINED BY THE MEDITATION OF ONE'S HEART

"Let the words of my mouth and the meditation of my heart be acceptable
in Your sight, O Lord, my strength and my Redeemer."
Psalms 19:14 (NKJV)

✦

Our hearts unconsciously affect everything we do. There is no greater understanding a believer must grasp than the unmatched power of a pure heart. Jesus tells us that "the pure in heart shall see God." He didn't say the rich; He didn't say the wise; He didn't even say those with great faith. Jesus said, "The pure in heart shall see God." The apostle John tells us, "If you say you abide in Him then you ought to walk as He did." Jesus is our example of true Godly character. Character is not something we can build independent of God; it is a result of God's Spirit coming alive in us. His Spirit demands that we do what is right.

Cultivation of true character is dependent upon our willingness to surrender our hearts to God. Because of the clarity of their hearts and right motivation, Moshe Dayan and his 42 co-prisoners had their prison sentences cut short as they were fatefully called upon to help the Allies fight the Vichy French, who were in control of Syria during World War II. Leading a group of commando-scouts, Dayan and his men set up a successful Australian invasion in the Syrian terrain. Their pliable hearts towards doing right affected everything they did.

The main issue lies not in the ability to be disciplined, but rather in the pliability of our hearts. David said, "Lord, I hide Your Word in my heart that I might not sin against You." As we fill our hearts with the Word of God, we soon see the character of Christ manifest in our lives.

DAILY CONFESSION
Father, I thank You that I guard my heart above everything else.
I see the importance of a pure heart, knowing it affects everything I do.

THE PROMISES OF GOD COME ALIVE THE MOMENT YOU PURSUE WISDOM AND UNDERSTANDING

"God said, because you have asked this and have not asked for long life or for riches, nor for the lives of your enemies, but have asked for yourself understanding to recognize what is just and right…behold, I have done as you asked, I have given you a wise mind…I have also given you what you have not asked, both riches and honor."
1 Kings 3:11-13 (The Living)

In most cases, a computer in the hands of a two-year-old child is nothing but a mere plaything, an intriguing mass of lettered buttons, and an attractive screen of colorful images. Furthermore, that same computer lays idle at the hands of the great-grandmother who loves gardening, baking, and sewing, seeing little rationale for even learning how to turn on the machine. Many times in life we may have the right tool in our hand, but if we don't know how to efficiently use it, that tool becomes utterly and hopelessly useless.

After covert military strategy was generously demonstrated by Captain Wingate (specifically revealing how to effectively use their weapons against the enemy), Moshe Dayan and Haganah wisely learned the power they possessed. Accordingly the Word of God is powerless to us if we do not fully understand why God sent it and the power it possesses to accomplish great things in our lives.

If we do not acknowledge that the Word of God is powerful and that it is the discerner of the human heart, then it is totally unable to help us. Understanding unlocks the power of the Word of God to flow into the life of the believer, just as the English captain unlocked strategic military power to surge into the life of Moshe Dayan. The more fully we give ourselves to the Word of God, the more fully understanding comes into our life.

DAILY CONFESSION
Father, I thank You that the wealth of
Your wisdom causes me to prosper in all areas of life.

EVERY RELATIONSHIP IS EITHER
DRAWING YOU CLOSER TO, OR FURTHER FROM,
GOD'S PERFECT WILL FOR YOUR LIFE

"I am a companion of all who fear You, and of those who keep Your precepts."
Psalm 119:63 (NKJV)

✦

Crashing like a rock into the field glasses he used for scouting the countryside, the enemy's bullet hurled tiny shards of broken glass directly into Moshe Dayan's left eye. Despite his ghastly injury, Moshe completed his mission in Lebanon. Following intricate operations to repair the damage, nothing was able to restore the general's sight. But General Dayan refused to mourn the past by relentlessly pondering the loss of his sight. On the contrary, his distinctive, shiny black eye patch became his trademark of courage, embracing his relationship to the world as the charming warrior from Israel. People who are relentlessly focused upon the past quickly become a weight that always deters you. You must break free from those relationships and boldly embrace those who will escort you into your future. Link yourself with those who are going somewhere. **Seek out those who have a vision for their lives; these are the people who will open the door to your destiny.** These individuals do not waste time, nor do they look for any short-term, special interest friends!

Every relationship you have either draws you closer to or drives you further from God's perfect will. Every person who surrounds you should push you like enthusiastic soldiers marching into the war, cheering you on to reach your objective. Jesus had an objective, "…I do not seek My own will but the will of the Father who sent Me." Jesus was more concerned about pleasing God than offending man. Why not tenaciously circulate among those who cause you to desire more of God, becoming a companion of those who help you draw ever closer to His will for your life?

DAILY CONFESSION
Father, I thank You that I am a companion of all who fear You
and those who keep Your precepts.

SACRIFICE IS THE ROAD TRAVELED ON THE JOURNEY TO YOUR DIVINE DESTINY

"Again, a second time, He went away and prayed, saying, 'O My Father,
if this cup cannot pass away from Me unless I drink it, Your will be done.'"
Matthew 26:42 (NKJV)

No one understood the principle of sacrifice more than Jesus. As you see in the verse stated above, Jesus' only road to His divine destiny was the cross, with the ultimate sacrifice – His life! God calls us to imitate Christ and rely on Him as our divine example. **God has a plan for every one of us...but that plan is only fulfilled as we willingly surrender our lives.** Jesus does not allow anyone to follow Him without them first being willing to give up their life.

Along with several thousands of Palestinian Jewish volunteers, Moshe Dayan (who served as liaison officer with the British in Jerusalem) helped organize a daring mission during World War II. Sacrificing all comfort and ease, these volunteers (clearly risking their lives) successfully parachuted German Jews into occupied countries, aiding in the return of downed British pilots. A great sacrifice—a wonderful mission...extremely hazardous, nonetheless.

Everything worth pursuit requires you to pay a price. Abraham became a friend of God, but it did not happen until he was willing to sacrifice his son. Paul is known as one of the greatest apostles of all time, but he was harshly beaten, hideously whipped, stoned nearly to death, and brutally persecuted. We all want to reach the destiny God has for us, but only those willing to pay the sacrificial price ever experience it.

DAILY CONFESSION
Father, I thank You that You placed within me the same spirit that dwells in Jesus.
I understand that the road to my divine destiny requires a sacrificial life.
I willingly give up my life to serve You all my days.

YOUR SEED IS THE PASSPORT INTO THE FUTURE

*"Remember this—a farmer who plants only a few seeds will get a small crop.
But the one who plants generously will get a generous crop."*
2 Corinthians 9:6 (NLT)

You can only act according to what you know. The Word of God plainly tells us, "God's people perish for lack of knowledge..." Many in the body of Christ have been taught that it is wrong to expect a harvest from an offering given to God. To fervently expect something is not greed; it is stable proof that we believe God's Word. In 2 Corinthians 9:6, God said, "...but the one who plants generously will get a generous crop." Those who do not expect a harvest do not understand this Scripture.

In everything we do, we expect a return; but the moment someone talks about money, we no longer feel it is appropriate to eagerly expect a return. When the Israeli soldiers fought, they fervently expected victory.

Remember, **God's greatest pleasure is to be believed.** His greatest pain is to be doubted. You see with almost every instruction, God subsequently follows it with a promise. Why? Because He created us to be reward oriented, understanding our intrinsic desire to excel, our intense desire to produce, and our natural desire for more. He put that yearning within us, and gave us the process through the seed, so that we might always attain the desires of our hearts.

DAILY CONFESSION
*Father, I thank You that I plant seed with an expectation of a harvest.
I never live in need, because I have been given seed. I sow generously
and I reap a generous harvest.*

YOUR MIND IS THE CANVAS UPON WHICH
YOUR THOUGHTS PAINT THE PICTURE OF TOMORROW

"For as he thinks in his heart, so is he."
Proverbs 23:7 (NKJV)

⬥

On May 14, 1948, with searing bombs raining over Tel Aviv, Prime Minister David Ben-Gurion, proclaimed the establishment of the State of Israel. Much of the world thought it could never happen, but men like Moshe Dayan knew otherwise. With Arabian forces occupying the Jewish quarter of Jerusalem, the second phase of Israel's War of Independence was in progress, armed with minds imagining celebrating the next Passover in an Israel that belonged entirely to them.

What you think today becomes a reality tomorrow. But you must stay long enough under the Word of God for it to transform you, creating a better tomorrow. When you understand the truth behind the origin of negative thoughts, you have the know-how to take control over them. As you take control, you are then able to worship the Lord your God with your entire mind and be free from guilt over wrong and negative thoughts that Satan brings your way.

For generations upon generations, the State of Israel was simply a propitious thought. But when God began to work inside His people, their minds became canvases upon which divine ideas were vividly painted.

All of God's power and promises are at our disposal, but only those who pay the price and saturate their mind with the Word of God experience the blessings of God.

DAILY CONFESSION
Father, I thank You that I am what I think in my heart.
I think Your thoughts and I act in Your manner!

HONOR IS THE DOORWAY
THROUGH WHICH ALL PROSPERITY WALKS

"'Honor your father and mother.' This is the first of the Ten Commandments
that ends with a promise. And this is the promise: if you honor your father
and mother, 'you will live a long life, full of blessing.'"
Ephesians 6:2-3 (NLT)

When I speak of prosperity, I do not only confine it to money. Money, you see, has only a small role to play on the diverse stage of prosperity. What I refer to is a full and abundant life. God has told humanity for more than four thousand years to honor their parents. And God promises a long, full life of blessings to those who do.

What is honor? And how do we honor? Honor is a term used to describe the act of making another feel valued. It also can be seen as giving another respect. We honor through our actions and our attitudes. Dishonor stems from one's heart, and eventually reveals itself in one's actions. Remember, **man looks at the outward actions, but God looks on our hearts.** Therefore, consider these two important questions: Do we honor with our hearts, or just our words? Do we value the gifts others give to us?

There are many people who do not have Godly parents. Nevertheless, the Scriptures do not exempt such people from honoring their parents. You can honor those who don't know the Lord just as you can those who do. Unsaved parents can be won to the Lord through honor. We owe it to them; maybe not for what they did or who they are, but because of what God did. We must begin today to honor our parents. Take some time to think about what you can do to show honor towards them. I guarantee it will make a huge difference in their lives, and you will be blessed for doing so.

DAILY CONFESSION
I honor my father and my mother and I will have a long full life of blessings.
I understand that I cannot live a full and abundant life apart
from honoring them.

WHATEVER CAPTURES YOUR FOCUS
CONTROLS YOUR LIFE

"Finally, brethren, whatever things are true, whatever things are noble,
whatever things are just, whatever things are pure, whatever things are lovely,
whatever things are of good report, if there is any virtue and if there
is anything praiseworthy—meditate on these things."
Philippians 4:8 (NKJV)

Your focus profoundly determines your life's direction. Ascertain what you would like to do, and focus precisely upon that objective, like a bullet to its target. And as we have so prolifically seen over these past few days, General Moshe Dayan intently focused upon the freedom of Israel since the time of his pre-teenage days. Nothing deterred him—not prison, nor a missing eye, nor the death of his only brother, Zohar, who was killed in the 1948 War of Independence. Undoubtedly, General Dayan knew that an idle mind becomes a negative mind. That is the reason it is so important to focus on God's Word and His will for your life.

What have you focused on lately? I personally have found it to be true, not only in my life but in the lives of others, that my moods are determined by what captures my focus. The enemy understands if he captures our focus, he alters our lives.

Very few individuals realize the power focus plays on their life. Until they do, they never experience the rewarding life God promised them. The emotions you feel, whether good or bad, reveal your focus. God does not and will not starkly force you to focus on His Word. It is your responsibility to focus your attention upon what He says. As you do, your feelings follow. This is the key to mastering any and all of your negative, unhealthy emotions.

DAILY CONFESSION
Father, I thank You that I think upon what is good, noble, just, and pure.
I meditate on whatever things are of good report.

POTENTIAL IS QUICKLY ACHIEVED BY THE WILLINGNESS TO CHANGE

"Jesus said to him, 'If you want to be perfect, go, sell what you have and give to the poor, and you will have treasure in Heaven; and come, follow Me.' But when the young man heard that saying, he went away sorrowful, for he had great possessions."
Matthew 19:21-22 (NKJV)

Having helped his people win their War of Independence, Moshe Dayan would now begin a new phase in his life. Retaining command of Israel's southern sector, in 1950 he was promoted to rank of Brigadier General, transferred additionally to command of the northern sector. Dayan was ready and willing to change into whatever personage his embattled nation needed. He could not refuse God. He dare not refuse his people.

Whenever we refuse to embrace change in any area of our lives, we hinder God from helping us grow. It is impossible to grow, however, when we refuse change. God calls us to purposefully walk and live as Christ did while here upon the earth. All of us have a distance to go, but the good news is that we have the ability to improve because of our relationship with Christ. If we willingly allow Christ to invade our lives, and if we follow His Lordship, as soldiers follow their general, we will mature in Him.

Our willingness to embrace change authorizes Heaven to promote us to a higher level (just as Brigadier General Dayan was continually promoted), giving us a superior future. As we seek to improve ourselves, we will soon achieve our God-given potential.

We cannot afford to allow our pride to prevent us from embracing the changes that are necessary for continual growth. In order to exceed our present status, we must be willing to pay the price of change.

DAILY CONFESSION
Father, I thank You that I am Your child and I walk as Christ walked. I speak as Christ spoke and I live as Christ lived.

YOU CAN'T CRUCIFY A DEMON, AND YOU CAN'T CAST OUT THE FLESH

*"I protest, brethren, by the boasting in you,
which I have in Christ Jesus our Lord, I die daily."*
1 Corinthians 15:31 (NASB)

Without a doubt, some people are doggedly possessed by demons prior to salvation. When they come to Christ, those demons are immediately cast out because demons can't dwell where God moves in! This is what happened to me the day I became born again in the mental institution. The majority of us, however, are not tormented by demons when we come to the Lord—but we do have a betraying flesh.

We are instructed to crucify our flesh daily because what it wants is contrary to what the spirit wants. Although a demon can be cast out, you cannot cast out your flesh; it must be crucified. People believe they can simply say, "In Jesus' name, I command you, flesh, to come in line." If we are honest with ourselves, we realize that we all have done this, and it didn't work. **The only way to defeat the flesh is to crucify it,** and that is never a painless process. And the only way to defeat the relentless Arab harassments and border raids which continually plagued Israeli farming settlements was to fight, continually beating down the enemy. In reality, though Israel was fully recognized as a new nation by the rest of the world, the surrounding Arab governments never acknowledged its existence, declaring to be at war with the Zionist state until it was annihilated. Therefore, General Dayan's Haganah became the modern Israeli army, prepared to take up the sword at a moment's notice.

And so we must also take the sword of the Spirit and withstand the desires and promptings of our flesh. Protect your passion for God like a sentinel guarding his nation's border. Discipline your body and make it your slave. Only then can you please God with your life.

DAILY CONFESSION
*Father, I thank You that I die daily to myself.
I take up my cross and follow wholeheartedly after You.*

MEDIOCRITY IS THE WILLINGNESS TO ACCEPT THE ORDINARY BECAUSE WE'RE UNWILLING TO STAND FOR THE EXTRAORDINARY

"Amaziah was twenty-five years old when he became king…Amaziah
did what was pleasing in the Lord's sight, but not like his ancestor David.
Instead, he followed the example of his father, Joash. Amaziah did not destroy
the pagan shrines, where the people offered sacrifices and burned incense."
2 Kings 14:2-4 (NLT)

Every woman alive knows it—either you are, or you aren't. Pregnancy is not a mediocre process; it is impossible to be "almost" with child. Either you are, or you aren't. As a natural example for us all, when God creates life, He never does it half way. How many of us can recall King Amaziah? Almost none of us, right? But who knows David? Virtually the whole world does, even those who are not believers. David stood for the extraordinary, but Amaziah accepted the ordinary, doing things half way. Notice, Amaziah wasn't displeasing to God. The Scriptures say that he did what was pleasing in the Lord's sight, which means that he must have had a certain degree of integrity and goodness to him. Nevertheless, he didn't do what it took to make things great, like his ancestor David did.

Mediocrity doesn't mean that we live a lazy, worthless life. No, mediocrity means that we let just a few things slip through the cracks on one hand, while we hold together everything else with the other, doing a balancing act. I wish I could say that God understands, but that just is not true. God gave us His grace so that we are able to become extraordinary, going all the way in every area of our lives. Ask yourself: What areas of my life have I allowed mediocrity to penetrate? While it may be difficult to stand for the extraordinary at first, it is the only way to make a lasting impact in your world.

DAILY CONFESSION
Father, I thank You for empowering me to stand for the extraordinary
so that You can be glorified in my life.

CRITICISM IS RESTRICTED TO THE POWER YOU GIVE IT

*"Sanballat was very angry when he learned that we were rebuilding the wall.
He flew into a rage and mocked the Jews, saying in front of his friends and the
Samarian army officers, 'What does this bunch of poor, feeble Jews think they are
doing? Do they think they can build the wall in a day if they offer enough sacrifices?
Look at those charred stones they are pulling out of the rubbish and using again!'"*
Nehemiah 4:1-2 (NLT)

Nehemiah set out to rebuild the dilapidated wall of Jerusalem, and
nothing was going to stop him. Nonetheless, it was no trouble-free
task. His greatest enemy, Sanballat, was on a constant tirade, trying to
destroy Nehemiah by crudely discouraging all of his builders. Soundly
determined to do God's will, even in the midst of vitriolic criticism,
Nehemiah led his team to complete the wall.

Sanballat's criticism would have been a great excuse for Nehemiah
to throw in the towel. He could have keenly listened to its banter,
firmly believing it, and then finally quit. But Nehemiah understood
that criticism would only hurt him if he allowed it.

On our journey to fulfill the will of God, we'll inevitably pick up
a few critics. On December 1, 1953, at age 38, Dayan became the
highest ranking Israeli commander with rank of Major General, the
role for which he seemed destined. Whether it was waiting in line for
his share of rations, or breaking his leg during paratroop training, all
criticism vanished as far as General Dayan's service was concerned—
the divine power of his assignment broke down (as it did with
Nehemiah) every wall and every critic. **When you hear criticism,
strengthen your resolve to complete your assignment so that you,
too, can glorify God.**

DAILY CONFESSION
*Father, I thank You that Your Word is the truth about me.
I decide from this moment on to shrug off criticism, look to Your Word,
and finish the tasks Heaven gives me.*

GOD WILL DO FOR YOU
WHAT YOU MAKE HAPPEN FOR OTHERS

"Knowing that whatsoever good thing any man doeth,
the same shall he receive of the Lord, whether he be bond or free."
Ephesians 6:8 (KJV)

From the very foundation of the universe, God established laws that could never be broken. One of those governing laws is the law of sowing and reaping. **This law is an avid expression of God's own faithfulness to mankind.** It is impossible for God to deny Himself, so He made it impossible for us to ever bypass the law of sowing and reaping. We cannot escape from the wondrous blessings, or the possibly grim consequences, of our actions.

In 1955, as an increase of tension broadened into an Egyptian naval blockade of Israel's shipping, Major General Moshe Dayan was called back from vacation, fully aware that sowing hostilities on the part of the Egyptians could very well reap the appetite for war. In an article published in "Foreign Affairs," General Dayan wrote, "...the air is heavy on both sides of the frontier, and peace hangs on a tenuous thread."

Now, some people are destined for misfortune because they totally ignore this divinely universal law. But you and I can be different. We can use this principle that, "whatever we make happen for others God makes happen for us," to better ourselves and those around us.

- *What do you desire for this life?*
- *Do you make that very thing happen for those around you?*

There is no surer way to experience the life of your dreams than by following this principle. May God help you to sow your life now, so that your future only reaps great rewards!

DAILY CONFESSION
Father, I trust that whatever I make happen for others,
You make happen for me. I thank You for giving me a right heart
as I sow into the lives of those around me.

EXCELLENCE IS A LIFELONG DISCIPLINE,
NOT A PAUSE IN THE LIFE OF MEDIOCRITY

"...and He will give you all you need from day to day if you live for Him and make the Kingdom of God your primary concern. So don't worry about tomorrow, for tomorrow will bring its own worries. Today's trouble is enough for today."
Matthew 6:33-34 (NLT)

There are all kinds of lists in the world: best-seller, government watch, crime statistical, animal endangerment, trendy dress, and weekly shopping lists. But excellence is not simply another list, filled with principles to be checked off as though on our daily "to-do" list. Nor is excellence reaching a particular destination. Excellence is a journey. It is becoming the very person God destined you to become.

Heaven's message is clear: **A casual attitude toward life leads us to a place of disappointment and defeat.** If we want to realize God's best and go further than our present state, we must answer His call, launching out on the jet that leads us to a lifelong mission of excellence.

Too often people say they want excellence in their lives, but they stop pursuing excellence because the price is too high. Many people become discouraged and quit the moment they realize excellence requires a daily striving for improvement. They are simply unwilling to pay the price to obtain the prize.

Excellence is something we must pursue continually, something we must earnestly seek, like water in a dry, barren land. It is the quest to become healthy in all areas of life. We must ask ourselves, "Why should I embrace this message of excellence?" Because the existence of God living within you demands that you improve—daily.

DAILY CONFESSION
Father, I thank You that I seek first Your Kingdom and Your principles. I never settle for just good enough because my desire in life is to walk the journey of excellence. I press toward the goal to win the prize for which You called me.

STOP STRUGGLING TO APPLY THE WORD TO YOUR LIFE AND BEGIN TO APPLY YOUR LIFE TO THE WORD

*"How shall a young man cleanse his way? By taking heed and keeping watch
[on himself] according to Your Word [conforming his life to it]."*
Psalm 119:9 (AMP)

Right this moment we need to stop using His Word as some sort of tool, erroneously attempting to "hammer out" all our negative circumstances. Instead, why not begin to use His Word as our guide, an informative, life-altering travel guide through life? Lately I have witnessed individuals neglect God's Word (and it is becoming more prevalent in the church today) until they need help in a certain area of their lives. Their marriage struggles so they discover what they need to do get their marriage back on track, but then they refuse to govern their business by God's Word. So, as their marriage begins to smooth out, their business begins to crumble and the cycle begins once again. This is not the way God intended life to be!

What does it mean to apply our lives to the Word? It means:

To live by it; to obey its every instruction; to pursue it, and seek the truth that it contains; to base every thought, word, and decision on it; to filter every relationship through it; to embrace the authority by which it stands; to see it as truth, and act accordingly.

God's Word must govern our lives. Jesus said it like this, "Why do you call Me Lord, Lord and do not do the things I say?" Israel's triumphant military could have never claimed Moshe Dayan as their Major General if they were not willing to apply their lives to the expertise of his training and education. And we cannot claim Jesus as our Lord yet be unwilling to apply our lives to His Word. The moment we build our lives around His Word is the moment He truly becomes the Lord of our lives.

DAILY CONFESSION
*Father, I thank You that I please You by heeding and keeping Your Word.
I pursue and obey Your instruction and apply my life to Your Word.*

FAITH IS THE MAGNIFYING GLASS THROUGH WHICH YOU VIEW GOD'S WORD

"So we don't look at the troubles we can see right now; rather, we look forward to what we have not yet seen. For the troubles we see will soon be over, but the joys to come will last forever." 2 Corinthians 4:18 (NLT)

The sky was a blackish, yellowish, grayish green that meant only one thing—TORNADO. Settled amidst the beauty of lush farmland, a father and his family loved living in the country—fresh, invigorating air, the relaxing ripples of the backyard pond, not a hint of crime, vast, animal-accommodating spaces, sheer, open land. Even though they lived in breathtaking surroundings all year long, whenever a storm threatened their peaceful existence, all they could picture were fierce, raging winds whirling into their two-story frame house like a freight train gone mad.

So what is magnified in your life – your seemingly insurmountable circumstance, or the matchless truth and everlasting power of God's Word? God's Word was true yesterday, and it still holds true today. **Regardless of the struggles we face, God's Word does not change.** I thank God that He does not lie; I know I can stand on His Word and watch Him set me free. He is faithful, and He desires to show Himself strong on our behalf.

There are two interesting aspects many people seem to ignore when believing God's Word during a time of contrary circumstances: 1) He never told us when, He just told us what He would do. 2) God is not a man that He should lie—what He said, He will do! The question is: Are you going to view His Word through the joyous eyes of the magnifying glass called faith, or the flawed blindfold called sight? We must choose today how we perceive life. **Our perception ultimately determines our destination.**

DAILY CONFESSION
*Father, I thank You that You don't lie. What You said,
You will do. I refuse to look at the troubles I can see.
I look at what I cannot see through the eyes of faith.*

ADMISSION STOPS PROSECUTION

*"'Because of what you have done, I, the Lord, will cause
your own household to rebel against you. I will give your wives to another
man, and he will go to bed with them in public view. You did it secretly,
but I will do this to you openly in the sight of all Israel.' Then David
confessed to Nathan, 'I have sinned against the Lord.'"*
2 Samuel 12:11-13 (NLT)

Just as Israel was relentlessly tormented by their Arab neighbors
with border disputes, village skirmishes, and perilous raids, so David
was equally tormented when hiding his sin. But when Samuel came
to prosecute David, David admitted his sin, and the prosecution
stopped. Once you fully admit that you were wrong, what else can be
said about you? Nothing. All accusations and prosecutions must stop
when you stand up and say, "I'm wrong. It's my fault."

Many people try to cover up their mistakes in the hope that no one
will expose them or that when they do, they won't be able to find the
guilty party. But that is not what integrity demands of us. When we
drop the ball, the first thing we must do is pick the ball right back up
by admitting to ourselves, and to our superiors, that we are wrong.

**While admission doesn't stop consequences, it does sever any
attempt by the enemy to speak fear into our life.** God promises that
our integrity delivers us. One of our responsibilities, then, is to own
up to our own shortcomings, no matter what it may initially cost. In
the long run, the cost is of greater worth than continuing to destruc-
tively hide our mistakes.

DAILY CONFESSION
*Father, I thank You that You deliver me when I walk in integrity.
I choose to take responsibility for my mistakes, knowing
that it saves me from destruction.*

THERE IS RARELY A DECISION IN LIFE, WHICH DOES NOT AFFECT THE LIFE OF ANOTHER

"Therefore let us not judge one another anymore,
but rather resolve this, not to put a stumbling block
or a cause to fall in our brother's way."
Romans 14:13 (NKJV)

Knowledgeable that his decision would affect the lives not only of his soldiers, but of the entire nation, on October 29, 1956, Moshe Dayan executed a daring, surprise attack near the southern end of the Suez Canal. With emphasis on the tactics and night maneuvers he learned from Captain Orde Wingate, within days, Israel's aptly-called "Hundred-Hour War" with Egypt was over.

Every decision we make brings with it a consequence, not only to our lives, but also to the lives of others. What we do affects other people. Before we articulate even one word, we must ask ourselves: What will the words I speak mean to this person? How will they precisely affect him or her?

Asking such questions is known as discretion. Discretion puts you in the position of another, helping you understand the explicit effect of your words and actions. **If we realize that what we are about to say will bring unnecessary pain or embarrassment, we should simply choose to keep quiet.** The above passage tells us that if we ever do anything that hurts someone or causes him or her to sin, we must determine never to do it again. We cannot allow ourselves to be brought under the power of anything that will adversely affect another person's life and their life's direction.

As we consider the affect we have on others, we are more conscious of the decisions we make.

DAILY CONFESSION
Father, I thank You that I do not judge others.
I do not cause my brother to fall or put a stumbling block in his way.
The words I speak build up and edify, pointing others toward You.

A PERSON'S ACTIONS DEFINE WHO THEY ARE;
IT IS RARELY YOUR PERCEPTIONS

"But be doers of the Word, and not hearers only, deceiving yourselves."
James 1:22 (NKJV)

⚓

With so many diverse people in our lives, how do we decide what position each individual fills? The answer is quite simple: permit each person to voluntarily determine who he or she desires to be in your life. They never do so by their words, or by their intentions—they do so only by their actions.

James tells us that we need to be doers of the Word of God and that we continually need to look at ourselves in the illuminated mirror of the Scriptures. What is in a mirror when we look at ourselves becomes a lens when we look at our relationships. You see, once we ourselves become doers of the Word of God, we must expect that of other people as well. While we may think one person is great and another is a hassle, **the truth of who they are in our lives cannot be defined by our perception or their personalities. It must be defined by their actions and the principles they choose to embrace.**

In 1967, the world saw Israel's new Defense Minister, Moshe Dayan, through a new lens, one that carried him once again into center stage. Aware of Egypt's mobilization on her borders, Dayan avoided outside help and began to act by readying his troops for another concentrated war. With each new crisis, it became acutely obvious the awesome role this man would perpetually play inside his nation's history. Yes, each person is defined by their actions, and when we see people through that lens of relationship, it becomes very clear the role each one is to play in our lives along with our role in theirs.

DAILY CONFESSION
Father, I thank You for helping me allow each person in my life determine who they are going to be, and for helping me judge according to Your Word, not my own perceptions.

SELF-CORRECTION IS PROOF
A PERSON'S CHARACTER IS AUTHENTIC

"Then Paul said to him, 'God will strike you, you whitewashed wall! For you sit to judge me according to the law, and do you command me to be struck contrary to the law?' And those who stood by said, 'Do you revile God's high priest?'"
Acts 23:3-4 (NKJV)

⚜

Authenticity…even the word itself has a genuine ring to it. And the very moment you decide to become a self-corrector is when your character is also deemed authentic. One of the chief reasons people compromise is because they have not made the resolute decision to confess when they yield to temptation or sin.

Just think for a moment how many things you would have heartily refused if you knew someone would eventually reveal what you did. Probably a number of things come to your mind. **Certainly there are times when we think we can get away with what we do behind closed doors, but truthfully, everything ultimately comes to the light.**

If you make the commitment to tell on yourself and be a self-corrector, you won't have anything to worry about when Satan comes to callously tempt you. Satan cannot destroy a self-corrector. Why not make the choice today to tell on yourself whenever you feel yourself moving in the wrong direction or toying with wrong thoughts?

Prove your character as authentic and remember that victory becomes real the moment you become a self-corrector.

DAILY CONFESSION
Father, I thank You that I always choose to bow my knee to Your Word.
I am a self-corrector therefore I prove my character to be authentic.

TRANSFORMATION IS THE RESULT
OF A CONSISTENT PURSUIT OF EXCELLENCE

"Brethren, I do not count myself to have apprehended; but one thing I do,
forgetting those things which are behind and reaching forward to those
things which are ahead, I press toward the goal for the prize of the
upward call of God in Christ Jesus."
Philippians 3:13-14 (NKJV)

They're open, 24/7—all-night gas stations, round-the-clock super-markets, year-round pharmacies. As believers, doesn't God also call us to faithfully press forward, twenty-four hours a day, seven days a week? Many believers are content to stay as ordinary as battery-run wall clocks, only enjoying fleeting moments of greatness, without ever living a fantastic life.

The common visit excellence momentarily, although in their minds, they think they do great all the time. They always think about the nice things they did last week or last month. At the same time, they wonder why they annually wait in vain for someone to finally recognize their vast achievements. But what they don't realize is that their pride and their refusal of correction make them utterly unap-proachable.

This is a sad observation, but it still stands true—**there is absolutely no advancement or promotion without embracing correction.** Without embracing the correction and modification that Captain Wingate made in Moshe Dayan's military life, certain battles might have never been won, and where would Israel be today? Remember, none of us are perfect. Every one of us has imperfections we must face. However, as long as we continue to pursue excellence, we are headed in the direction that will consistently make us more like Jesus.

DAILY CONFESSION
Father, I thank You that I press on to take hold of that for which
Christ Jesus takes hold of me. I do not count myself to have apprehended.
But this one thing I do, I assign to oblivion those things that are behind me
and I press on to the things before me.

LIFE IS NOT A CONTEST TO BE WON, BUT A JOURNEY TO BE ENJOYED

"So I decided there is nothing better than to enjoy food and drink and to find satisfaction in work. Then I realized that this pleasure is from the hand of God."
Ecclesiastes 2:24 (NLT)

How many people do you know that zealously work for retirement but never take the time to enjoy themselves along the way? Finally, that fateful day arrives when they retire, but sixty days later, they curiously die from the stress of overworking all their lives. **Enjoy every moment of every day, no matter what season of life you're in right now.** If you can't afford the luxuries of culture, be content knowing this is the worst off you will ever be. Focus on what you do have, and thank God for all His wonderful blessings.

Also, be careful not to always look so far into the future that you view your present disdainfully. Don't hate where you are right now just because you would rather be somewhere else. The mind always searches for what it does not possess. The child who has all the latest toys still wants the one another child has! The young valet parking attendant dreams about one day having the car of the wealthy business owner who frequents the restaurant. But that same business owner yearns to make more money this year than he did last year. There is an endless search for achievement, but **true fulfillment is only attained through visualizing life as a journey that is to be enjoyed, rather than an arduous race to be won.**

Following his victorious campaign in which the Old City of Jerusalem was returned to the nation of Israel, Moshe Dayan became Israel's Prime Minister, having enjoyed each one of his distinct leadership roles, no matter where those roles took him. In life, enjoy where you are at the present moment, but don't set up camp there.

DAILY CONFESSION
Father, I thank You that I enjoy the fruit of my labor and I live for You and experience the fullness of the abundant life You give me.

THE EXCELLENT FOCUS ON WHAT
THEY'RE GOING "TO" WHILE THE AVERAGE COMPLAIN
ABOUT WHAT THEY'RE GOING "THROUGH"

"…who for the joy that was set before Him endured the cross,
despising the shame, and has sat down at the right hand of the throne of God."
Hebrews 12:2 (NKJV)

Palestine of the ancient Hebrews; modern-day Palestine; now—
first-century Palestine of Jesus is firmly set before us. Intended as a
type of public humiliation, Roman execution by means of crucifixion,
was reserved for slaves, foreigners, robbers, and troublemakers.
Undoubtedly, the whistles of the mockers' cruel taunting, the slap of
the soldiers' violent whips, and the slivers of the wooden cross as it
backed up against His mutilated form attempted to create obstacles
within the Savior's mind. But Jesus, our greatest example, boldly
demonstrates the power of focus. James 1:2 tells us that life brings
many storms and tests our way. However, **only those who focus on
the promises of God survive.** Not understanding your purpose causes any obstacle to appear insurmountable. It is important to ask ourselves: "Where am I headed in life…What do I want to accomplish,
possess, and become?" Those who have no clear purpose have no
internal fortitude to press beyond their current circumstances.

We must always remember—**our lives move in the direction of our
focus.** The road to Jerusalem was consistently before Jesus' eyes, and
nothing could deter Him. Although what we go through may seem
too difficult to overcome, it is imperative that we meticulously focus
on the victory that awaits us. Just as an athlete focuses on running the
race to win the prize, ignoring sore muscles and irritating cramps, his
mind relentlessly concentrates upon his feet traversing the finish line.
So we must possess a clear, distinct image of the joyous victory.

DAILY CONFESSION
Father, I thank You that as Christ, I endure the trials of life
and focus on the joy set before me.

DOUBT IS THE ENEMY
ASSIGNED TO THROW OFF GOD'S TIMING

"That you may not be sluggish, but imitators of those who through
faith and patience inherit the promises."
Hebrews 6:12 (NAS)

⚔

A boasting serpent with long, twisting fangs; a whimsical creature of bright, dazzling colors; or a lying, slimy snake who bends about branches as easily as the wind; however he materializes inside your mind, our foe is adorned in a most deceitful costume called DOUBT. From the beginning of time, **Satan has attempted to convince us that God is not going to come through for us. Remember, God told us what was going to happen, He just never told us when.**

God's timing is the right time no matter when it is. We live in a world that is governed beneath the economy of evil, but God gave us the power and authority to live above the world's system. He gave us His Word so we can walk by faith, and not by sight. If Satan can keep us walking by what we see, he will destroy us. But, if we stay in the realm of faith, we can thwart all of his diabolical strategies.

The Scriptures tell us in Matthew 11:12, "And from the days of John the Baptist until now the Kingdom of Heaven suffers violence and the violent take it by force." That is exactly what we must do. The reason we are called to seize God's Kingdom by force is because Satan attempts to snatch it right from our fingers this very moment. The enemy tries to stop anyone from experiencing the promises of God. He puts up roadblocks, sends every demon, and ruthlessly lies to you every day about how God is not going to keep His Word. We must stand strong (as stalwartly as Jesus did) and continue to press, knowing that God is faithful to His Word. Through faith and patience, we will receive what is promised.

DAILY CONFESSION
Father, I thank You that I am full of faith and patience.
I receive what is promised, for You are not slack concerning Your promise.

CHARACTER IS THE SAIL
THAT CHARTS THE COURSE OF YOUR LIFE

"Vindicate me, O Lord, for I have walked in my integrity.
I have also trusted in the Lord; I shall not slip."
Psalm 26:1 (NKJV)

⚓

Think carefully about this timely principle for just a moment: "Character is the sail that charts the course of your life." Keeping that in mind, consider if you will the great English revivalist, George Whitefield. So fiery and convicting were his sermons that both the American and English clergy refused to allow him inside their pulpits. Did Whitefield withdraw his sail, becoming embittered at his brothers, slandering them and deciding to resign? No, and because he demonstrated good character, God gave George Whitefield a better idea—preach outdoors! And it was all in God's plan since by utilizing vast, open fields, multitudes of various sects and denominations could freely attend his meetings, many of whom otherwise would have never entered any house of worship whatsoever.

Regardless of the winds of adversity and compromise, if your sail is aimed in the direction of God's Word you will always remain in line with His will.

By embracing the standards outlined in the Word of God, your sail will never drift; no, it is firmly set to override any adverse current that floats along. And by doing as David and revivalist Whitefield, being solidly resolute causes you to purpose in your heart never to deviate from God's path.

Do you truly believe character is important? If so, make the choice today to set your sail with God's Word. Embrace His principles and set your course towards Heaven.

DAILY CONFESSION
Father, I thank You that You vindicate me, for I walk in integrity.
I trust in You and I shall not stumble.

PROGRESS IN LIFE IS MOST OFTEN DETERMINED BY HOW ONE RESPONDS TO FAILURE

"Peter said, 'I swear by God, I don't know the man.'
And immediately the rooster crowed."
Matthew 26:74 (NLT)

"Then Peter stepped forward with the eleven other apostles
and shouted to the crowd, 'Listen carefully, all of you, fellow Jews
and residents of Jerusalem! Make no mistake about this.'"
Acts 2:14 (NLT)

☀

One of the things I enjoy most about the Word of God is the fact that God customarily uses men and women exactly like you and me. In God's Word are numerous accounts of great men and women who failed, made mistakes here and there, but tenaciously refused to quit and give up. Joseph, the husband of Jesus' mother, Mary, almost failed, thinking of leaving Mary upon discovering that she was about to have a child. However, following a divine visitation, Joseph passionately pushed through his nagging doubts, refusing to yield to impending failure of what God desired for him to accomplish.

Proverbs tells us, "Though a righteous man falls seven times, he gets back up." I have a question for you – how are you going to respond the next time you fail? The reason I ask is because you have a strategic choice in the matter, just as Joseph did. See, we make far too many hasty, unwise decisions during the ardent heat of the battle. Instead, we must make the uncompromising decision today how we are going to respond to life's setbacks.

Our progress only continues if we steadily refuse to allow failure to hold us down. Remember, God does not call the perfect; He calls the willing and obedient.

DAILY CONFESSION
Father, I thank You that I am not a failure and I refuse to allow life's setbacks to hold me down. I do not quit! I diligently push through troubles of tomorrow. I am perfect in Christ.

LOVE IS THE PROOF THAT
GOD IS AT WORK IN YOUR LIFE

*"If we love our Christian brothers and sisters, it proves that we have passed
from death to eternal life. But a person who has no love is still dead."*
1 John 3:14 (NLT)

Love for Mary...love for his God, both simultaneously motivated Joseph to act. A carpenter by trade, his sandaled feet straddled the dirt of the ninety miles necessary to enroll in the census decreed by the Roman ruler, Caesar Augustus. Tenderly caring for her needs, without that love, Mary might have never reached Bethlehem alive! When we are outside of love, we are outside of the will of God, no matter how justified we feel. We read in 1 John 3:14 that "if our life has been changed, it will be proven by the love we show towards others (author's paraphrase)."

Most of us would deny the fact that we hate anyone because hate is such a strong term. But the truth is, if we do not actively exercise the love of God towards the people around us, we express hate towards them.

I have seen people in the ministry brutally criticize, step on others, and defame those with whom they work in order to accomplish their ministry goals, as if God's call was solely to build a big ministry. We must understand, however, it is never right to disrespect people, no matter how just the cause. **Even though offenses come, we must be certain that they do not come through our hands.**

If we do not strive to walk in love with the people around us, we prove that our lives have yet to be touched by God. Without love, whatever we do results in destruction and failure in the end. Without such love, the world might not have seen the Savior's birth. Jesus said it like this: "You will know them by their love..." The question you must ask yourself is: Do others know me by my love?

DAILY CONFESSION
*Father, I thank You that I prove I am changed by the love I show towards
my brothers and sisters. I imitate You and love others as You love me.*

Intimacy In Relationship Is Solely Dependent Upon The Depth Of Truth You Can Openly Share

"I no longer call you servants, because a master doesn't confide in his servants. Now you are My friends, since I have told you everything the Father told Me."
John 15:15 (NLT)

Every time the child moved within her body, she sensed the unusual, the divine. Nevertheless, young and unfamiliar with motherhood, Mary urgently needed a friend she could rely on. Her cousin, Elizabeth, became that trusted friend.

God made us in His image and likeness. He ties our identity to His own nature. **Part of the nature of God that we share, then, is the unending desire for real, genuine relationships.** Perhaps, even more than we want right relationships, God wants them for us. Out of need, desperation, loneliness, hurt, or naivety, many people often find themselves in relationships that are painful, burdensome, and even dangerous.

Without delay, we need to reevaluate the quality and purpose of our relationships:

- *Do you have friends with whom you feel uncomfortable sharing the deep secrets of your heart?*

- *If the above is true then ask, what makes these people your friends?*

Your closest relationships must be those with whom you have virtually absolute security in sharing your deepest dreams, greatest desires, and erratic uncertainties, knowing that they will support you and carry out the Word of God together with you through every stage of your life.

DAILY CONFESSION
*Father, I thank You that I become who
You desire me to become in all my relationships, and that
You reveal to me the people with whom I can build true friendships.*

TRANSFORMATION IS THE REWARD A MAN
RECEIVES FOR EMBRACING GOD'S THOUGHTS

*"Don't copy the behavior and customs of this world, but let God transform
you into a new person by changing the way you think…"*
Romans 12:2a (NLT)

✦

Passing through the gate of Bethlehem's marketplace as helmeted
Roman soldiers stood guard, merchants vociferously hawked their
goods—food, cloth, and provisions of all types. Four and a half miles
south of Jerusalem, the tiny hamlet set in the hills of Judea was about
to be transformed, renewed in spirit and in mind through the person-
ages of Joseph, his wife, and the holy Child she carried. The subject
of mind renewal is one that should never fade away from our
Christian foundations, since all of us desire to be successful in life.
God put within us a longing for more, and an innate passion for
growth. All of us have the distinct desire for improvement in our
lives; we must understand that we do not attract what we want; we
attract who we are. God gave us an avenue through which we can
become the person who attracts the very things we desire.

**By using God's Word to renew our minds, He gave us the ability
to transform our lives.** What a powerful thing! To realize and understand transformation causes one to exceed above the rest. "And why is
that?" you might ask. It is because transformation belongs only to those
who pursue it and work hard to achieve it. We are not transformed
overnight; it is a process very few are patient enough to endure.

As we begin to saturate our mind and embrace the thoughts of God,
transformation is the result. God tells us, "…be transformed by the
renewing of your mind…" Transformation comes only by renewing
our minds with God's Word. May God help us to be diligent and press
on until the outcome we desire is finally attained!

DAILY CONFESSION
*Father, I thank You that I no longer live or think like the world.
I am transformed because I diligently renew my mind to Your Word.*

HEAVEN'S WORDS ARE RUDDERS OF THE SHIP
WHICH GUIDE YOU THROUGH THE STORMS OF LIFE

"Finally, brethren, whatever things are true, whatever things are noble,
whatever things are just, whatever things are pure, whatever things are lovely,
whatever things are of good report, if there is any virtue and if there is
anything praiseworthy—meditate on these things."
Philippians 4:8 (NKJV)

Rome's invincible legions (tough units of 6,000 professional fighting men) enforced peace throughout the empire, among which was the tiny town of Bethlehem. These soldiers possessed razor-sharp swords, edged with blood dried from their latest victim, tangible proof they were fully prepared for the next battle, the next war. Each of us is in a battle, a raging war that is being fought upon the battlefield of our mind. God gave us twin tactical weapons with which to fight–His Word and our mouth. But we must faithfully use these weapons to pull down and bring into captivity every traitorous thought to the obedience of Christ.

The thoughts you harbor in your mind are potent seeds that soon develop and produce after their own kind. If a thought is not constructive, it is destructive. There is no middle ground. There are no neutral thoughts—although Satan wants you to believe otherwise!

All self-limiting thoughts of weakness, impending failure, unhappiness, or poverty are harmful and self-destructive. If God did not say it, then we are not authorized to think it. Those thoughts are fatal enemies and trenchant thieves, attempting to hinder our future progress. The key is to counterattack with the ruthlessness of the Roman soldier, and substitute those thoughts with God's Word whenever they try to gain ascendancy in our minds.

DAILY CONFESSION
Father, I thank You that I think upon Your Word. I choose to meditate upon
what is pure, noble, just, lovely, and that which is of a good report!

EVERYTHING IN YOUR FUTURE WILL BE CREATED BY SOMETHING IN YOUR PRESENT

Moses said, "God, I can't talk."
And God replied, "That's all right, you have a rod."
Exodus 4…(Author's paraphrase)

David said, "God, I can't use this armor."
And God replied, "It's all right, you have a sling shot."
1 Samuel 17…(Author's paraphrase)

The widow of Zarephath said, "I don't have enough for my son and I."
And Elijah said, "It is enough."
1 Kings 17…(Author's paraphrase)

⁂

Whatever you possess in your present is more than enough to create a future. So, what do you have in your hand? When you let go of what is in your hand, God lets go of what is in His hand.

Elijah, a remarkable, Old Testament prophet, understood this principle as much as any other person in all of scripture as he stared into the pallid face of an impoverished peasant woman about to eat her last meal. Her son lie on his bead, shriveled and withered, death only a faint breath away. Broken as a shattered clay pot, she had nowhere to turn. Isn't it interesting that God did not send her a miracle of food, or even give her money but instead brought an opportunity to sow a seed?

Elijah understood this law and was able to change this woman's life by recapturing her focus and teaching her the principle of sowing and reaping. The seed within her hand was the solution to her life. And as Joseph and Mary treaded through the town of Bethlehem, God's Seed, planted divinely through His Spirit, was about to change the world—forever. And the same is true for you and me. The solution to every problem we face lies within the seeds we hold. We must sow what we have if we desire Heaven to deliver what God has.

DAILY CONFESSION
Father, I thank You that I sow abundant seed and I reap an abundant harvest.
I expect my harvest to come knowing that I planted in faith.

NEVER EMBRACE ANYONE WHO IS UNQUALIFIED
TO GIVE YOU A PROMOTION

*"Bondservants, obey in all things your masters according to the flesh,
not with eyeservice, as men-pleasers, but in sincerity of heart, fearing God."*
Colossians 3:22 (NKJV)

✦

What is God's will for us in the workplace? Have you yet realized that He wants you to clearly understand the way His Kingdom works within a structure of authority? After that, **God wants you to eagerly pursue pleasing the authority over you in the workplace.** He wants a smile to come to that person's face every time he or she thinks of you.

At the time of Jesus' birth, Caesar Augustus was in power. The term "Augustus" means revered, a title that the Romans previously used only for their gods. Without a doubt, all the citizens of the empire deeply respected their ruler, soldiers, masters, and superiors.

Are you criticized when you try to please your superiors? Yes, you often are. However, you are only criticized by the people who have stopped their forward progress. In time, you will grow out of those critical relationships if you are willing to endure it. You can look forward to being celebrated in time to come by those who are interested in your promotion.

DAILY CONFESSION
Father, I thank You that I look to please those who can bring Your promotion into my life. I thank You that You make me sensitive to their needs, wants, and desires.

REAL JOY IS DEPENDENT UPON THE PURSUIT OF GOD YOU CAN COMFORTABLY MAINTAIN

"…in Your presence there is fullness of joy."
Psalm 16:11 (NKJV)

✦

Heaven and earth would never be the same. A broad smile illuminated the Father's face; innumerable angels sang their melodious tunes, rejoicing as if frenzied, celebrating without bounds. Joy caused the stars to sparkle with a supernatural glitter, conveying great joy to shepherds who tended their herds each night. The presence of God finally came, bringing unspeakable, unquenchable joy.

Joy seems hard to come by for many people today. Why is that? I have discovered only one answer – neglect of time in God's presence. The Bible tells us, "The joy of the Lord is our strength." If the devil can steal your joy, he can defeat you. **We cannot fight the enemy without divinely-empowered strength.**

I have taught this principle over the years – "Satan cannot destroy you; he can only distract you." Satan eternally attempts to get believers to look at their circumstances. Whenever we look at our circumstances, joy begins to evaporate from our very midst, like puddles on a blistering hot day.

Joy only comes by having our focus on God's Word and in His presence. If you want to overcome the enemy, begin to worship God and mediate on His Word day and night. As you do, joy rises within you, and no devil in hell is able to defeat you!

DAILY CONFESSION
Father, I thank You that my feet are firmly planted on the Rock, Jesus Christ. In Your presence is fullness of joy. I refuse to be distracted by circumstances around me. I am strong because I have Your joy and I passionately pursue Your presence.

HONESTY IS A MAJOR INGREDIENT
IN THE FOUNDATION OF ALL PERSONAL EXCELLENCE

"Good people are guided by their honesty;
treacherous people are destroyed by their dishonesty."
Proverbs 11:3 (NLT)

While the shepherds' hearts were flooded with great joy, the rest of Bethlehem slept, unaware that the true Savior of the world had come, wondrously called, "The Way, The Truth, and The Life." How can we excel in any area of life without possessing the awesome virtue of honesty? We must be truthful with where we are, where we want to go, and with our Creator. **When we walk in honesty, it causes us to progress in life like never before, and likewise prevents us from going backwards.** As we cultivate honesty in our lives, excellence is a daily by-product. Many times, people are unwilling to be honest with where they are in life because they know the report would be dismal. Remember, we cannot disregard our actions of disobedience and then haughtily claim we are the righteousness of God. When we evaluate our present position, we discover the truth hidden in the preconceived actions of yesterday.

Examining ourselves causes us to come to grips with the truth. When we embrace the truth our actions declare of us, we begin to move in the direction God desires for us. We cannot change what we don't know. We can only move forward as we are willing to change. God Himself placed leaders over us who see the weaknesses we possess. They understand if our weaknesses are not addressed, our progress comes to a halt. Our leaders prove their love by their willingness to tell us the truth at the cost of our disliking them. Truth hurts, but it liberates us if we learn to embrace it. Ask yourself, and ask those above you, exactly what you need to change. Your response determines the excellence in which you walk.

DAILY CONFESSION
Father, I thank You that I am guided and directed by honesty.
I choose to be honest with You, myself, with those You place above me.

THE WORD OF GOD IS THE GREATEST MAP
IN LIFE'S JOURNEY OF SUCCESS

*"All Scripture is inspired by God and is useful to teach us what is true
and to make us realize what is wrong in our lives. It straightens us out
and teaches us to do what is right. It is God's way of preparing us in every
way, fully equipped for every good thing God wants us to do."*
2 Timothy 3:16-17 (NLT)

The moment our ears catch the initial strains of the alarm clock's chatter and our eyes focus upon the glimmer of the sun's first light, we choose what kind of attitude we will display. We may think others have the power to decide our attitude, but that is never the case. By continually grafting the Word of God into who we are, we skillfully learn how to handle exasperating situations that would have previously set us ablaze. Like scrutinizing our appearance in the bathroom mirror following a morning shower, we methodically begin to visualize ourselves becoming more patient, making wiser decisions, and most importantly, avoiding evil.

We must, therefore, rely on God's Word to lead the way toward the success we desire. If God's Word does not direct our steps, our destination will not be pleasant. I have come across many people who are unhappy with the way life has turned out for them. They desire a great future but refuse to follow the guidelines established in God's eternal Word to make it happen.

When we take His Word and live in accordance to the instructions given to us, we have no choice but to see great things happen. The Word of God transforms us when we begin to get our daily dosage of God's success plan. Remember, transformation is a process; we must be patient as we progress on our journey toward success.

DAILY CONFESSION
*Father, I thank You that Your Word fully equips me for every good work
that You have for me to do.*

YOU'RE EITHER A PRISONER TO YOUR PAST
OR A PIONEER OF YOUR FUTURE

*"Brethren, I do not count myself to have apprehended; but one thing I do, forgetting
those things which are behind and reaching forward to those things which are ahead,
I press toward the goal for the prize of the upward call of God in Christ Jesus."*
Philippians 3:13-14 (NKJV)

✦

With the advent of the Messiah, every individual of Jewish ancestry either remains a prisoner of their religious past, or through Jesus, becomes a pioneer of a God-planned future. Which is it for you: Will you allow the enemy to imprison you to your past, or will you put on the armor of God and fight for the future God promised you? **Just because we are saved doesn't mean we are guaranteed a good future.** We are promised a future, but so were the children of Israel. They were presented with the Promised Land but never entered it because they were prisoners of their past.

Put yourself in the shoes of an eighteen-year-old who just graduated from high school. Your wealthy uncle comes and informs you that he would like to pay for your college education (all four years). Wouldn't you be excited? Sure you would. That is exactly what God did for us. He gave us salvation free of charge, without having to do anything to acquire it. But just because you have a scholarship to college doesn't mean you are exempt from attending a variety of classes, doing hours of homework, and studying for final exams. Unless you are diligent to do those things, you won't make it through all four years.

In the same way, God delivered you from your past and promised you a great future. But unless you put in the time to mediate on His Word, go to church, love people, and obey Him, you won't possess that great future. It remains true: You're either a prisoner to your past, or a pioneer of your future.

DAILY CONFESSION
*Father, I thank You that I forget the things behind
and reach forward to those ahead.*

YOUR VALUES OF TODAY WILL DETERMINE
YOUR FUTURE OF TOMORROW

*"Now it shall come to pass, if you diligently obey the voice of the Lord your God,
to observe carefully all His commandments which I command you today...and all
these blessings shall come upon you and overtake you..."*
Deuteronomy 28:1-2 (NKJV)

⚜

You can try for several days, but you probably won't find this perfume at your local shopping mall. Myrrh, a well-known gum resin extracted from the Arabian Balsamodendron Myrrha, was used as an exquisite perfume, an ingredient for holy anointing oil, as well as for embalming. It was one of Christ's material rewards following His birth, and an overwhelming prophecy of His future. God's Word contains principles that when applied, cause one to experience a life of blessings. Although each of us desires to be blessed, few accurately apply God's principles to their lives. We must be willing to do what God said if we expect to experience what God promised. Remember, God never promised us a reward without first completing an instruction.

God is a God who loves to reward! That is what He loves to do. But He does not hand out an I.O.U. to just anyone. He is very selective in who He blesses. **We determine whether or not God rewards us.** God made this very clear in Deuteronomy 28. Our future is only as bright as the principles we embrace. What a powerful principle! **We are responsible for the outcome of our future.** What God desires, and what actually happens, may not always align. There is a reason for it, and God is not the problem. Although God desires to bless all of us, He can only do so upon our obedience. The principles by which we live starkly determine the future we experience. Whatever future we desire, we must faithfully apply the principles to bring fruitful results.

DAILY CONFESSION
*Father, I thank You that I am diligent to heed Your voice
and act upon the principles outlined in Your Word.*

DOUBT IS THE VEHICLE THAT LEADS YOU DOWN THE ROAD OF POVERTY

"If any of you lacks wisdom, let him ask of God, who gives to all liberally and without reproach, and it will be given to him. But let him ask in faith, with no doubting, for he who doubts is like a wave of the sea driven and tossed by the wind. For let not that man suppose that he will receive anything from the Lord."
James 1:5-7 (NKJV)

- *What caused much of Israel to reject Jesus Christ, the Messiah?*
- *What forced the Romans to eventually crucify an innocent man?*
- *And what is the wave that tosses us to and fro?*

DOUBT! Doubt puts a chokehold on any blessings God wants to bring to our lives. The moment we look upon the circumstances of our lives, we dilute the faith that we possess. When Peter focused on the fierceness of the waves and the howling of the wind, he began to sink—and so do we if we allow doubt to crowd our faith in whatsoever God said.

If we focus on the circumstances of life rather than keep our attention on God's Word, faith remains dormant. Doubt is given power the moment we choose to take our eyes off the truth of what God said.

But faith comes alive the moment we choose to believe the promises of God, regardless of what we go through. **Doubt remains powerless as we commit to live by faith and not by sight,** for we are recreated in Christ to dwell there.

DAILY CONFESSION
Father, I thank You that I bury doubt by believing Your Word. I ask You in faith for what I need, not doubting, and I expect to receive what I ask of You.

HAPPINESS IN LIFE IS IN DIRECT PROPORTION TO YOUR WILLINGNESS TO TRUST THE CHARACTER OF GOD

"I reflect at night on who You are, O Lord, and I obey Your law because of this. This is my happy way of life: obeying Your commandments."
Psalm 119:55-56 (NLT)

As the lamplight flickered in her weary eyes, something quickened intensely within the old prophetess. This night was different from a thousand others—an inexplicable happiness flooded her soul. Had the long-awaited Messiah indeed come? Having reflected upon His laws and His character for most of her life, Anna knew for certain, her God could not lie.

Understanding the character of God is the foundation of Christianity. There is one Scripture upon which every person's life hinges—Numbers 23:19, "God is not a man, that He should lie. He is not a human, that He should change His mind. Has He ever spoken and failed to act? Has He ever promised and not carried it through?" Who God is does not change us until we make the decision to trust His character. God is not a man; He does not lie. God is faithful to His Word. As these truths become the core of our belief system, obedience becomes easy.

We must choose to trust the character of God. When we do, we are no longer affected by our deceptive emotions and led wildly astray because of them. Emotions are essential in order to feel out the circumstances of life, but we should never trust in them to live. Satan is a deceiver who uses our emotions to cause us to stumble. God asks us to trust in His unchanging character so that we don't stumble. We must search out and study the character of God, as did the prophetess Anna. As we do, we are empowered to prove to the world truly who He is.

DAILY CONFESSION
Father, I thank You that I choose to meditate on Your age-old laws.
Your Word brings comfort to my soul as I reflect upon You
throughout the night watches.

YOU WILL NEVER DISCOVER YOUR FUTURE WHILE STARING AT YOUR PAST

"...I am still not all I should be, but I am focusing all my energies on this one thing: forgetting the past and looking forward to what lies ahead, I strain to reach the end of the race and receive the prize for which God, through Christ Jesus, is calling us up to Heaven."
Philippians 3:13-14 (NLT)

The Nativity—a familiar scene of the Savior's tranquil birth—gives hope to the world by His eventual death, the means through which the darkness of our past is forever erased. And that is exactly why many today do not even wish to celebrate the Nativity scene: they instead choose darkness over the Light. But God went to great lengths to bestow upon us a new future, and is willing to grant it to anyone who embraces it. Enthusiastically He tells us, "For I know the plans I have for you...they are plans for good and not for disaster, to give you a future and a hope." God has a good future awaiting us. But how do we possess that great future? One way is to learn from others' mistakes. Consider the Israelites. They incessantly looked back on their past rather than hopefully toward their future. They were unwilling to fight for the very freedom for which they prayed.

The future God has for us does not come because we want it—we must continuously fight for it. It takes great effort, but the rewards are well worth the cost. The apostle Paul said it like this, "I am focusing all my energies on this one thing: forgetting the past and looking forward to what lies ahead..." **Only by focusing on where we are going do we escape where we are. Our entry into the future is dependent upon our departure from our past.** We need to open God's Word and begin to see the tomorrow He has for us. It is a bright and wonderful future!

DAILY CONFESSION
Father, I thank You that I do not look back, for there is no future in my past. I press forward to the bright future of hope and blessings You have for me.

THE GREATEST ACHIEVERS YOU'LL EVER MEET ARE THE GREATEST LEARNERS YOU'LL EVER FIND

"Intelligent people are always open to new ideas. In fact, they look for them."
Proverbs 18:15

"The wise person makes learning a joy; fools spout only foolishness."
Proverbs 15:2

⚶

At the time of Christ's birth, Rome had illustriously become the world's alternative to God. As the master of the world, Rome began to fall into unearned wealth through slavery, immorality, laziness, and obsession with worldly pleasures. They had achieved much, but learned little. Wisdom in the Roman Empire was as scarce as the reading of the Law. As Christians, however, we can be so grateful to God for where He takes us. He gave us wisdom and insight from His Word that we otherwise could not discover. **Our present situation is a reflection of how well we use the knowledge God gave us. Nevertheless, if we are to achieve more, we need to learn more.**

Knowledge—it floods today's world with the force of the Seven Seas! The trouble we have is deciding what we want to learn, and then devoting ourselves explicitly to it. The best way to solve this dilemma is to determine what you really need in order to be more successful at your current assignment.

Your goal is never simply raw information. On the contrary, you must refine raw information into wisdom and understanding in order to apply it to your life. From there, the sky is the limit! Make the choice to dedicate yourself to learn what it takes to excel in a specific area of life. Don't look back. Once you make the choice, stick to your commitment.

DAILY CONFESSION
*Father, I thank You for helping me
hear new ideas and put them into practice.*

YOUR ACTIONS
ARE A PHOTOGRAPH OF YOUR VALUES

"So likewise, whoever of you does not forsake all that he has cannot be My disciple."
Luke 14:33 (NKJV)

⚔

"That sunset is so beautiful I just had to take a picture!" Scanning the horizon, centering the camera, "click," the photograph was in her memory, a picture of that gorgeous action of God. Having securely saved it, now it would be irrefutable proof for posterity of His value of beauty.

Jesus also has irrefutable proof of what we truly value in life by looking at our actions. He calls everyone to choose how they invest their time, proving their internal values. And here is how He determines the value He has in the eyes of others. He says, "Whoever does not forsake all that he has cannot be My disciple." The moment we forsake everything—that is, every desire that conflicts with God's way of doing and being right—to follow Jesus, is the moment we prove we treasure Christ above everything else.

We cannot deny that our actions reveal our true values. We cannot say we value health yet live a lazy, gluttonous lifestyle. We cannot say we value our spouse, yet ignore him or her. We value what we do, not what we think we do. If you are at a place in your life where your actions do not prove what you want to value, then you must reconsider how and where you spend your time. **As we keep our values before our eyes, our actions cannot help but correspond.** Above all, we can prove that we value Christ through obeying His Word and by spending quality time in His presence.

DAILY CONFESSION
Father, I choose to forsake all, proving I value a relationship with You above anything the world has to offer. I imitate You and live a life of love, just as Christ loved me and gave Himself for me.

PROMOTION STEMS FROM ACTIONS, WHILE FRUSTRATION COMES AS THE RESULT OF INTENTIONS

"But if you keep looking steadily into God's perfect law—the law that sets you free—and if you do what it says and don't forget what you heard, then God will bless you for doing it."
James 1:25 (NLT)

⚜

The Jews intended to believe in the Messiah. They also intended to follow God with all their hearts, intending to learn the Scriptures and the prophecies therein. But obviously, many of them failed to do so since they crucified the very same Messiah that was eagerly awaited for so many generations. Their intentions faltered—big time!

The blessing of God comes to the person who follows through with his intentions. While we may think our good intentions should bring us promotion, it's only when there is real progress that we can expect promotion in life. **Dormant intentions only serve as a source of frustration.** We must avoid the temptation to believe that we are being cheated or treated unfairly when we don't receive promotion, even though we have such grandiose intentions.

So, where do we begin?

- *First*, let us admit that we have ample room to grow in this area.

- *Second*, let us determine which of our good intentions deserve our concentrated attention.

- *Third*, let us pull out all the stops and go after a solid performance, measuring our success by our actions, and no longer by our mere intentions.

DAILY CONFESSION
Father, I thank You that I look steadily into Your perfect law, the law that sets me free. Help me to always be a doer of Your Word, and I know that I am blessed because of it.

FOR ENJOYMENT SAKE, PEOPLE OF THIS WORLD CHOOSE CONFORMATION, WHILE THOSE WHO BELIEVE IN GOD CHOOSE TRANSFORMATION

"And do not be conformed to this world, but be transformed by the renewing of your mind, that you may prove what is that good and acceptable and perfect will of God."
Romans 12:2 (NKJV)

Marked by peculiarities of dress, ritualistic religious practice, and strict regulations, the most significant Jewish spiritual faction in the time of Christ was, by far, the Pharisees. Their name means "the separated ones," and held an assumed allegiance to God within the minds of the Jews at Christ's birth. However, with the advent of the Messiah, could these minds be transformed? Your mind can only hold one thought at a time. Therefore, the easiest way to get rid of negative thoughts is to replace them with positive thoughts. The most effective way to do this is with your spoken words.

Your mind must entertain what your mouth says. The mind is never empty; it is always occupied with a thought. Spoken words override unspoken thoughts. **By substituting your thoughts, you can replace troubling thoughts with a God-thought that has the power to transform your life.**

You can't be filled with nagging fear, superfluous doubt, and increased worry when you constantly meditate upon God's Word. As long as you don't allow negative thoughts to be planted into your mind, you'll discover true peace, joy, and happiness. The transformation of your life is distinctly linked to your avid commitment to change the way you think.

DAILY CONFESSION
Father, I thank You that I am not conformed to this world but I am transformed by the renewing of my mind. My mind is renewed by Your Word.

LOVE IS NOT WHAT YOU SAY;
LOVE IS WHAT IT COST YOU TO SAY IT

"For God so loved the world that He gave His only begotten Son,
that whoever believes in Him should not perish but have everlasting life."
John 3:16 (NKJV)

Fully aware of the consequences, Mary candidly realized that her perceived unfaithfulness following her betrothal to Joseph was considered adultery by the Jews. Therefore, Joseph had two options: expose her by trial before a court, or file for a certificate of divorcement. But long before, conscious of what it might cost her, Mary simply stated, "...be it unto me according to Thy Word." In other words, Mary said that she would believe and obey exactly what was told to her, even though it seemed utterly illogical and physically impossible.

What are you willing to do to show God just how much you love Him? Don't talk about it any longer; prove it through a seed of time, commitment, and obedience. Look what Jesus said about the Pharisees, "These people draw near to Me with their mouth, and honor Me with their lips, but their heart is far from Me." He also tells us, "Why do you call Me Lord and not do the things I tell you?"

Obedience is the only thing God truly requires of you. He is a faithful and loving God, but few are quick to obey His instructions. Sometimes what God tells you may seem illogical or even ridiculous, just as it did in Mary's life. It may, at times, even keep you from getting something you desire. But only when you obey Him without hesitation does your obedience fill Heaven's streets with a divinely effervescent aroma.

DAILY CONFESSION
Father, I thank You that You loved the world so much that
You gave Your only Son so that I may live eternally with You.

THERE IS NO SUBSTITUTE FOR BECOMING THE EXPERT IN YOUR PURSUITS

*"The governors reported to the vice-regents, who made sure
that everything was in order for the king. But Daniel, brimming with
spirit and intelligence, so completely outclassed the other vice-regents and
governors that the king decided to put him in charge of the whole kingdom."*
Daniel 6:1-3 (The Message)

Read again how The Message says in Daniel 6:3, "...Daniel...so completely out-classed the other[s]..." That's pretty impressive. I hope the same can be said of me. Do my spirit and my attitude put me head and shoulders above others? It is erroneous to think that we can accomplish all that God has planned for us without becoming the absolute best we can be in our chosen field of endeavor. The Scriptures tell us that we are to do everything as if we were doing it for the Lord Jesus Christ. **We actually contradict God's Word when we allow ourselves to slump into mediocrity or just-good-enough performances.** Once Joseph was fully persuaded that Mary would give birth to the Messiah, he did his best as an earthly Jewish father—carefully watching over mother and Son, taking the Child to the temple, and following God through specific dreams. God demanded Joseph's best, and His grace empowered Joseph to accomplish it. God's life within us demands our very best, and His grace empowers us to give it!

There is no way around it; God wants our best, and that's what will take us to the next level of:

- *A place of promotion*
- *A sphere of influence*
- *A life of prosperity*
- *A new area of fulfillment*

Make the choice to move in the right direction and embrace change in your life.

DAILY CONFESSION
*Father, I thank You for pouring out Your grace on me to help me become
my absolute best in the areas to which You assigned me.*

PROSPERITY IS AN INTERNAL RECOGNITION
BEFORE IT IS EVER AN EXTERNAL POSSESSION

"Beloved, I pray that you may prosper in all things and be in health,
just as your soul prospers."
3 John 2 (NKJV)

No one could dissuade them. Peering into Jesus' eyes, holding Him closely, and tending to His needs, Joseph and Mary were intrinsically aware—they were prosperous in a way that no other parent could even hope to understand. They sought God with all their hearts, inwardly knowing that they held the Messiah in their hands.

Prosperity does not solely consist of one's possessions. God did not design prosperity so we could attain nice cars, expensive jewelry, or fancy homes; He designed it so we would have more than enough to fulfill the assignment given to us. God has nothing against anyone enjoying material things, but we must seek to fulfill His will first before we can ever seek to enjoy the pleasures of this life. Jesus said, "Seek first the Kingdom of God and His righteousness, and all these things shall be added unto you."

Although the world's superstars, the country's top athletes, high-paid fashion models, and television's pop artists may have lots of money and toys of a fantasy world, they are far from experiencing true prosperity. **The prosperity God desires for His people dwells within the pages of His Word.** As we continue to plant the seed of God's Word into our hearts, we soon see it manifest in our lives. His Word contains the provision we need for every area of our lives.

The Bible tells us that, like Joseph and Mary, the diligent prosper. Those who diligently receive and fervently act upon the Word of God soon see abundant provision.

DAILY CONFESSION
Father, I thank You that I prosper and am in health even as my soul prospers.
I choose to speak and meditate upon Your Word knowing that I make
my way prosperous.

You Will Never Attract What You Want; You Only Attract What You Respect

"Anyone who loves a pure heart and gracious speech is the king's friend."
Proverbs 22:11 (NLT)

"Please place all your valuables inside the hotel safe," warned the flyer placed conspicuously on the fifth-floor hotel suite's polished desk. Removing her watch and rings, and ignoring the four major credit cards she considered safe inside her wallet, she disregarded the instructions. And money, well, she really didn't know how much money she brought with on her latest trip out West. What was money anyway?

To respect something is to find it valuable. What we respect always moves towards us; what we disrespect moves far from us. This is the case of many people's financial status. It is possible to disrespect money. We disrespect money by doing three things:

- *Refusing to pursue financial counsel*
- *Refusing to sow*
- *Refusing to meditate upon Scriptures pertaining to finances*

I have heard people say, **"Money doesn't make you happy." But neither does poverty!** The purpose of money is not to make God's people happy. He alone is our sufficiency for happiness. Ecclesiastes 10:19 tells us, "Money is necessary because it solves problems." When we respect money, we attract it to our lives.

Money is not only a tool, it is a weapon used to advance the Gospel to the ends of the earth. If we see money as having a purpose greater than possessions, we begin to attract more of it to our lives.

Daily Confession
Father, I thank You that You are my sufficiency. I find money valuable and choose to respect it, knowing that I then attract it. I thank You for giving me the tool to take Your Gospel around the world.

THE DAY YOU DIE TO "SELF"
IS THE DAY YOU BEGIN TO LIVE FOR GOD

"And you cannot be My disciple if you do not carry your own cross and follow Me."
Luke 14:27 (NLT)

⚜

The day Mary forfeited her reputation, dying to self, was the day she fully began to live for God. The day Joseph forfeited his feelings and pride, also dying to self, was the day he fully began to live for God. **There is a great price to pay for those who desire to live for God.**

Living for God does not just happen through your confession; it must become evident in your actions as well. Jesus qualifies His true disciples as "those willing to die to themselves, take up the cross, and follow Him." John the Baptist said it best when he made the statement, "I must decrease and He must increase." The apostle Paul said, "for me to live is Christ and to die is gain."

These were two men who changed the world by their sacrifice. Why? Because the moment you die to self is the moment you begin to live fully for God. God cannot use a man who is unwilling to die to his own desires and wants.

We must realize that our greatest enemy is the one we see in the mirror. We hold ourselves back from truly being used by God. You may hear a man confess, "Lord, whatever it is You want for my life, I will go anywhere, but please don't send me to Africa." God cannot use a man like that. We must be willing to surrender our entire lives, as did Mary with her reputation and Joseph with his feelings, if we truly desire to be used by God.

DAILY CONFESSION
Father, I thank You that I am crucified with Christ; it is no longer I who live but Christ lives through me and in me. I am a disciple of Christ. I willingly lay down my life for the cross of my King.

MONEY IS THE VEHICLE BY WHICH GOD
FINANCES BRINGING THE WORLD TO HIMSELF

"And you shall remember the Lord your God,
for it is He who gives you power to get wealth, that He may establish
His covenant which He swore to your fathers, as it is this day."
Deuteronomy 8:18 (NKJV)

✦

The iron boot of Rome was distinctly felt throughout Israel. Roman standards waved proudly over the nation's citadels, while Roman tax collectors gathered funds from almost every village and town. Jewish fathers were required to teach their sons a trade, so Joseph taught Jesus the skill of carpentry, grooming Him to become the well-known woodworker of Nazareth. Jesus' example demonstrates that God gave us the power to get wealth so His covenant can be established. He desires His children to walk in abundance so that we can be financially equipped to generously fund the Gospel. So what is Heaven's plan for the Church? To be so well established that the economy does not hinder the progress of the Church. God intends for His Church to flourish, regardless of the geopolitical temperature.

The covenant God made to Abraham cannot be established until we embrace the fact that God gave us power to generate wealth. Money is not evil. We must rid ourselves of that kind of thinking. On the contrary, **money is not only a tool God uses to show His goodness to the world by lavishing His people with worldly possessions; its primary purpose is to finance the Gospel.** When we begin to allow God to express His kindness and generosity through us, we begin to see financial abundance throughout the body of Christ. Money is a seed to be sown, not a possession to be hoarded. Remember, fear hoards while love gives. Choose today to become the greatest sower the Kingdom of God has ever known!

DAILY CONFESSION
Father, I thank You that You give me the power to get wealth.
I prosper in everything I set my hand to in order to establish
Your covenant and finance Your Gospel.

IMPROVEMENT IS GUARANTEED TO THOSE WHO ARE WILLING TO MAKE EVEN THE SLIGHTEST CHANGE

"Therefore we also, since we are surrounded by so great a cloud of witnesses,
let us lay aside every weight, and the sin which so easily ensnares us,
and let us run with endurance the race that is set before us,"
Hebrews 12:1 (NKJV)

⚜

The air was different in Palestine…lighter, friendlier, and more joyful. A magnificent improvement was happening to the people of Israel, a new Force was silently stirring among the people. During the time that Israel had been held captive by the Babylonians, idolatry cursed the Jews. But now, the Sabbath day was kept, the synagogues were filled, the Scriptures were read, and the rabbis were heard. Most Jews had been willing to change, but who would they now follow—the Sadducees, the Pharisees, or the Herodians? No doubt, Mary pondered meekly inside her heart: Will they eventually embrace the changes that my young Son will bring?

Unless you embrace the process of change, you will not grow. **All significant change begins when you make the choice to dismantle the weights of life that hinder you from achieving your dreams.** Those weights come in all different forms: wrong relationships, laziness, procrastination, negative attitude, mediocrity, stagnation, and apathy. Letting go of these weights is not exciting, but the rewards of doing so definitely are.

Positive change is not as automatic as the washing machine in your laundry room. Change, you see, is a decision. It's not an easy task, but those who make the choice never regret it. The Jews who eventually received the change of Jesus Christ were never the same. Once you decide what you want and who you want to become, relentlessly pursue the necessary change.

DAILY CONFESSION
Father, I thank You that I am surrounded by a great cloud of witnesses.
I am a new creature, all things have passed away, all things have become new.

EXCELLENCE IS THE ANTIDOTE USED TO STOP
THE DEADLY DISEASE CALLED MEDIOCRITY

"Do you see a man who excels in his work?
He will stand before kings; he will not stand before unknown men."
Proverbs 22:29 (NKJV)

While mediocrity of spirit plagued the scribes and chief priests in Jerusalem as they ignored the Messiah's birth, the Wise Men of the East paid attention to the spark that lit the Middle-Eastern air. A priestly class, most likely from the region of Persia, they lived in spiritual excellence—potently able to interpret dreams, blessed with supernatural visitations. Mediocrity cruelly infects all of mankind. In our contemporary culture, there is a magnetic pull towards mediocrity. People foolishly attempt to get by in life with the attitude of "just good enough." That mentality eventually debilitates a person's potential. **The moment we do not press forward, we move backward. We must continually rise above the temptation to accept the status quo.**

The individual who does not desire to excel is deceived into thinking that going further is not worth the effort. However, God wants more for us. The desire to excel is really the desire for a fuller, richer, and more abundant life, which stems from God. When God enters a life, He deposits a relentless desire for betterment. Many quickly reject that desire, either because they have been taught conversely or because they consciously choose laziness.

Nevertheless, we must give our attention to principles of excellence. As in our example of the Wise Men of the East, people of excellence are tools God uses to influence kings and great men across the entire globe. If we neglect to become more, we reject our duty to allow God to express Himself through us.

DAILY CONFESSION
Father, I thank You that I am a person who excels in my work.
I will stand before great men and kings. I continually press forward
to a fuller, enriched life that glorifies You.

IT IS NOT WHAT HAS BEEN DONE
TO YOU THAT DECIDES YOUR FATE IN LIFE BUT
HOW YOU RESPOND THAT DETERMINES YOUR DESTINY

*"And David was greatly distressed; for the people spake of stoning him,
because the soul of all the people was grieved, every man for his sons and
for his daughters: but David encouraged himself in the Lord his God."*
1 Samuel 30:6 (KJV)

"I can't believe divorce happened in my family," the devout woman stated to her sister-in-law on the telephone one afternoon. "Who would have ever thought it?" But indeed, after several years of marriage and three handsome sons, for some reason, the husband and wife grew distant. Refusing to take sides or gossip about either family member, the sister-in-law wisely decided to step back and pray.

Whenever life doesn't go the way you planned, step back and ask yourself: How can I respond to the situation? Remember, **you are in charge of your attitude, so you cannot blame your response on anyone or anything but yourself.** Understanding why you feel the way you do relieves a lot of your frustration.

Attitude is not based on circumstances or people. It's all about how we choose to respond! A wife cannot blame her troublesome depression on her husband. An employee can't blame his shoddy attitude on the boss. There's always something positive to focus on. Discover it, and you are on your way to fulfilling your destiny!

DAILY CONFESSION
*Father, I thank You for giving me the power to determine my attitude.
I choose to have the same attitude as Christ Jesus, knowing that
He trusted You even through death on a cross.*

YOU ARE GOD'S INSTRUMENT
CREATED TO HEAL HIS PEOPLE

"The Spirit of the Lord is upon me, for He has appointed me to preach
good news to the poor. He has sent me to proclaim that captives will be released,
that the blind will see, that the downtrodden will be freed from their oppressors."
Luke 4:18 (NLT)

Having followed the most unusual star the world had ever beheld,
upon finding the Christ Child, the Magi, the Wise Men of the East,
humbly knelt, placing the gifts of myrrh, frankincense, and gold at
Jesus' feet. Could they feel even then the healing strength that
already characterized the young babe?

Today, God calls us to continue and complete the work of Jesus
Christ and to bring His will to the nations. **We are ambassadors of
God's Kingdom, commissioned on earth to rescue humanity.** We
are not here simply to idly relax and enjoy vacations.

God shed His love abroad in our hearts by His Holy Spirit, and
expects us to love others as He loves us. We must never forget what
God said in His Word, "Love never fails." Remember,

- *People are hurting.*

- *People are crying out for someone to come and help them.*

- *People want to be free, but they don't know where to turn.*

We must help those who are wounded and hurt. Jesus gave us the
necessary tools to bring liberty to those in bondage: authority,
instruction, love, anointing, and His Holy Spirit.

It is time we take our place as instruments of God and begin to
allow Him to love and heal His people through us. If God is going to
do anything in the lives of others, He is going to use those of us who
are ready and willing.

DAILY CONFESSION

*Father, I thank You that You gave me Your love that I may love others as You love me.
Your Spirit is upon me and anoints me to preach the Gospel to those who haven't heard.
I am called to proclaim that the captives are released, the blind see, and the downtrod-
den are freed from their oppressors. I am anointed to love and heal Your people.*

YOUR FUTURE PROSPERITY
LIES IN THE PRESENT CONFINES OF YOUR MIND

*"Beloved, I pray that you may prosper in all things
and be in health, just as your soul prospers."*
3 John 1:2 (NKJV)

✦

Prosperity has more to do with your mind than with your pocket-book.

- *Do you believe God wants you to prosper?*
- *Do you believe prosperity is your right as a believer?*
- *Or do you believe God wants people to be poor and needy?*

Whatever you believe is evident in your life. Let me explain. People hold many beliefs about life intransigently formed by past experiences and rigidly directed by various people. After years of sustained thought, those viewpoints become beliefs that govern and ultimately control your life. **You and I are stringently governed by the core beliefs we hold. We act in accordance to what we truly believe, not just what we say we believe.** If we believe God wants us poor, or that poverty is our destiny, life proves that for us. But if we believe God wants us blessed, life proves this to us as well.

We are a living prophecy of what we believe. What do you believe? Whatever it is, it just might be the very thing that precludes God's blessings from your life. The Israelites believed they were grasshoppers in the sight of the giants and therefore never seized the Promised Land. Your future prosperity lies in the present confines of your mind. Believe and receive what God has for you.

DAILY CONFESSION
*Father, I thank You that above all things I prosper
and walk in health even as my soul prospers.*

LIFE IS NEVER DEFINED NOT BY WHAT YOU CAN GET, BUT BY WHAT YOU CAN GIVE AWAY

"In the same way, the Lord gave orders that those who preach the Good News should be supported by those who benefit from it. Yet I have never used any of these rights. And I am not writing this to suggest that I would like to start now. In fact, I would rather die than lose my distinction of preaching without charge… What then is my pay? It is the satisfaction I get from preaching the Good News without expense to anyone, never demanding my rights as a preacher."
1 Corinthians 9:14-15, 18 (NLT)

What an incredible man Paul was! The situation described here is a result of the shortcomings of the Corinthians. Though Paul was their spiritual father, the one who freely gave of himself so they could hear the Gospel, they did not treat him justly. Instead, they unwisely gave honor to people who did much less for them in comparison to Paul. And what was Paul's response recorded in the Scriptures above?

- *He never demanded his rights.*

- *He diligently worked to add to the Corinthians, not to use them for his opportunistic gain.*

Do you go to work adding value, or are you like crawdads in a bucket? Every time one crawdad almost makes his way out of the bucket by walking all over the other guys, another crawdad reaches up, pinches his leg, and pulls him right back to where he started.

You can live that way if you choose, but you will have nothing to show for it. Instead, be the one to propel others to their promotion. **Go to work to add value, not to use others.**

YOU MUST NEVER ALLOW YESTERDAY'S VICTORIES TO CLOUD TODAY'S PRIORITIES

"No, dear brothers and sisters, I am still not all I should be, but I am focusing all my energies on this one thing: forgetting the past and looking forward to what lies ahead."
Philippians 3:13 (NLT)

⚓

"Something's wrong with the scale; I couldn't have gained five pounds," she grimaced, stomping hard enough to cause the digital numbers to flicker. "Well, stop and think," countered the husband, tapping his fingers on his chin. "Do you think it could've been the party? Didn't you say, 'I ran two miles this morning so a couple of pieces of chocolate cake shouldn't hurt me?'" Suddenly, she remembered.

After great success, why do we often feel as though we can depart from the disciplines that carried us to that success? A woman aspiring to become more fit has a productive workout, then indulges in unhealthy foods and rationalizes her shortcoming with her recent success. A minister has a great day vibrantly teaching the Word of God, and then falls into sin the next day. A believer powerfully shares the Gospel with an unbeliever, and then neglects to pray and study the Word. Satan's counterattack to our success is to tell us we don't need to maintain the practices that brought us success. He seeks an opportune time, and immediately after success is often a time of least resistance to his suggestions.

After God does something awesome through our life, or following a great accomplishment, we must faithfully continue to reach new levels in all areas of life. God desires us to develop further, even as we reach milestones. The enemy tempts us to slow down and relax after our accomplishments. We must refute that temptation and use our victory as a launching pad for even greater things in the future.

DAILY CONFESSION
*Father, I thank You that I don't look back,
but I press forward to attain a greater prize. I do not slack or relax.
I press on to greater things.*

NEVER ATTEMPT TO TAKE AUTHORITY OVER SOMETHING FOR WHICH YOU ARE NOT RESPONSIBLE

"Jesus replied, 'If I want him to remain alive until I return,
what is that to you? You follow Me.'"
John 21:22 (NLT)

⚜

King over Judea at the Savior's birth, Herod attempted to use his authority by quizzing the Wise Men concerning the Child's whereabouts by craftily asking for information upon their return via Jerusalem. Nonetheless, God intervened, warning them not to meet Herod at the palace, but to travel to their country another way, halting Herod's plan to do business outside of God's desires. Deviously, and with great pride, Herod took responsibility over that which did not concern him.

The journey of promotion is abruptly halted when this principle is violated. It often shows a superior that the current responsibilities are not enough for the employee. Rather than fulfilling his or her own duties with excellence, the employee decides to spend his or her time in someone else's business.

Let's look at another Biblical example. The moment Peter stepped outside of his responsibility, Jesus quickly rebuked him. We see how seriously the Lord takes this issue. It wasn't that Jesus tried to keep something good from Peter by not telling him about John; Jesus tried to lead Peter on a path that would be best for him. Jesus understood that getting involved in someone else's business is self-sabotage! Peter had to focus 100% on his responsibility, which meant that he could put no thought into what another person had to do.

DAILY CONFESSION
Father, I thank You that I mind my own business,
and that I do the things I am commanded to do. I refuse to compare myself
with those around me, knowing that I do everything as unto You.

ANY STATEMENT LEFT UNCHALLENGED
IS ESTABLISHED AS TRUTH

"I told you the truth I heard from God,
but you are trying to kill me. Abraham wouldn't do a thing like that.
No, you are obeying your real father when you act that way."
John 8:40-41 (NLT)

✦

First Century Jerusalem—King Herod to the Wise Men of the East: "...Go and search diligently for the young Child; and when ye have found Him, bring me word again, that I may come and worship Him also."

God could not leave King Herod's hideous lie unchallenged. Herod had no intention whatsoever of worshipping the King of all kings. Now, God knew that something drastic had to be done, so He gave one of the Wise Men a dream, alerting them of Herod's false intentions.

As a grown man, Jesus understood that any lie left unchallenged is established as truth in the minds of those who hear it. That principle is true for us, too. Satan comes to steal, kill, and destroy. He knows that if he can cause us to believe a lie, he is able to control our lives. **We must confront and counterattack every wicked and deceitful thought with the Word of God, which is why it is imperative that we study the Scriptures.** Only when we have the truth can we fight and conquer deception.

Remember, deception believes a lie to be true. Therefore, people do not know they are deceived. They think they are doing the right thing, but the enemy artfully blinds people from the truth. We must pursue God's truth and pay any price to press into the Word of God. As we grow in the knowledge of God and confront the lies of Satan, we walk in greater depths of truth and freedom.

DAILY CONFESSION
Father, I continue in Your Word. I am a disciple of Jesus Christ.
Therefore I alter my life in accordance to Your Word.
I know the truth and the truth makes me free.

TOO MUCH TALK AND
NOT ENOUGH ACTION IS AS WORTHLESS
AS A PERFUME THAT HAS NO FRAGRANCE

"Work brings profit, but mere talk leads to poverty!"
Proverbs 14:23 (NLT)

Talk is as cheap as second-hand goods! Nevertheless, we must become men and women who no longer simply talk about what we are going to do. Instead, we must carry it out. For far too long, we have talked about what we are going to accomplish; now it is time to back up our words with corresponding actions. **God proves everything He says with action—He always fulfills what He promised. We must do the same.**

We see in the above Scripture that work brings profit, but mere talk leads to poverty. That principle holds true for all areas of life. Getting fit, building Godly habits, and investing resources—these are things we can begin immediately.

We must go beyond knowing that we should do something and actually do it. People are often content to simply know something—they then feel they don't have to do it.

The apostle James tells us, "But be ye doers of the Word, and not hearers only." Hearing the Word does nothing for us when action is absent. We must put action to our words; this leads us to the promotion God desires for us.

DAILY CONFESSION
Father, I thank You that I am a doer of Your Word.
I am not one who merely talks. I put action to what I say and
I will enjoy the promotion You have in store for me.

REGARDLESS OF WHAT YOU ARE GOING THROUGH, REMEMBER, GOD'S WORD IS ALWAYS TRUE

*"So don't worry about tomorrow, for tomorrow will bring
its own worries. Today's trouble is enough for today."
Matthew 6:34 (NLT)*

✦

Here is a comprehensive definition of worry:

- *To strangle*
- *To harass*
- *To treat roughly with continual biting or tearing with the teeth*
- *To annoy*
- *To bother*
- *To cause to feel troubled or uneasy*
- *To make anxious*

Now, does that sound like something you want?

Worry is really believing more in your circumstances than you do God's Word. Yes, it is true many don't see worry as something that is terribly wrong, but is this true? Is it acceptable to worry? Doesn't God's Word command us to be anxious for nothing?

God does not lie. He cannot lie. In fact, it is impossible for God to lie. If I am worried over a given situation, it is because I don't believe what God said concerning my circumstance. Jesus said in Matthew 6:34, "Do not worry…" Understand, Jesus doesn't make suggestions; His words are not to be disregarded. He commanded us to never worry about another thing again, and if He commanded us not to worry, rest assured, He soundly gave us the ability to obey Him. May we bring great pleasure to the Father by trusting in Him with all our heart!

DAILY CONFESSION
*Father, I thank You that I am free from worry because
I trust in the Words You speak.*

FUTURE SUCCESS IS UNDENIABLY LINKED TO THE UNDERSTANDING OF YOUR IDENTITY IN CHRIST

"I have been crucified with Christ; it is no longer I who live,
but Christ lives in me; and the life which I now live in the flesh I live
by faith in the Son of God, who loved me and gave Himself for me."
Galatians 2:20 (NKJV)

✦

"It has to be Him!" the devout Jew tottered toward the young family of three, his face aglow as the noonday sun. Having received the divine message that he would not die until he personally witnessed Israel's "salvation," Simeon's new identity arrived inside this otherwise obscure temple dedication. Have you yet realized, along with Simeon of old, that God sees you in Christ, He sees greatness in you, and He has a destiny for you? When He looks at you, He sees success and a winner. He sees Jesus, His Son!

You are not destined to lose, because He made you victorious through Christ. If God made you a winner, then what are you waiting for and what keeps you from success? God waits for you to believe it about yourself. It doesn't matter what God believes about you; what really matters is what you believe about you. Which are you going to believe, your past or what God says?

What you meditate on and routinely contemplate soon manifests into action reflecting the thoughts you harbor, good or bad. **Your life is an outer image reflecting your inner projection.** Every thought God has concerning you is written on the pages of His Word. He tells you who you are, what you have, and all you can do through Jesus Christ. You are born into the family of God through the incorruptible seed of the Word of God. You are a child, an heir of God! It is time to step into your rightful place, knowing your identity, just as Simeon did.

DAILY CONFESSION
Father, I thank You that I am crucified with Christ.
I no longer live, but Christ lives in me. I now live by faith
in Your Son who loved me and died for me.

HEAVEN SMILES UPON THOSE WHO POSSESS
"HUMILITY OF HEART"

"God be merciful to us and bless us, and cause His face to shine upon us."
Psalm 67:1 (NKJV)

An unassuming teenage virgin; an inconspicuous carpenter; a discreet birth; an unobtrusive Child—these people, and these circumstances possessed great humility of heart, refusing the nauseating pride that this world deceptively offers. We must never forget that Heaven shines favorably upon anyone willing to humble themselves. And humility takes on many forms.

However, for it to be genuine, humility must always first reside in the heart. Remember, God looks at our heart, while man looks on the outward appearance. Humility is proven by the attitude with which we serve another.

What is your attitude when you do what you have been asked to do? **God delights in the humble; He moves towards the humble looking to manifest His power and glory through their lives.** Humility is the open door that allows God to work, first in us, and then through us. Heaven desires to shine brightly upon believers, but until we humble ourselves, we are never able to experience God in this most excellent way.

NEVER TAKE AN INSTRUCTION FROM A PERSON WHO IS UNABLE TO GIVE YOU A PROMOTION

*"Then he said to the man of God, 'Come home with me and eat some food.'
'No, I cannot,' he replied. 'I am not allowed to eat any food or drink any water
here in this place.' But the old prophet answered, 'I am a prophet, too, just as you
are. And an angel gave me this message from the Lord: 'Bring him home with you,
and give him food to eat and water to drink.'" But the old man was lying to him."*
1 Kings 13:15-19 (NLT)

✦

When the package is opened and the shiny appliance is set upon
the kitchen counter, the box is tossed into the trash, leaving behind
the dilemma of knowing exactly what to do with that little booklet of
irritating instructions. More often than not, that multi-lingual set of
garble called the "instruction manual" is stored in some unknown
locality or thoughtlessly hurled away with the box.

The man above was given a precise instruction from God, yet when
another man came and gave him a new instruction, he thoughtlessly
"hurled away" what God initially told him to do. The point is clear.
**If we accept instructions from people who are not responsible for
the outcome of our future, we find ourselves in a lot of trouble we
could have avoided.**

"Arise, and take the young child to Egypt." This was a simple, yet
life-saving instruction from God, the only one with the authority to
promote Joseph, Mary, and Jesus into the destinies He had in mind.
God designed the earth in such a way that Godly promotion only
comes by submitting to authority and following their instructions. On
the job, at home, or wherever you spend your time, make a decision
not simply to decline instructions from those who cannot promote
you, but also to carry out your instructions from right authorities
promptly and with excellence.

DAILY CONFESSION
*Father, I thank You for giving me Godly authorities.
Help me carry out my instructions from the people You empower to promote me.*

FINANCIAL FREEDOM OFTEN MASKS
ITSELF IN FISCAL STUPIDITY

*"Remember this—a farmer who plants only a few seeds will get a small crop.
But the one who plants generously will get a generous crop."*
2 Corinthians 9:6 (NLT)

✦

**Money is not evil. If it were, any amount you possess would be
wrong.** This lie causes many to reject the very tool needed to fulfill
the Great Commission—"Go into the entire world and preach the
Gospel." Now that takes money! Always keep in mind these three
important things:

- *God did not intend for anyone to live in continuous poverty,
  perpetual debt, or stubborn lack.*
- *God placed within us an inherent desire to prosper and brazenly
  excel.*
- *God gave us a desire to press beyond our present financial plateau.*

Therefore, we must rid ourselves of the thoughts that contradict
God's Word. Although money doesn't produce happiness, what we
can use it for does. Every time I sow in the kingdom of God, joy floods
my soul. I know that my money is some way helping another experience the love of God. Let us ask ourselves this profound question:
How can I focus on meeting the needs of others when I am in debt
and have no money to pay my own bills?

We are the engineers of our own prosperity. God shows us what we
need to do to cultivate a prosperous life. It was never God's intention
for mankind to live in poverty. What father would wish that upon his
children? As we apply 2 Corinthians 9:6 and Joshua 1:8 to our lives,
we soon make our way prosperous and we have good success.

DAILY CONFESSION
*I am a generous giver and I reap a generous crop.
I observe to do all that is instructed in the Word of God knowing
that my way is prosperous and I have good success.*

YOUR SEED IS THE GREATEST TOOL
TO ACHIEVE A TRANSFORMED LIFE

"Jesus also said, 'Here is another illustration of what the Kingdom of God is like:
a farmer planted seeds in a field, and then he went on with his other activities.
As the days went by, the seeds sprouted and grew without the farmer's help,
because the earth produces crops on its own. First a leaf blade pushes through,
then the heads of wheat are formed, and finally the grain ripens. And as soon
as the grain is ready, the farmer comes and harvests it with a sickle.'"
Mark 4:26-29 (NLT)

As a child, do you remember tossing about those winged "helicopter" seeds, watching them whirl and float through the air? In reality, those winged creatures were maple seeds, carried upon the wind, divinely planted, and grown in diverse habitats. The scriptures tell us that when we plant a seed, it grows up and produces fruit, even though we don't know how.

God engineered the laws of the universe so that every seed we sow matures and produces a harvest. Some people argue that they have no means to sow, but that simply isn't true. The problem is we look at what we don't have, rather than what we do. Let's begin this moment to look at everything we do have. Because when we resolve to do so, we are always ready to eagerly give.

Now think of how powerful a seed is. Though small at first, it can overturn the concrete in our greatest cities. **Your seed—your time, heart, money, attitude, words, and skills—can radically transform your life if you let it.** But like Jesus said, you have to be willing to let your seed fall to the ground and "die" so that something can come of it. In fact, you must be willing to make your whole life a seed, dying to yourself so that your life can produce fruit for others. And that's a harvest worth waiting for.

DAILY CONFESSION
Father, I thank You that as I sow my life, I reap an eternal harvest.
I sow today and stand firm expecting a harvest from my seed.

THE KEY TO LIFE RESTS
IN THE DELICATE ARMS OF BALANCE

"In all matters requiring wisdom and balanced judgment,
the king found the advice of these young men to be ten times better than
that of all the magicians and enchanters in his entire kingdom."
Daniel 1:20 (NLT)

What does it mean to have balanced judgment? Picture a large, impressive diamond. If you look at it from a distance, it appears rather flat. But once you clutch the diamond inside your hand, you can examine at it from all angles and realize how truly intricate it is. **Balanced judgment is the ability to consider all the facets of an issue and then be able to synthesize one complete, diamond-like understanding.** That understanding encompasses everything about the issue. It allows a person to know which facet is most important at the moment in order to skillfully answer the questions at hand.

Our ability to balance our lives comes from having a complete, multifaceted view of everything life entails. If we get trapped in the world of business, we forget the facet of family. If family time becomes overemphasized, we begin to overlook the facet of service to God and humanity. Jesus' life was fully balanced right from the start. Each phase of His life was firmly planned; each circumstance sensibly cultivated. He was born in Bethlehem for a purpose, and fled to the foreign soil of Egypt for another.

And as we look steadily into the Word of God and do what it says, all the facets of life become much clearer—we are able to see how big, or how small, each one is to become according to God's standards, and then we truly are able to have balance in our lives.

DAILY CONFESSION
Father, I thank You for giving me Your Word, which shows me
how to balance my life. In all matters requiring wisdom I thank You
that the Holy Spirit leads me into all truth.

EXCELLENCE IS LITTLE MORE THAN THE PASSIONATE PURSUIT OF DISTINCTION

"Therefore 'Come out from among them and be separate,' says the Lord.
'Do not touch what is unclean, and I will receive you.'"
2 Corinthians 6:17 (NKJV)

Have you ever wondered why you possess the apt ability to tally the tip at a restaurant in five seconds flat, while tipping a palm-sized golf ball into a grassy hole seems an utter impossibility? In what very distinctive ways has God set you apart from those around you? No two people are fashioned exactly alike by our artistic Creator. You are unique – an exceptional handiwork of esteemed value. God put something extraordinary on the inside of you that no one else has; He gave you an assignment that belongs exclusively to you. What is it, you may eagerly ask.

Romans 12:2 says, "but let God transform you into a new person by changing the way you think. Then you will know what God wants you to do, and you will know how good and pleasing and perfect His will really is." Notice it says, *then* you will know God's will...

As you obey God and continually renew your mind with His Word, you will begin to step into the pathway of your distinction, assignment, and destiny. It is important that you pursue His Word at all cost. Never settle for status quo. You are superb! The Bible says, "...seek and you will find..." Go after it. Seek God with all your heart. By learning His ways, His distinction will be made clear inside your life.

DAILY CONFESSION
Father, I thank You that I come out from among the world and I separate myself.
I refuse to touch what is unclean and I receive You. I am excellent and therefore
passionately pursue Your distinction in my life.

YOU WILL SUFFER BOTH THE CONSEQUENCES AND THE REWARDS OF THOSE WHO ARE CLOSEST TO YOU

"He who walks with wise men will be wise,
but the companion of fools will be destroyed."
Proverbs 13:20 (NKJV)

⚜

If you want to have a successful and purposeful life, you must relentlessly fight the constant pressure of negative people coming into your life, struggling as formidably as you would a thief leaping past the threshold of your back door. You must **Stop Them— IMMEDIATELY! The only way one can maintain a stable life is through pursuit and maintenance of right relationships.** You cannot afford to get involved with the wrong types of people. As we see in the above passage, Solomon warned, "He who walks with wise men will be wise, but the companion of fools will be destroyed."

That word "destroyed" does not necessarily mean dead or absent from life. It describes the death of one's purpose. The moment you or I move toward the direction of a wrong relationship is the moment our purpose begins to fade away like the moon at dawn.

- *God knew Herod was a danger to His Son.*
- *God realized Herod was hazardous to His plan.*
- *God, therefore, refused to allow even the Wise Men to continue any further companionship with the treacherous king.*

And that is why it is vital to qualify every person who comes into your life. Find those who are wise. Link yourself to their life. Serve them. Help them fulfill their dreams, and watch in amazement as God fulfills yours.

DAILY CONFESSION
Father, I thank You that I walk with wise men and I am wise,
for I know the companion of fools will be destroyed.

THE ONLY TIME IT IS RIGHT TO LOOK DOWN UPON ANOTHER IS THE MOMENT YOU ARE BENDING OVER TO PICK THEM UP

"Be kindly affectionate to one another with brotherly love,
in honor giving preference to one another."
Romans 12:10 (NKJV)

Only a select few—lowly shepherds, an elderly prophetess, a distant cousin, a devout Jew, and later...Wise Men from a foreign nation—only this delegated remnant honored Christ, the Son of the living God. Only they acknowledged His lowly birth, while the rest of the world slept. But because He was indeed great, "The Greatest," there was no need to boast. There is never a need to boast or brag of a higher status, because true greatness never boasts. Whenever you find anyone who sings his own praise, you can be certain insecurity and doubt float around as swirling debris inside his heart.

Allow your actions to convey to people your greatness, and be content without drawing attention to yourself. Rather, make a practice of sincerely highlighting the achievements of others. Whenever you are tempted to boast, realize that there is a possibility you are probably not as great as you think you are.

As you begin to experience promotion in life, refuse to look down upon another. Remember where you came from, and remember that you have much to learn. See others as greater than yourself, taking the posture of a servant. Your responsibility in life is founded upon unfeigned love—caring for the welfare of others more than your own. Walking in love causes your higher status to become a hand up for another. Samuel Milton Jones said, "What I want for myself I want for everybody."

DAILY CONFESSION
Father, I thank You that I am kindly affectionate toward others
with brotherly love. In honor I give preference to others.

SUCCESS IS DEPENDENT UPON THE UNSWERVING CONTINUAL PURSUIT OF YOUR DREAMS

"Where there is no vision, the people perish:
but he that keepeth the law, happy is he."
Proverbs 29:18 (KJV)

✦

One common mistake many individuals make in their pursuit of success is to focus on the very thing they don't desire. Many people want to live happy and fulfilled lives, but how many truly do? Most people want to succeed and impact the world, but few ever do. In order for you to succeed and accomplish the things God has for you to accomplish, you must point your life in the direction of your desired destination. It is not enough to say you want these things. **Unless you become clear and adamant about what you want out of life, you'll never attain it.**

- *Where do you want your life to go?*
- *Which direction are you pointing your life?*
- *Are you moving toward or away from God?*

Just as soon as King Herod died and God allowed Joseph and Mary to leave Egypt safely with Jesus, their lives were pointed back in the direction of Judea. They dare not remain on foreign soil one moment longer than necessary. Make the choice today to point your life in the direction you desire to go.

Remember, you cannot control the winds, but you can govern the sails. God gave us the power to choose the outcome of our lives. The question is: Will you point your life in the right direction? I believe you will!

DAILY CONFESSION
Father, I thank You for the vision You gave me.
I keep that vision before my eyes and I make the decision
to point my life in the right direction.

YOUR ACTIONS ARE PROOF OF WHERE
YOUR HEART HAS ALREADY BEEN

"A good man out of the good treasure of his heart brings forth good things,
and an evil man out of the evil treasure brings forth evil things."
Matthew 12:35 (NKJV)

* *Why do we find the little girl continuously perusing the doll section of the toy store?*

* *Why is the schoolteacher the first to arrive and the last to leave?*

* *How is it that Jesus was always found in the temple debating the Scriptures?*

We go where our heart goes. Solomon encourages us to guard our heart above all else, for out of it spring the issues of life. There is no greater aspect of our lives than the purity of our heart. God can work within us only to the degree that we keep our hearts pure. Jesus stated, "A good man out of the good treasure of his heart brings forth good things."

Nestled in the seclusion of the hills of Galilee, Nazareth was the place where the angel announced the Messiah's birth to Mary. Now, with pure hearts, Joseph and Mary returned to their former residence that was to be home to Jesus until His thirtieth birthday.

What is stored in your heart? And what path has your heart already traveled? We must continually check the condition of our heart, because our life moves in the same direction. **We must realize that our actions always follow the path where our heart has already been.** We can protect our heart and fill it to overflowing with ingredients that lead us down the path God desires for us.

DAILY CONFESSION

Above all else, I guard my heart knowing that the wellsprings of life flow out from it. I bring forth good things out of the good treasure that lies within my heart. I am pure and God moves mightily in my life.

YOUR HEART IS WHERE YOU CONSTRUCT
THE PILLARS OF YOUR LIFE

"For as he thinks in his heart, so is he. 'Eat and drink!'
he says to you, but his heart is not with you."
Proverbs 23:7 (NKJV)

Alter your thoughts, and you will be amazed at the rapid transformation of your life. Solomon understood this principle, stating, "As a man thinks in his heart, so is he."

- *Any thought dwelt upon soon becomes a belief system.*
- *A belief system expresses itself in habit.*
- *Those habits determine our circumstances.*

Although we cannot directly choose our circumstances, we can choose our thoughts, and so indirectly determine our circumstances. Any pattern of thought, whether good or bad, cannot fail to produce results in the character of an individual. The enemy understands if he gains control of our mind, he easily determines our destiny. The outcome of every life starts with a thought. Criminal or Olympian—both begin as thought. We can use this principle to create a great future.

Success is not a matter of environment. If it were, all the people in certain neighborhoods would instantly succeed, and all those in other neighborhoods would immediately fail. It is true that some environments may be more favorable than others. Nevertheless, when two people in the same environment have different outcomes, it indicates that success is the result of the way one chooses to think. What kind of future do we desire? We cannot allow ourselves to believe or expect a future contrary to what we think. As we think, so we are. Choose your thoughts wisely, for by them you become a living expression of Heaven, or you fade away into the sea of insignificance.

DAILY CONFESSION
Father, I thank You for giving me the necessary tools to create
a successful future. I understand that my mind is the workshop of my life,
so I choose to think only what is written in Your Word.

A MAN'S CHARACTER IS CROWNED THE MOMENT
HE EMBRACES HIS "DUTY" TO OBEY

"No, O people, the Lord has already told you what is good, and this is what He
requires: to do what is right, to love mercy, and to walk humbly with your God."
Micah 6:8 (NLT)

✦

On many occasions, it was young Jesus who performed the duty of reading the Scriptures on the Sabbath day. His Godly character was expressed by His great desire for the Word of God, making it His custom, when His peers might have been out doing other things. Godly character always expresses itself in conduct, inspired and guided by principle, integrity, and wisdom. **The Christian life is something we are called to undertake, not because of a requirement, but because we willingly accept the invitation to give up our lives, desires, and opinions for those of Jesus Christ.**

The word "duty" brings a sour face to many who hear it. Nevertheless, the moment we give our lives to Christ, we step under his umbrella of Lordship, cheerfully accepting our mission and its instructions. The crown of a man's character is granted the moment he accepts his call to duty. We must choose our steps carefully and pursue God's Word fervently, esteeming the duty of obedience above the relationships and opinions of others.

As we embrace the authority of God and of those under whose jurisdiction we must abide, we bravely pioneer the slender trail of obedience, regardless of what it may cost us. We are called to obey, regardless of how we feel, what we think, or what others do not do. Like Jesus, we must choose to please Heaven as our custom, knowing that we prove our love by following His instruction. We must move from the attitude of "have to" and embrace "want to" if we are going to fulfill the call on our lives.

DAILY CONFESSION
Father, You told me what is good and what You require.
I continue on the path of obedience regardless of the cost. I do right,
I love mercy, and I walk humbly with You.

Promotion Is The Avenue
By Which Favor Expresses Itself

"Then pharaoh said to Joseph, 'See, I have set you over all the land Egypt.'"
Genesis 41:41 (AMP)

✦

"Please, take this as a seed for your business," the honey-haired woman wrote on the note to her brother, tucking the antique necklace securely inside the envelope, praying for favor, a harvest, and most of all, her younger brother. *Seven Years Later:* "There's more jewelry here than most antique stores have," the woman told her daughters, opening box after box, all colors, shapes, sizes, and styles. "Where did all this jewelry come from?" one of the woman's daughters questioned, intrigued by the sheer massiveness of it all. "From your uncle, my brother," the woman pondered, finally remembering that day long ago when love, and God, told her to send one necklace to her brother, to help him succeed.

Favor is an intriguing aspect of life. It is the desire within an individual to help another succeed. Over the years of ministry, I noticed that promotion and favor go hand in hand. Coming from one who has employees, I can say that although one may get the job done, it does not guarantee them a promotion.

The missing ingredient is favor from both man and God. In the Gospel of Luke, we learn that Jesus grew in favor with both God and man. You can actually increase favor on your life. You can grow the desire in another to help you succeed. How do we increase favor on our life? The favor of God rests upon your life if you look to please God through submitting and bringing pleasure to your boss, spouse, pastor, or any authority God places in your life.

Once the favor comes, promotion is soon to follow. May the world one day hear of the promotion God brings into your life.

Daily Confession
*Father, I thank You that I am obedient to my leaders
and I submit to them, continually recognizing their authority over me.*

YOUR PURPOSE IN LIFE IS SOMETHING YOU DISCOVER, NOT SOMETHING YOU DECIDE

"But we know these things because God has revealed them to us by His Spirit, and His Spirit searches out everything and shows us even God's deep secrets."
1 Corinthians 2:10 (NLT)

Extending his hands over the uneven tabletop, it would take just a little more work until finally finished. Chairs, chests, tables, beams, and doors—the scent of the forest ran deep within Joseph's blood. But as his firstborn grew into a man, Joseph began to discover that he was more than a carpenter—he was the earthly father of the King of kings.

Everything is created for a purpose. We were created for a purpose just as well. Let's consider Jesus and His cousin, John the Baptist. They didn't choose what God wanted for their lives. They searched until they discovered their purpose in the Word of God.

God placed a calling on each and every one of us. All of us are called to obey. There is no exemption from obedience. Only upon the road of obedience do we discover our purpose in life. The Creator decides, while the creation discovers. Many Christians attempt to tell the Creator what they are going to do. This is not the way it is intended to be. Our purpose is discovered, not decided.

This does not mean we sit and wait for God to tell us what to do. We must take action and begin to move in the direction of the desires within our heart. Action causes our purpose to become clear. What this means is along the path we walk, we avail ourselves to the written Word of God, spiritual authorities, and the Spirit. We ask the question, "Father, does this bring You pleasure?"

DAILY CONFESSION
Father, I thank You for revealing secret things to me by Your Spirit. Through my obedience to You, I discover Your purpose for my life and fulfill what You called me to do.

EMBRACING SHORT-TERM PAIN
WILL CREATE LONG-TERM PLEASURE

"An inheritance gained hastily at the beginning will not be blessed at the end."
Proverbs 20:21 (NKJV)

✦

As one of the smaller wonders of the ancient world, Herod's temple dazzled the Jews with its grandeur and magnificent architecture. At age thirteen, Jesus and His family joined much of the nation, traveling to Jerusalem for the annual Passover festivities. Denying themselves comfort, the pilgrims from Nazareth slept on mats under the stars, traipsing over rocky hills and thorny scrub in order to maintain this long-term tradition inside their family.

Today, people lose in life, not because they are destined to lose, but because they live with a short-term mindset. Happy and successful people sacrifice today in order to enjoy the benefits of tomorrow. They use their present as an investment for their future. They live with the end in mind. They are strategic about their success rather than reliant on a lofty hope that life will turn out the way they want. If you haven't already noticed, you don't get out of life what you want; you only get what you put into it. You reap what you sow. What are you willing to do to ensure happiness and success at your final destination?

The majority of people want to enjoy short-term benefits while simultaneously hoping to partake of long-term pleasures. It is no different than the individual who eats unhealthy foods yet expects to enigmatically retain a slim figure and a strong body. If you desire to live a happy and successful life, accept short-term self-denial. It is a choice few are willing to make, but it guarantees you a bright and fulfilling future.

DAILY CONFESSION
*Father, I thank You that I wait patiently for my inheritance.
I refuse to gain my inheritance too hastily, and therefore
I expect You to bless me in the end.*

ABUNDANCE IS THE REWARD OF THE SOWER, WHILE LACK IS THE CONSEQUENCE OF THE HOARDER

"There is one who scatters, yet increases more; and there is one who withholds more than is right, but it leads to poverty. The generous soul will be made rich, and he who waters will also be watered himself."
Proverbs 11:24-25 (NKJV)

⬥

Erected in the shape of a trapezoid, the temple was bounded on the east by the Valley of Kidron, on the west by the valley of Tyropoeon. Entrance to the entire temple enclosure was gained by two gates on the southern end and four gates on the west. Built with abundance and beauty in mind, prior to Jesus' ministry, crucifixion, and resurrection, the temple was the divine connection between the people and God. There is also a divine connection between Kingdom laws and the abundant life God promised. Sowing and reaping is a divine law God established in this universe. As a law, it works repeatedly. For us to live in abundance, however, we must accurately apply the laws of God's Word.

God's Kingdom functions according to principle, not desire. Regardless of what we want, we only receive in proportion to the principles we follow. Receiving God's blessings requires us to comply with God's manner of doing things. His principles produce for anyone willing to apply them. **The secret to our harvest is contained within the law of sowing and reaping. What we faithfully plant, we faithfully harvest.**

Fear is the underlying factor keeping many believers from taking the steps toward a life of sowing and expecting a harvest. When Satan uses fear to cause us to withhold our seed, He controls the outcome of our lives. We must face fear head on by sowing in faith, knowing God does not lie. The moment we sow is the moment abundance is scheduled for our future.

DAILY CONFESSION
Father, I thank You that as I scatter, I increase. I refuse to withhold; I am a generous, cheerful, prompt to do it giver whose heart is in my giving.

YOUR THOUGHTS ARE THE COMPASS THAT GUIDES THE SHIP OF YOUR LIFE TO ITS DESIRED DESTINATION

"…bringing every thought into captivity to the obedience of Christ…"
2 Corinthians 10:5 (NKJV)

⚓

"What was he thinking?" A young mother glanced over at her husband, wondering how her son could possibly think he could get away with stealing the neighbor's new soccer ball without anyone discovering it. "Maybe he thought about it since he saw it the other day," her husband wisely replied. Whatever you allow to harbor in your mind and dwell upon in your thoughts are seeds that develop and produce after their own kind. All thoughts that suggest weakness, failure, unhappiness, or poverty are harmful and self-destructing.

- *We must see those thoughts as enemies attempting to break out into manifestation.*
- *We must counterattack those thoughts whenever they try to gain ascendancy in our minds.*
- *We must avoid them as we would thieves…for they truly are…and of the highest degree.*

Our minds must be kept free from devastating bitterness, resentment, hatred, suspicion, and everything that does not line up with God's thoughts. The apostle Paul tells us, "I see another law in my members, warring against the laws of my mind, and bringing me into captivity to the law of sin which is in my members." We are in a battle, and we must choose to get on the battleship called "Godly Thinking" if we are ever going to experience Heaven's best. God gave us the weapons with which to fight. We are to pull down and bring every negative thought into the obedience of Christ. If He did not say it, then we should not think it.

DAILY CONFESSION
Father, I thank You that I watch over my thoughts and I make sure to think only what You think. I understand my thoughts are the compass that guides my life to its desired destination.

YOUR MIND IS THE VEHICLE
WHICH DELIVERS YOU TO YOUR DESTINY

"And do not be conformed to this world, but be transformed by the renewing of your mind, that you may prove what is that good and acceptable and perfect will of God."
Romans 12:2 (NKJV)

What is the difference between an over-achiever and an under-achiever? The under-achiever never changes the picture that is painted onto the canvas of his mind.

If we want to escape from the habits and ideologies created by our parents, grandparents, and great-grandparents, we must renew our minds. What kind of life do we desire? God's Word produces for us when we take His thoughts and saturate our minds with them on a daily basis. Let me add a note of caution here: many Christians meditate on the Word and confess it for countless hours yet never receive any benefit from it. Why is that? Because they never act on it!

Although thousands flooded Herod's Temple at the time of the Passover, giving sacrifices and listening to the Scriptures that were read, without the thought transformation that demonstrated that faith, their religious actions were as worthless as the ashes from their sacrifices!

We must pressurize the Word of God that dwells in our hearts. It has to work! God is absolutely faithful to His Word, and He is not a respecter of persons. We must stick with the Word as tenaciously as children stick to their parents in a huge crowd, encouraging God's thoughts at all costs. As we meditate on the Scriptures and speak the Word of God with our mouths, our new actions lead to our breakthrough.

DAILY CONFESSION
Father, I thank You that I am not conformed to this world but I am transformed by the renewing of my mind. I am transformed by replacing my old thoughts with Your thoughts.

TRUTH WITHOUT LOVE IS CRUELTY,
BUT LOVE WITHOUT TRUTH IS HYPOCRISY

"But, speaking the truth in love, may grow up in all things
into Him who is the head – Christ…"
Ephesians 4:15 (NKJV)

✦

Before we ever begin to shine the light of correction upon another, we must first take the time to honestly evaluate whether or not we tell ourselves the truth. For instance, are we unapproachable about any area of our lives? Do we realize our own need for change?

Jesus could not lie—it was utterly impossible! So when the Passover celebrations ended and the family traveled back to Nazareth, Jesus remained in the Temple, absorbed completely by the Word of God. On the third day, when it was recognized that the boy was absent, His parents went back to search for Him. When asked about His actions, Jesus did not give excuses but simply questioned in return, "Didn't you know I would be about My Father's business?" God requires honesty with others. He may lead us to talk to someone who just doesn't seem to understand the severity of his situation. If that person doesn't recognize the potential consequences of his wrong behavior, we may come to the point where we cannot let the lie go on any longer—we must confront that person with the truth.

Proverbs 27:6 tells us, "Faithful are the wounds of a friend." Many Christians want to spend all their time telling a person how great he is instead of loving him enough to tell him the truth he needs to hear, even if it hurts. **Let us choose to be a true friend, speaking the truth in love, and working at building up one another in the things that matter to God.** One last thing: Why not look to 1 Corinthians 13:4-8 for the attitude we must possess so that we may begin to speak the truth in love?

DAILY CONFESSION

Father, I thank You for revealing to me what I need to change about myself.
As You do, I choose to be a faithful friend who speaks the truth in love.

YOUR WORDS ARE MESSENGERS SENT TO CREATE YOUR FUTURE

"…he will have whatever he says."
Mark 11:23 (NKJV)

⚓

God engineered our bodies with chemical messengers so we can respond to the demands of our environment. Adrenaline is one such messenger; it prepares the body for intense action and dangerous situations. Suppose a person's adrenal glands malfunctioned and didn't supply adrenaline when it was needed. The muscles would never know they were supposed to go into action. Accurate messengers are vital to a person's safety and well-being.

In the same way, our words function as spiritual messengers. They harness the power to create the outcome we desire in any situation. They have the power to change circumstances and create futures. They even cause our dreams to materialize before our eyes. The first thing Jesus asked when a frantic Mary finally found her Son was, "How is it that you sought Me?" In other words Jesus calmly said, "Why are you so worried? Didn't you realize that at age thirteen, the consecrated age of the Jews, I would create the future God planned all along?"

We fashion our future with our words. We only achieve success after we use our mouths and declare with confidence the promises of God. Remember, words are messengers; they carry defeat and bring worry and death or transmit victory, peace, and life. This is stated very clearly in Proverbs 18:21, "Death and life are in the power of the tongue; and they that love it shall eat the fruit thereof." If we don't like the situation we are in, we must change what we say. With our words, we determine the outcome of our lives. We frame our world for defeat or change what we say and frame our world for victory.

DAILY CONFESSION
Father, I thank You that as You framed the world with Your Word,
I frame my world with my words.

YOU MUST NEVER NEGLECT
YOUR PRESENT RESPONSIBILITIES WHILE ATTENDING
TO YOUR FUTURE ASPIRATIONS

"His lord said unto him, Well done, thou good and faithful servant:
thou hast been faithful over a few things, I will make thee ruler over
many things: enter thou into the joy of thy lord."
Matthew 25:21 (KJV)

Something was happening in early, nineteenth-century England—a drastic change for the better! Following various revivals, Englishmen began to depend less and less on superstitious charms and astrology to make their crops grow, instead, they put more and more faith into God's principles. These men accepted responsibility by seeking ways to use their land in the most efficient manner possible, going far beyond their ancient traditions.

All growth requirements change. God expects change of us, just as a parent of his child. Like those English farmers, we must reach for more, pushing beyond what we have always done. The challenge we face, though, is maintaining our same level of excellence in our current responsibilities, as we boldly step into new ones. Even if we could do a great job at the next level of life, we will never have the freedom to enter that place if we neglect the duties of our present assignment.

This pitfall is very dangerous, and is often very well disguised. It is so tempting to imagine all the bliss of something new. And then, just as we are about ready to lay hold of that new thing, the ground beneath our feet falls out from under us like a jagged land fault, solely because we did not complete the very thing for which we were responsible. Let us, therefore, strive for growth while we flawlessly carry out the tasks we were asked to complete.

DAILY CONFESSION
Father, I thank You that You are faithful. I fulfill all my current
responsibilities as if I were doing them for You, and I trust that
You make my future dreams a reality!

NEVER GET CAUGHT UP IN THE TRAP OF KNOWING TOO MUCH YET DOING TOO LITTLE

"But be doers of the Word, and not hearers only, deceiving yourselves."
James 1:22 (KJV)

♠

The most intriguing section of the temple was also the most intimate location in the grand edifice. Just as a veil shielded females' countenances for purity's sake, a veil (or thick curtain) separated the holy of holies from the rest of the temple. And although the Jewish priests were very knowledgeable in the Scriptures, entering past the veil was only for the elect, established for one who truly knew how to be intimate with the holy God. Intimacy with any person thrives on time spent together, disconnected from the pressures of life.

Our personal intimacy with God is very similar. Many contemporary believers know much about the Word—they know what it says, but they don't necessarily adhere to it. Sure they say they do, but their lives don't reflect it. This is a dangerous trap, because it is very easy to equate knowledge with action, though the two are quite separate.

Consequently, many believers know that they should spend ample time in solitary prayer, yet they don't do it. Instead, they turn on Christian television to hear about the awesome power of life-changing prayer or pick up the latest best-selling book on intimacy with God. They could even write books about the presence of God and how glorious it is, yet they don't experience it for themselves. **Students are taught theory in schools, but their complete training comes when they enter the workforce and face real-life problems and circumstances.** In the same way, the presence of God can only be outlined by theory. Its fullness requires experience by real, consecrated, consistent, solitary prayer.

DAILY CONFESSION
Father, I thank You for showing me the path of life.
In Your presence is fullness of joy, and at Your right hand
are pleasures forevermore.

YOU ARE DESTINED TO WIN,
WHETHER OR NOT YOU DO IS UP TO YOU

*"If you keep quiet at a time like this, deliverance for the Jews will arise from
some other place, but you and your relatives will die. What's more, who can say
but that you have been elevated to the palace for just such a time as this?"*
Esther 4:14 (NLT)

✦

"For such a time as this…" Could that same phrase be said of you
and me? I believe so. For such a time as this, we have been put on this
earth to make a difference. We have been given all the tools we need
to make a significant impact on the lives of those around us. The
question is, are we?

Whether or not we like it, just as Jesus daily realized His destiny was
approaching, so it is that our moment of destiny is coming closer all
the time. Until then, we have only brief tastes of what our lives will
represent. We must learn to take each of those little opportunities and
use them to the fullest, and in time, we'll arrive at bigger things.
There is no turning back time, and no making up for lost opportunities. We must pursue these four things:

- *Character*
- *Excellence*
- *Understanding*
- *Relationships*

These are the four requirements necessary for our grandest moment
of destiny. God is working in us, but ultimately, the choice is ours!

DAILY CONFESSION
*Father, I thank You that You placed me here for such a time as this.
Create in me the willingness and determination to accept
Your transforming power in my life.*

WHATEVER CAPTURES YOUR FOCUS
CONTROLS YOUR LIFE

"Finally, brethren, whatever things are true, whatever things are noble,
whatever things are just, whatever things are pure, whatever things are lovely,
whatever things are of good report, if there is any virtue and if there is
anything praiseworthy—meditate on these things."
Philippians 4:8 (NKJV)

"Is it ten o'clock already?" Shutting down the computer, the newly-married husband lost track of time once again. Stuffing the game disk into the cabinet filled with DVD's, instructions, and other amusing games and attachments, his thoughts and focus were so settled upon the strategy of the game's newest edition (coming out during the holidays) that he could hardly sleep!

Your focus determines the direction of your life. Ascertain what you would like to do and vigorously focus on that objective. What have you focused on lately? Whatever it may be, it controls the bulk of your life. The enemy understands if he can draw your attention to something other than God's Word and God's will, he can shut down your productivity.

An idle mind becomes a negative mind. That is why it is so important to focus on God's Word. Realize, too, that God will not force you to focus on His Word; it is entirely your responsibility. As you do, your feelings in life keenly follow. This is the key to mastering your negative emotions. Once you have a secure grip on your emotions, you can begin applying yourself to accomplish worthwhile things for the Kingdom of God.

DAILY CONFESSION
Father, I thank You that I think on things that are good, noble, just, and pure.
I fix my thoughts on things of good report, excellence, and virtue.

YOUR ENJOYMENT OF LIFE
IS IN DIRECT PROPORTION TO YOUR COMMITMENT
TO THE PRINCIPLES OF HEAVEN

"Happy are those who obey His decrees and search for Him with all their heart."
Psalm 119:2 (NLT)

- *Where does your commitment lie with God?*
- *If there were to be a trial, would you be found guilty of a life committed to God?*

These are two questions we must ask ourselves if we truly want to enjoy life. Jesus told us, "I come to give life and life more abundant." Do we want that kind of life? It won't come to just anyone…there is a requirement.

You must commit your life to Christ Jesus. He must reign (like a king reigns over a nation) as Lord in your heart, directing your every decision. Our commitment to God goes no deeper than our commitment to His Word. There are believers who claim they are committed to God but refuse to do what God commands in His Word. Jesus says, "Why do you call Me, 'Lord, Lord,' and do not what I said?"

Though many Jewish priests were committed to studying the Scriptures, during His ministry Jesus told the Pharisees, "You honor Me with your lips, but your hearts are full of all kinds of evil."

Your commitment to God is proven through your passionate pursuit of obeying His Word. It must be your greatest desire. If you ever truly want to enjoy life, obedience is the safest and best route to take. It may just be the only route you can take.

DAILY CONFESSION
Father, I thank You that I am happy because I am one of integrity
who follows after Your law and obeys the written Word. I enjoy life
as I passionately seek after You with all my heart.

IN ORDER TO PROTECT GOD'S INVESTMENT IN US, WE MUST OBEY THE INSTRUCTIONS HE'S GIVEN US

"Keep your heart with all diligence, for out of it spring the issues of life."
Proverbs 4:23 (NKJV)

We are to keep God's commandments at all times. "Keep" means to guard, to protect, and to defend. Keeping God's commandments is a constant effort. We cannot walk with Jesus one day, live like the devil the next day, and then live for Jesus again the day after that.

We must protect God's Word in our lives. Suppose a person says, "God, I love You, but I am not going to show up at church today," or, "God, I love You, but I am still going to retaliate against that person for what he did to me." Such a person is viciously deceived, thinking they love God while bypassing His Word.

Solomon wrote, "Watch over your heart with all diligence, for from it spring the issues of life." The New Living Translation says that the heart "affects everything you do." We perish if we walk the picket fence of life, blustering in all directions like the wind in the trees. Let us rather commit ourselves to the pursuit of His Word and live the life God has for us.

DAILY CONFESSION
Father, I thank You that I am committed to the pursuit of Your Word.
I keep my heart with all diligence, for it affects everything I do.

IN LIFE YOU MUST GET RESULTS,
NEVER GIVE REGRETS

"So, dear brothers and sisters, work hard to prove that you really are among those God has called and chosen. Doing this, you will never stumble or fall away."
2 Peter 1:10 (NLT)

There is a great fallacy in much of Western culture. We mistakenly believe that we are entitled to a certain quality of life without ever working for it. We grew up in an era of relatively great prosperity, especially compared to the rest of the world. Consequently, we think we simply deserve a lot of things.

While it is true that we have a degree of entitlement to the rewards for which our parents and grandparents worked, we must never rely on that for our future prosperity. Jesus did not, and could not rely on Joseph and Mary for the success of His ministry. No, He was in the temple, interacting with people and discussing the Scriptures. Whether:

- *On the job*
- *At home*
- *In relationships*
- *In service to God*

We must always remember that results are expected. **Whatever we promise, we must deliver, and more.** As we do so, we can expect to continually increase in both our quality of life and in our influence as people of integrity.

DAILY CONFESSION
Father, I thank You that You live inside of me,
and that I have the ability to get results in every area of my life.

Your Willingness To Reach Will Determine The Wisdom You Walk In

"Tune your ears to wisdom and concentrate on understanding. Cry out for insight and understanding. Search for them as you would for lost money or hidden treasure."
Proverbs 2:2-4 (NLT)

"I love all who love Me. Those who search for Me will surely find Me."
Proverbs 8:17 (NLT)

⚜

Wisdom is available to everyone. Unfortunately, pride keeps many people from reaching for God, causing them to stay imprisoned in their situation. Ask anyone who is in debt, without a job, or in a troubled marriage, "How much time do you spend pursuing God's Word?" Their answer will be the same—little or none at all.

As His ministry began, Jesus, "Wisdom Himself," saturated the pages of God's Holy Word, dumbfounding Israel's scholarly priests with practical lessons for the young and old. And as He walked in that wisdom, respect for His ministry grew. Solomon tells us, "Wisdom is the principal thing."

Without wisdom, we cannot fulfill the will of God for our lives, nor can we live above the circumstances of life. Wisdom is the ability to accurately apply God's Word to every situation. What kind of life do we want? Our answer determines the type of action we need to take. We must take the wisdom of God and apply it, like lotion of aloe, to those areas where we need improvement.

The Word of God can be applied to all situations, but only those willing to embrace God's thoughts experience true wisdom from Heaven.

DAILY CONFESSION
I tune my ears to wisdom and concentrate on understanding.
I search for them as I would search for lost money or hidden treasure.
I love wisdom and humble myself by reaching for God's understanding.

IF ANY RELATIONSHIP DOES NOT GIVE BIRTH TO CHANGE, THEN ANY FURTHER ASSOCIATION IS UNNECESSARY

"As iron sharpens iron, so a man sharpens the countenance of his friend."
Proverbs 27:17 (NKJV)

If the relationship between Joseph and Jesus had not given birth to change, foretelling something new, then their close association as parent and child would have been completely unnecessary. So, with schooling behind Him, wood chips now intriguingly clung to Jesus' fingertips, the pegs hammered straight, just as Joseph instructed. Change and growth compellingly marked the relationship between Joseph and Jesus, the carpenter and his apprentice. Joseph's firstborn Son was willing to learn how to work as an adult, convincing others by His presence to live honest and pure.

If you are not changing and growing as a result of your relationships, then what is the point of continuing them? Is there something beyond the fishing trips and the shopping sprees? **We must not allow mediocrity to penetrate our lives through the influence of mediocre relationships!** Such influence may appear benign, but like cancer, it is indeed deadly.

If you are going to be thrust into a dynamic future, then you must surround yourself with dynamic, excellent individuals who might sometimes even make you feel uncomfortable, as was often the case with the master and his apprentice—father and Son. These individuals compel you, by their very presence, to unearth the excellence within yourself. Embrace their correction and allow them to be honest with you. By doing this, change is inevitable.

DAILY CONFESSION
Father, I thank You as iron sharpens iron,
I sharpen those I call friend.

HUMAN CONSEQUENCES EXIST
EVEN IN THE FACE OF DIVINE FORGIVENESS

*"From this time on, the sword will be a constant threat to your family,
because you have despised me by taking Uriah's wife to be your own.
But you have given the enemies of the Lord great opportunity
to despise and blaspheme Him, so your child will die."*
2 Samuel 12:10, 14 (NLT)

✦

As He matured into a man, Jesus undoubtedly began to realize His mission on earth—to provide forgiveness for the sin of all mankind. But God's forgiveness through Christ does not override the consequences that come from my sin. Just because I repent for my sin does not mean I won't experience the consequences of that sin. This was the case for David. When Nathan confronted David over his sin with Bathsheba, David repented and made this declaration, "I have sinned against God and God alone." Although David repented, the sword did not leave David's family and his infant son also died (2 Samuel 12:10, 14).

Forgiveness does not mean God wipes away the consequences of our sin—it simply means He wipes away the memory of the sin we committed, like marks wiped away from a glass (Psalm 103:12). But I must face up to the consequences of my decisions and accept them, knowing they are a result of my own construction. I go to God to clear the shame, guilt, and memory that stem from my lack of obedience, but I do not expect God to remove the harvest of my wrongdoing.

God is just, and the law of sowing and reaping works both ways. Life returns to me exactly what I put into it. And that is a truth I must embrace, otherwise, I get angry at God for not removing the varied consequences of my choices.

DAILY CONFESSION
*Father, I thank You that You forgive me.
I understand that human consequences exist, even in the face of
divine forgiveness, and I humbly accept the harvest of my decisions.*

THE BRIDGE TO GOD'S WILL CAN NEVER BE CROSSED
UNTIL THE BRIDGE FROM YOUR WILL IS FINALLY BURNED

"Again, a second time, He went away and prayed, saying, "O My Father,
if this cup cannot pass away from Me unless I drink it, Your will be done."
Matthew 26:42 (NKJV)

His unmistakable scent; his legendary stride; his fury, his anointing—when Elijah appeared at Elisha's field, no one could mistake what had happened. The coat of the fiery prophet Elijah was symbolically presented to Elisha, signaling to everyone that Elisha was to follow the prophet of God. At the time, Elisha's livelihood was his team of oxen and his plow. When the man of God arrived, however, Elisha burned his plow until it became ash and roasted his oxen for a commemorative meal. There could be no retreat, just as there would be no retreat for Jesus when it came time for the Father's will to be done on the cross. Jesus, as well as Elisha, walked confidently into the will of God. The will of God is not as mysterious as it may seem.

First Thessalonians 5:16-18 tells us exactly what God's will is for our lives: "Always be joyful. Keep on praying. No matter what happens, always be thankful, for this is God's will for you who belong to Christ Jesus." God's will is contained in those explicit instructions: Don't be like the world… Embrace God's way of thinking… Always be joyful… Keep on praying… And always be thankful.

We fulfill God's will when we follow these commands. To live in such a way means we must be thoroughly finished with our own way of living. We must burn the bridges to our own righteousness, troubles, and time constraints. The bridge of God's Word that lies in front of us transports us to God's will. The secret, nonetheless, is to remain firmly on the bridge.

DAILY CONFESSION
Father, I thank You that I am not conformed to this world,
but I am transformed by the renewing of my mind, and
I prove what is Your good, pleasing, and perfect will.

EVERYTHING IN YOUR LIFE WILL REMAIN A SEED UNTIL YOU CHOOSE TO SOW IT

*"I tell you the truth, unless a kernel of wheat falls to the ground and dies,
it remains only a single seed. But if it dies, it produces many seeds."*
John 12:24 (NIV)

In recent years, archaeologists have discovered seeds that are thousands of years old. To the surprise of many, when these seeds were planted, they began to grow. We can be ensured, therefore, that our seed is entirely dormant until we place it in the proper soil. While the seeds were in storage, they were only seeds. Yet, once they were planted, the seeds "died," but a new plant grew in its place.

Early in His ministry, Jesus informed us that this would happen. Yet, the seeds of our lives remain just that, mere seeds, until we strategically plant them in fertile soil. What seeds are you holding in your hand? What have you been unwilling to release?

Take a look around your life. Everything you have is a potential seed, but the only way to receive a harvest is to sow. Be aware, though, that the Scriptures speak of seed, time, and harvest.

Your harvest takes time, and you must be prepared to wait. Rest assured that, just as crops often spring up without the farmer's knowledge or assistance, your seed also grows up and brings you a harvest at the appointed time.

DAILY CONFESSION
*Father, I thank You that You give seed to the sower
and that You cause my harvest to come so I can sow again.*

SEEDTIME IS THE ONLY REQUIREMENT
THAT HEAVEN PUBLISHES FOR AN ABUNDANT HARVEST

"While the earth remains, seedtime and harvest, cold and heat,
winter and summer, and day and night shall not cease."
Genesis 8:22 (NKJV)

"Are we there yet?" For anyone who has ever been around children, that irksome refrain is as familiar as gum on the bottom of their shoes. But even as adults we can generally agree that waiting on God is not easy. I have come to understand in my own life that waiting gives me an opportunity to prove my reliance on God. **It is *not* our ability to wait, but our attitude during the waiting process that catches the attention of God.**

God requires us to sow a seed wrapped in our faith, and to hold fast to our confession for He who promised is faithful. Always remember that the sequence of sowing is: 1) Seed 2) TIME 3) Harvest.

God's timing is always perfect for the harvest of our seed. He is never too late; He is never too early. Let us not worry about what God is going to do — He will always do His part. What we must take care of is our part. Always remember that your seed, when planted in the right soil, always produces a harvest.

DAILY CONFESSION
Father, I thank You that You cause my seed to harvest in due time.
I understand that a man who sows sparingly harvests sparingly, but a man
who sows generously harvests generously. I choose to sow knowing that whatever
I sow is what I reap. Lord, I thank You that Your timing is perfect.

DECEPTION BECOMES EVIDENT THE MOMENT THAT TRUTH ENTERS THE ROOM

"And you will know the truth, and the truth will set you free."
John 8:31-32 (NLT)

⚔

As a carpenter, Jesus knew a great deal about the art of measuring, various kinds of wood, the construction of houses, and the shape of rooms. Additionally, there were yokes to make for the oxen and tools for the farmers. And as an attentive servant of the people of Nazareth, spending hours creating objects for their daily use, Jesus knew the difference between deception and truth. In fact, Jesus has this to say concerning Satan, "He is a liar and the father of all lies." Although Satan cannot destroy us, ignorance can. **God gave us His Word so we would walk above any deception Satan brings our way.** The enemy attempts to twist and pervert the truth of God's Word. As the father of lies, he convinces many that God is the one who is the liar.

We must never take ignorance lightly. Contrary to popular belief, what we don't know will eventually hurt us. God's Word states, "My people perish for lack of knowledge." Not knowing what the Word of God says concerning an issue opens the door to deception. Remember, deception believes something to be true when it is not. Some of the most confident men and women are misled without even realizing it. The Scriptures are given to us so we may know the thoughts of God in every area of our lives. As we press into the truth of God's Word, we have the ability to clearly identify and ruthlessly expose the deception of the enemy.

God's Word is truth. We must keep it before our eyes and meditate upon it day and night. As we continue in the Word, deception flees because the darkness of deception cannot withstand the light of truth.

DAILY CONFESSION
Father, I thank You that I passionately pursue the truth of Your Word.
I am truly Your disciple because I obey Your teachings.

WISDOM MUST BE CHOSEN;
UNDERSTANDING MUST BE PURSUED

"Wisdom is supreme; therefore get wisdom.
Though it cost all you have, get understanding."
Proverbs 4:7 (NLT)

✦

"Why Mom? Why Mom? Why Mom?" Even preschool children are on a quest for wisdom, and for many years, my passion was to know what God thought and said about any given subject. Now, I want to know why God said what He said. I have come to understand that wisdom is *what* God said...understanding is *why* God said it. If we as believers can understand why God said something, we will have no trouble doing what He plainly instructed us to do.

I must make this clear: **You cannot begin to pursue understanding until you first choose wisdom.** One must willingly do what He said before one can qualify to ask God what He meant by His statement.

You see this mistake in many young people as they are trained in the way they should go. Their father may say, "Son, I want you to take out the trash right now." The son may respond, "Why now? Can't I do it later?" At times, the body of Christ acts the same way. I truly believe that God will not grant me understanding until I first obey His Word with unquestioned compliance.

We must first choose wisdom, and then passionately pursue understanding if we desire to mature into the likeness of Christ Jesus.

DAILY CONFESSION
Father, I thank You that I choose wisdom as it is the principal thing.
Though it cost all I have, I passionately pursue understanding.

YOUR SEED OF TODAY WILL CREATE
YOUR HARVEST OF TOMORROW

"But this I say: he who sows sparingly will also reap sparingly,
and he who sows bountifully will also reap bountifully."
2 Corinthians 9:6 (NKJV)

As Roman flags fluttered in the warm breezes of Palestine, restlessness indignantly characterized the land, oozing like olive oil from a fractured lamp. An unpleasant reminder that Israel was not yet free, faint whispers of a King, a Liberator, the long-awaited Messiah, rode on the coattails of those breezes: hopeful, ready, uncertain. And as John began sowing the seed, baptizing in the River Jordan, Jesus and Heaven prepared to reap the harvest. The law of sowing and reaping persistently governs your entire life, whether or not you realize it! As with any law, you can either work it to your advantage, or experience the consequences it may bring. **God gave each of us a method to create the future He called us to live; He does not just give us what we want because we ask for it.**

Your seed of today creates your harvest of tomorrow, therefore:

- *What kind of relationships do you desire to attain?*
- *What kind of life would you like to live?*
- *How much money would you like to acquire?*

God tells us, "Whatever a man sows that shall he reap." So often we erroneously believe that God is going to make our relationships work, give us a fantastic life, and shower finances on us like a steady drizzle in the middle of spring. But if we are honest with ourselves, we know this is not the case in our personal life. God told Joshua, "You will make your way prosperous and you will have good success if you meditate, speak, and act on My Word." What you sow you certainly reap. We must always remember, however, we can never harvest from a seed never sown. Choose to sow your life today!

DAILY CONFESSION
Father, I thank You that I sow bountifully and therefore I reap bountifully.

A SEED NEVER SOWN
WILL PRODUCE A HARVEST NEVER GROWN

"…for whatever a man sows that and that only is what he will reap."
Galatians 6:7 (AMP)

Any farmer knows that it is foolish to expect a harvest from seed he never sows. In all of life, there is no such thing as a harvest that did not first begin as a seed. There are many today in the body of Christ who continually beg God for a harvest, although there was never a time when they ever sowed a seed. Though diverse in appearance and habits, John and Jesus were of the same family, the same seed, planning the same harvest. And it is interesting to note that as John's fundamental ministry was to prepare Israel for Jesus' ministry, so must we prepare for the harvest God so intricately planned.

Never complain to Heaven about a harvest from a seed you have never sown. In fact, even those who sow never need to approach God about their harvest. The law of sowing and reaping is intact. If you sow, you will reap. You don't need to spend many hours in prayer for a harvest.

- *Just sow the seed*
- *Wait in faith*
- *And expect that the harvest will come*

Soon, you will find it coming to the shoreline of your life, sailing upon every wave.

DAILY CONFESSION
Father, I thank You that I understand that whatever I sow is what I reap.
I choose to sow the right seeds today that will produce the future You desire
for my life. I won't grow weary in well doing, for I know that in due time
I will reap a harvest if I do not faint.

THE CLOSER WE WALK WITH GOD, THE MORE OUR HEARTS WILL BEAT AS ONE

"Jesus answered and said to him, 'If anyone loves Me, he will keep My Word; and My Father will love him, and We will come to him and make Our home with him.'"
John 14:23 (NKJV)

Following His baptism, Jesus was led to the wilderness where His spirit and flesh were allowed to be tested by the enemy. Have you realized that the spirit and flesh are in constant contention, much like the relentless conflict between the Arabs and the Jews? Neither is willing to compromise; there is no middle ground. The difficulty we face is that for all the years before we came to Christ, our flesh was the only voice that directed our lives. When we came to Christ, our old sinful selves were crucified, and we were given a new mandate: to walk in the spirit, and in doing so, to starve the lusts of the flesh.

Any effort we make to draw near to God sounds an alarm in the fortress of our flesh. To illustrate, slowly read the following sentence aloud: "I am going to fast for the next three days." Now, the moment you said that, what thoughts crossed your mind? Were they thoughts of experiencing God's presence to a new fullness, or thoughts of panic and hunger?

Both the spirit and the flesh have a distinct voice. We need to strengthen our spirit so that its voice reverberates in our hearts with the blast of a trumpet, and so that our flesh can hardly utter a peep. Remember the adage, the dog that wins the fight is the one that is fed the most. Walking with God is not an emotional or surreal concept. It is very real and very normal. Intimacy with God is not super-spirituality. Rather, it is a confident assurance that we live in accordance with God's commands, that our will (just as that of the Lord Jesus Christ) is totally submitted to His.

DAILY CONFESSION
Father, I thank You that I walk in the Spirit and let the Lord Jesus Christ control my life, and I do not fulfill the lusts of the flesh.

YOU CAN NEVER WASH AWAY THE CONSEQUENCES OF WRONGDOING WITH THE TEARS OF SORROW

"If you are willing and obedient, you shall eat the good of the land;
but if you refuse and rebel, you shall be devoured by the sword;
for the mouth of the Lord has spoken."
Isaiah 1:19-20 (NKJV)

⚶

Two months had miserably passed since the shock of his death. Awakened by the gunshots, five quick blasts, upon opening her back door, there he was, her husband of twenty years, lying on the cold driveway, a mess of blood and flesh emulating from what had been his head. "I want to get out but I can't," she had heard him whisper into the telephone a few days before his death. Somehow, some way, he got in with the wrong crowd. Now, although the holes from the bullets that hit the garage were being filled in and repaired, the consequences of his actions would remain.

Radically condemning the Jewish "establishment" of that day, John the Baptist called Israel into a "new beginning," a baptism of repentance from years of stubborn sin. And although scores were baptized, cleansing their lives of wrongdoing, the consequences remained. **It is essential to realize that living the life God intended begins by recognizing there are consequences for our actions, just as there were consequences for the man who got involved with the wrong crowd.** Of course, we live in a society today where consequences for a lack of self-control are few and far between.

But we need to realize that even though society hands out very few consequences for wrong behavior, there are great consequences in the Kingdom of God, and those consequences don't go away with the wind.

> **DAILY CONFESSION**
> *Father, I thank You that I am willing and obedient*
> *and I eat the best of the land.*

PROGRESS IS GUARANTEED THE MOMENT
YOU COMMIT YOUR LIFE INTO THE HANDS OF GOD

"He must increase, but I must decrease."
John 3:30 (KJV)

✦

Like a careless match setting a house wildly aflame, ultimately rendering it into nothing but a useless pile of rubble, it is only a matter of time before we see those who have yet to commit their life to God cry out for help. Although they may have all the worldly possessions one could want, in reality, their life is little more than a brittle heap of scorched ash.

God always begins His strategic work on the inside before He ever manifests the final product on the outside. True progress is when one commits his or her life and plans to the Lord, allowing Him to exclusively lead. And as soon as you commit your work to the Lord, somehow through Him, your plans begin to favorably succeed.

Choose today to give God not part, but your entire life. He deserves it, doesn't He? God desires to make you great; all He requests is your heartfelt compliance! John the Baptist said (and we must do the same), "I must decrease and He must increase." That means the more we pursue God, the less we desire the pleasurable things this world offers, thereby allowing the progression of His will to be accomplished.

DAILY CONFESSION
Father, I choose to decrease so Jesus may increase in my life.

THE WAY YOU TREAT A RELATIONSHIP
WHEN YOU NO LONGER NEED IT REVEALS
THE MOTIVES OF YOUR CHARACTER

"And Lot lifted his eyes and saw all the plain of Jordan, that it was
well watered everywhere (before the Lord destroyed Sodom and Gomorrah)
like the garden of the Lord, like the land of Egypt as you go toward Zoar.
Then Lot chose for himself all the plain of Jordan, and Lot journeyed
east. And they separated from each other."
Genesis 13:10 (NKJV)

The way you treat a relationship when it no longer saves your life, pays your bills, or soothes your broken heart candidly reveals the motive you had for it, right from the very start. It is impossible to escape your motives once you establish them as the direction for your life. With pure motive of heart, John the Baptist "made way for the Christ" since Jesus' baptism by John was a starting point for apostolic preaching and the new, exhilarating era of salvation.

John's meekness in his attitude toward Christ, making way and standing aside as the Son of God commenced His ministry, revealed the true motive of his character—humility, selflessness, and sacrificial purity.

Carefully examine your motives before entering any relationship, but especially a relationship with an authority figure. If there is even a shred of selfishness in your heart, any thought of "What's in it for me?" you would be wise to stop pursing that relationship until you purify your motives. Otherwise, you'll run into a dead end and be at a regretful loss to appropriately recover.

DAILY CONFESSION
Father, I thank You that You purify the motives of my heart.
I choose today to lose myself so I can be a person who adds value
to those with whom I am in relationship.

PREPARE FOR WHAT YOU WANT
OR SETTLE FOR WHAT YOU'VE GOT

"But we all, with unveiled face, beholding as in a mirror the glory
of the Lord, are being transformed into the same image
from glory to glory, just as by the Spirit of the Lord."
2 Corinthians 3:18 (NKJV)

His thoughts resting upon God as his feet sunk into the desert sand, John's garment scratched against his weathered skin, Heaven's voice echoing louder than all the wild animals in the barren wilderness combined. Realizing that change was apparent, that his long years alone were about to end, he was willing for God's change, prepared to become the vessel through which the Holy Spirit could perform His vital work. **Instead of always wanting our circumstances or the people around us to change, we must be willing for God to change us on a daily basis.** Only then can we become the kinds of vessels through which the Holy Spirit can help others.

It is God's plan for us to continually be in a state of transformation as we become increasingly more like Jesus. Unfortunately, the vast majority of Christians refuses to change. We want our circumstances to change but we do not want to change. In fact, statistics show that in America, more than ninety-three percent of the population refuses to change.

We must be willing to change if we want to excel and win in this life. We must embrace change every day, as did John the Baptist, so we can be significant in the lives of those we serve and in the heart and mind of God as He leads us into the fullness of what He plans for us. Take a moment and ask yourself this question: What single change have I avoided and postponed for a later time?

DAILY CONFESSION
Father, I thank You that with an unveiled face,
I behold Your glory as in a mirror. I am transformed into
the same image from glory to glory by Your Spirit.

YOU CANNOT REGAIN THROUGH REPENTANCE THAT WHICH YOU LOST BY DISOBEDIENCE

*"Then the Lord spoke to Moses and Aaron, 'Because
you did not believe Me, to hallow Me in the eyes of the children of Israel,
therefore you shall not bring this assembly into the land which I have given them.'"*
Numbers 20:12 (NKJV)

When we observe the lives of Adam, Moses, David, Samson, Judas, and even Lucifer, we see that Scripture continually exemplifies this principle. Still, there are many people who truly believe God is a God of the second chance. The Scripture, however, does not support this teaching. God is a God of fresh starts, but never will we regain the same position as the day we disobeyed God. If one were to fail a class, he would not start where he failed; he would have to repeat the entire class. Although he had a fresh start, he could not regain the position he once held in that class, nor could he recoup his time.

Let's take a closer look at Moses. God told him to speak to the rock, but Moses decided he was going to disobey God. Out of frustration, instead of speaking to the rock, he struck it with all his might. Then notice what God said, "Because you did not believe Me, to hallow Me in the eyes of the children of Israel, therefore you shall not bring this assembly into the land which I have given them." God did not allow Moses to enter the Promised Land because of his disobedience. Just one act of disobedience kept Moses from enjoying the pleasures of Canaan.

We must clearly understand—God is serious about our obedience; life is not merely a game to Him. **He can only reward the obedient.** He desires for all of us to possess the Promised Land, but only those who choose the avenue of obedience enjoy the fruit of Canaan.

DAILY CONFESSION
*Father, I thank You that I am willing and obedient,
therefore, I eat the best of the land. My obedience proves
my trust in You and I choose to obey Your instruction.*

GRATITUDE IS THE HARVEST YOU RETURN
TO THOSE WHO HAVE SOWN INTO YOUR LIFE

"And one of them, when he saw that he was healed, returned, and with a loud voice glorified God, and fell down on his face at His feet, giving Him thanks."
Luke 17:15-19 (NKJV)

Openly acknowledging Jesus of Nazareth as the Lamb of God, the hoped-for Messiah, John the Baptist was grateful for the role God gave him, exceedingly thankful, even as his own ministry began to decrease, while Christ's would exponentially increase! Jealousy would have no part within this divine connection that set the stage for God's greatest Gift to all mankind.

Perhaps more than any other man in all of Scripture, David also understood gratitude. In Psalm 119, David penned, "I will thank You by living as I should." You and I cannot repay God for what He does for us. There is nothing we can do to return all God bestows upon our lives except to be grateful. Gratitude, however, is different than repayment. We live for God out of gratitude for what He does for us. **There is no greater way to express our reverence to God than to possess a heart of gratitude.**

Our reverence toward God and His Word is not a form of repayment; it is the proof that we recognize we owe Him our very lives. Please carefully consider these three questions:

- *Is it too costly for you to be thankful?*
- *What are the things for which you are thankful?*
- *Like David, why not thank the Lord by living as you should?*

Let me remind you of the words of the apostle Paul, "And so, dear brothers and sisters, I plead with you to give your bodies to God. Let them be a living and holy sacrifice—the kind He will accept. When you think of what He has done for you, is this too much to ask?"

DAILY CONFESSION
Father, I am thankful for all You do for me. I know I cannot repay You, but I choose to show my gratitude through living as I should.

LOYALTY WAS BIRTHED
TO PROTECT A MAN'S INNOCENCE,
NOT TO KEEP THEIR SIN SECRET

"He who rebukes a man will find more favor afterward
than he who flatters with the tongue."
Proverbs 28:23 (NKJV)

♠

Many people have become masters at avoiding or distorting the truth because they refuse to confront others over their sin. It seems as though many Christians play a game with each other. We've all heard the phrase "there is 'honor' among thieves." Well, there's that "false honor" among Christians, as well. It's an unspoken understanding that says, "We're not going to discuss the real issues. And as long as all of us do not discuss the real issues, the real issues don't exist."

A "real issue" existed, however, for John the Baptist. Having confronted the leader for his sinful relationship with his brother's wife (and a long list of additional transgressions), just as Jesus' ministry began, Herod the tetrarch decided to shut away John in prison.

John, you see, had no experience in avoiding or distorting the truth—walking in love for John meant to repent from sin! And as the daylight was slowly eclipsed by the darkness of the dungeon, by doing what was right through loyalty to the commandments of God, John knew that he ultimately possessed eternal favor from Heaven.

Many times we fool ourselves and call it walking in love, not realizing we consent to another's spiritual demise. So don't overlook someone else's sin in the name of loyalty. Confront their sin and help them walk free from the chains that bind them.

DAILY CONFESSION
Father, I thank You that I am willing to rebuke a man and find more favor
afterward. I refuse to flatter with my tongue.

THE PRICE TAG OF SUCCESS
IS STAMPED WITH THE WORD "DILIGENCE"

"The plans of the diligent lead surely to plenty,
but those of everyone who is hasty, surely to poverty."
Proverbs 21:5 (NKJV)

⚜

As buses and trucks spewed out exhaust and a dusty haze clouded the street lights, she wouldn't give up; neither would she listen to excuses. Attending church since a mere toddler, when the young mother moved into a new neighborhood in the city, she diligently questioned her neighbors, faithfully searched the area newspaper, and patiently checked the telephone book, praying that God would lead her small family into the right place to worship. It took a little discipline, hard work, and time, but it was well worth it, since years later, those very same children repeated their mother's diligence, searching for a place to worship in whatever city they lived. Diligence requires discipline, hard work, and time. In other words, it requires a marked effort. **For us to delight in the promises of God, we must continually apply diligence to our efforts.** God's system is not arranged in such a way that a one-time action produces lasting results. God's way of progress requires diligence, faithfulness, and patience.

The same principle applies for any endeavor. We cannot expect to be physically fit by exercising one week out of the year. To see positive results, we must continue for several months, and for lasting results, we must make exercise a part of our daily lifestyle! All of us want to achieve more and do great things, but we only experience true greatness by diligently applying God's principles to our lives.

Diligence bridges the gap between discipline and reward. Anyone can discipline himself for a day, but only discipline coupled with diligence causes us to lay hold of Heaven's reward.

DAILY CONFESSION
I refuse to have a slack hand knowing it leads to poverty.
I walk in plenty and not in lack because I diligently
apply God's principles to my life.

WHATEVER YOU REFUSE TO CONQUER
WILL ULTIMATELY CONQUER YOU

"I say then: Walk in the Spirit, and you shall not fulfill the lust of the flesh."
Galatians 5:16 (NKJV)

⚜

Consider the example of Jesus. Prior to beginning His earthly ministry, the Bible says He was led of the Spirit into the wilderness. Jesus was physically tested as the tempter called upon Him to change the stones into bread. Jesus was tested as the tempter tried to cause Him to doubt His authority and His position in God, calling upon Him to throw Himself down and be rescued by angels.

The tempter tried Jesus by placing all the world's kingdoms before His eyes in an effort to trade earthly riches for worshipping the devil. But only after Jesus' character was tested and proven in the wilderness did He return in the power of the Holy Spirit to fulfill His divine purpose on this earth.

In the same way, **before you can go forth in the power of the Spirit, you must first go to the wilderness.** You don't have to go there the same way Jesus did, because He already defeated every challenge you could ever encounter in the wilderness.

Nonetheless, in faith and through His power, we are called to conquer the obstacles that come our way in the wilderness, because whatever you refuse to conquer ultimately conquers you.

DAILY CONFESSION
Father, I thank You that I walk by Your Spirit
and I do not fulfill the lust of my flesh.

GOD'S WILL CAN ONLY BE DISCOVERED ON THE ROAD OF OBEDIENCE

"I can of Myself do nothing. As I hear, I judge; and My judgment is righteous, because I do not seek My own will but the will of the Father who sent Me."
John 5:30 (NKJV)

"For I have come down from Heaven, not to do My own will, but the will of Him who sent Me."
John 6:38 (NKJV)

I hear it quite frequently, "What is God's will for my life?" All of us want to know what career we are to pursue, who we are to marry, and where we are to live. But we must understand that God's unknown will may only be discovered by those who choose to travel upon the road of obedience. God called humanity to simply obey; it is His will for our lives. As John the Baptist walked down the highway of obedience, and Jesus walked upon the road of obedience, we too must submit ourselves to the instructions that lie within the pages of God's written Word, putting a sound conclusion to infinite searching and exhaustive wondering.

Jesus came with one purpose: to obey the instructions of His Father. Our calling in life is to please the One who chose us. When we focus upon obeying the Word of God, we no longer are distracted with the perpetual curiosity of God's unknown will. As we obey, we are assured that He leads and guides our steps.

It is only a matter of time before we enter His perfect will for our lives. Let us renew our minds to the call that is placed upon our lives to passionately obey God's known will—His written Word.

DAILY CONFESSION
Father, I know that I can do nothing of myself. As I hear, I do. As I see, I imitate. I passionately pursue the call You placed on my life, seeking Your will, not my own. You are my Father, and I thank You for working through me.

THE FUTURE YOU CREATE IS DEPENDENT
UPON THE FAVOR YOU ATTRACT

"So David said to him, 'Do not fear, for I will surely show you kindness
for Jonathan your father's sake, and will restore to you all the land of Saul
your grandfather; and you shall eat bread at my table continually.'"
2 Samuel 9:7 (NKJV)

Very few understand the subject of favor. Many think favor is "luck" or "good fortune" and perhaps even "chance." They do not understand that we are the determining factor for the favor that comes into our lives. God does not sit up in Heaven and tell Jesus, "Let's show favor to Jimmy today, but as for Barbara, we are not going to show favor."

He gave us principles by which we can live our lives. By executing those principles, favor increases, and neglecting to do them, in turn, causes favor to decrease.

What is favor? Favor is the desire that someone has to help you succeed. It is when someone has a desire to participate in your future. John the Baptist needed the favor of Jesus—His Godly character of meekness and His eternal strength—to persevere through the greatest of trials to come. He desperately needed Jesus in order to help him succeed, to take him where he had never been in his God-given assignment on earth.

We desperately need those who can take us to where we haven't been. Understand this about favor: it can only come from those who can promote us. We must seek to please those God called us to serve, and when we do, we see the favor we need to enter the future we truly desire.

DAILY CONFESSION
Father, I thank You that as Jesus increased in wisdom and stature and
in favor with You and men, so do I. I apply the necessary principles
to my life to cause the favor I need to come to fruition.

WHATEVER YOU REFUSE TO CONQUER
WILL ULTIMATELY CONQUER YOU

"How long shall I bear with this evil congregation who complain against Me? I have heard the complaints which the children of Israel make against Me. Say to them, 'As I live,' says the Lord, 'just as you have spoken in My hearing, so I will do to you.'"
Numbers 14:27-28 (NKJV)

✤

"She's always been such a good student," the middle-aged mom pondered aloud to her husband, concerned about their freshman daughter. "She does great on the tests, answers well in class, participates with her classmates; it's just the homework where she lacks." Straining his ears, the husband listened (just to be sure) and in seconds, their problem would be solved. "It's easy, honey. All we have to do is eliminate the negative distractions—music (like the stuff that's blasting in her room now), television, movies, friends, phone calls. That's what's doing it." And sure enough, as soon as those negative elements were removed, factors that could have destroyed the way to their daughter's future, they saw victory in her grades the next term.

And if we refuse to eliminate negative things from our lives, those things ultimately destroy us, and we do not find a place of repentance. The moment we choose to obey is the moment we declare we want God's will more than our own.

It is also God's desire for us to be pleasing to others. In our modern society, everyone wants to know the reasoning instructions. "Why do you want me to do this? Why do you want to do it that way?" The question is constantly "Why?" There is little willingness to submit, and that spirit has subtly crept into the church. We must be serious about stopping negative influences from penetrating our lives. Remember, we are all susceptible to the negative flow of society, so we must remain diligent to fill ourselves with the overcoming power of the Word of God.

DAILY CONFESSION
Father, I thank You for making me
more than a conqueror in Christ Jesus.

PURITY IS THE MASTER KEY
THAT UNLOCKS THE DOOR OF GOD'S HEART

*"Who may ascend into the hill of the Lord? Or who may stand
in His holy place? He who has clean hands and a pure heart, who has not
lifted up his soul to an idol, nor sworn deceitfully. He shall receive blessing from
the Lord, and righteousness from the God of his salvation. This is Jacob,
the generation of those who seek Him, who seek Your face."
Psalm 24:3-6 (NKJV)*

✦

"God, I want nothing more than You." That's the attitude of one who
possesses a pure heart. Please bear these thoughts in mind...

- *Purity* has no extra agenda, and no ambition for personal gain to the
  detriment of another.

- *Purity* is so consumed by God's love for other people that it is willing to
  endure any hardship for others' benefit.

- *Purity* realizes that in God exists the fullness of life, joy, happiness, and
  purpose, so it is content to have God, even if everything else is cast off.

- *Purity* realizes that this life is fleeting and eternity beckons.

- *Purity* says to God, "I will obey You no matter what it costs, and I'll
  do it even if I don't get credit. I want Your approval on my life. I don't
  need any special awards or any extra attention. I just want You."

God's heart is touched by such an attitude. When a child of His
approaches Him like this, He cannot help lavishing His love upon that
child. He eagerly searches for someone to whom He can entrust the
secrets of His Word, and only a person with a pure heart (one who does
good and right with God's revelation) uniquely qualifies. All others
must remain in the outer courts of God's presence until they cultivate,
like a shiny pearl produced from an oyster shell, a pure, shiny heart.

DAILY CONFESSION
*Father, I thank You that I have one desire—the thing I seek most—to live
in Your house all the days of my life, delighting in Your Word.*

YOUR RESPONSE TO A MAN OF GOD DETERMINES HEAVEN'S RESPONSE TO YOU

"So she went away and did according to the word of Elijah;
and she and he and her household ate for many days."
1 Kings 17:15 (NKJV)

People of all sizes, shapes, and circumstances hovered around the mountain's rocky base, not only Galileans, but folks as far away as Jerusalem, Judea, and beyond the River Jordan. Gathered to hear the Teacher, this prophet and carpenter from Nazareth, their respect for the Teacher caused a hush to settle over the crowd. His words meandered into their ears and wafted down into their hearts and souls, "Blessed, Blessed, Blessed." The Teacher said the word "blessed" nine times in all. What a strange way of speaking! What an odd way of delivering a religious message. But with each compelling sentence, the people's response was one of sheer, unwavering respect for the Man of God who thundered before them.

- **Whatever you respect is whatever steadily increases inside your life.**

- *Stay very sensitive to respect and honor the men and women God assigns to lead your life.*

- *Look for opportunities to express that respect and honor, for before honor can become a harvest in your life, it must first be your seed.*

Grasp and live this concept and you will operate at the highest levels of life.

THE MAIN INGREDIENT TO ENJOYING
THE REWARDS OF LIFE IS GENUINE COMPLIANCE

"If you will only obey Me and let Me help you, then you will have plenty to eat."
Isaiah 1:19 (NLT)

Obedience simply means doing what God instructs us in His Word. It means to live up to the knowledge we receive. God told Abram, "Abram, I want you to move from your comfortable situation and go to a new country." Abram obeyed God. If God talks to us about something, we must do it. Our Heavenly Father expects each of His children to yield to Him with wholehearted obedience.

The entrance into this new life with Christ demands the vow of absolute obedience. As Christians, we must surrender our whole being, exactly as Jesus did, to be, think, speak, and act according to the will of God; it is not enough to just agree with Him. It is only through obedience that our agreement is proven, and in doing so, we have access to God's favor and abundant blessings. As Jesus continued His sermon, distinct commands were given. Instructions such as:

- *Rejoice, and be exceedingly glad when persecuted.*
- *You are the salt of the world, so don't lose your flavor.*
- *You are the light of the world, so don't hide your light.*
- *You know it's not right to kill, but neither should you be angry without cause.*

Jesus knew that God requires obedience. Every act of our obedience is an added ingredient unto a just reward. Jesus said in Matthew 7:21 that obedience is the very essence of salvation. Obedience opens the door to all that God has to give—most importantly, an intimate relationship with God Himself.

DAILY CONFESSION
Father, I thank You that You reward me for the good I do.
I choose to be willing and obedient knowing that I will eat the best of the land.

THE PROOF OF SERVANTHOOD
IS THE WILLINGNESS TO ABANDON ALL
TO BECOME A TOOL IN THE HAND OF ANOTHER

"I have no one else like him, who takes a genuine interest in your welfare.
For everyone looks out for his own interests, not those of Jesus Christ. But you
know that Timothy has proved himself, because as a son with his father
he has served with me in the work of the Gospel."
Philippians 2:20-22

Long before Timothy was the renowned pastor of the church at Ephesus, he was a young man serving with his spiritual father, Paul. In those years of maturing, he chose to make himself a competent tool in the hand of the man of God. He didn't do so because he wanted to be the pastor of a big church or because he knew it would lead to fame. He simply did what the Spirit of God inside of him whispered to him: Become a tool.

Paul writes that there was no one like Timothy. Everyone else was interested in their own welfare—in what they could get out of preaching the Gospel. That was not so with Timothy. He simply wanted to become whatever God desired him to become. And though Timothy did not realize it, his decision to do so prepared him to be entrusted with the lives of thousands of believers. He became a servant—a true servant. He laid aside his own agenda and readily picked up the agenda of another.

I'm certain that the celebration in Heaven when Timothy finished his course was an outstanding spectacle to see. May the same hold true for us as we become a tool in the hand of the One we serve.

IN THE GAME OF LIFE, PRINCIPLE, NOT EMOTION, WILL DECIDE YOUR FATE

"He went a little farther and fell on His face, and prayed, saying, 'My Father, if it is possible, let this cup pass from Me; nevertheless, not as I will, but as You will.'"
Matthew 26:39 (NKJV)

⚜

Just how important are the decisions we make? They are the determining factors of the success or failure of our future. **The choices we make today determine who we become tomorrow.** We make thousands of decisions every day, many of which we don't even think about. Other decisions can alter our life for better or for worse. To create the future God desires in our lives, we must select our decisions by principle, and not by emotion. Without Godly principles, we are like a ship with no one to man the sails. The wind fatefully decides the ship's course.

Without principles, the circumstances of life have complete control over our direction. For example, many people do not tithe because they are in debt and cannot afford to give God ten percent. They claim that when things get better, they will tithe. God assures us things will not get better for them until they tithe. Another example is a teenager who promises to stop partying when he gets out of high school. Unfortunately, things only worsen for that young person in the meantime, making it almost impossible to escape the party scene later in life.

We must never make decisions based upon present circumstances, but rather on the ultimate outcome we desire. Whatever we find in the Word of God, we must embrace as truth and apply our lives to it.

DAILY CONFESSION
Father, I thank You that I live by Your principles and every Word that proceeds out of Your mouth. I am a doer of the Word and not a hearer only.

THE GREATEST RESPONSIBILITY PLACED UPON ANY MAN IS ADHERENCE TO THE WORD OF GOD

"Here is my final conclusion: fear God and obey His commands,
for this is the duty of every person."
Ecclesiastes 12:13 (NLT)

✦

In a southern California city is a glamorous movie theatre whose towering spotlight flickers and floats across the desert sky, drawing people to their nightly showings. That spotlight is proof something is going on. Our unwavering obedience and positive attitude draw Heaven's spotlight—proof that something exciting is going on—not in some old movie theatre, but inside the hearts of His people! The Bible never says, "If you love Me, you will eat the best of the land." It says, "If you are willing and obedient, you shall eat the best of the land." Our obedience is the only proof that we trust God. The success of our life by Heaven's standard depends on our obedience to the written Word of God. The more accurately we obey, the greater the rewards.

Picture this: a mother asks her son to take care of the dishes while she is out. She comes home to find a beautiful bouquet of flowers, a sweet "I Love You" card, and a sink full of dirty dishes. Is she to believe her son loves her because of the flowers and card? Perhaps, if he did the dishes, but his disobedience to her specific instruction speaks louder than the sacrifice he went through to buy the flowers and the card. Obedience is better than sacrifice.

Solomon had everything, yet in Ecclesiastes 12:13 he came to one conclusion: fear God and obey His commands. **Obedience to the Word of God is the one responsibility for which every man has to give an account on the Day of Judgment.** God places such a high emphasis on obedience because our actions prove exactly who we are.

DAILY CONFESSION
Father, I thank You that I fear You and keep Your Word.
I prove my trust in You and my love for You by doing what You ask of me.

THE PURSUIT OF EXCELLENCE AWAKENS
THE PROCESS OF TRANSFORMATION

"Do you see a man who excels in his work?
He will stand before kings; he will not stand before unknown men."
Proverbs 22:29 (NKJV)

Stand before kings? Hard to believe, you might say, but it has happened in my life. I have had the privilege of standing before many great men and women, including kings, queens, and presidents of different nations. The verse above says, "Do you see a man who excels? He will stand before kings; he will not stand before unknown men."

Your pursuit of excellence awakens the remarkable process of transformation. You may say, "Dr. Thompson, not me. You don't know me, I am just an ordinary Joe."

Please listen carefully: If God can take a man who did drugs, became an alcoholic by the age of fourteen, embezzled stereo equipment, and was institutionalized at a mental hospital, and cause him to stand before some of the greatest men and women on the face of the earth, then He can certainly do it for you.

But **with every great achievement there comes a great price to be paid.** As you pursue excellence, which is the continual pursuit of improvement, God takes you—an ordinary person—and does extraordinary things through your life. Now, the question is, do you believe it?

DAILY CONFESSION
Father, I thank You that I excel in my work
and I will stand before kings and not unknown men.

A SOFT HEART IS THE ONLY ENVIRONMENT
IN WHICH GOD'S PRESENCE CAN DWELL

"Keep your heart with all diligence, for out of it spring the issues of life."
Proverbs 4:23 (NKJV)

✦

Like precious metals being reduced to a fluid, usable state, the very nature of God's presence is refinement. God purifies our motives, decisions, relationships, actions, and shortcomings when we meet with Him. Consequently, God must have a soft heart with which to work. Soft means tender, pliable, and responsive to impression. James says God resists the proud, but gives grace to the humble. Pride, however, is not simply a smug look and an arrogant attitude. Pride in a more subtle (but possibly more dangerous) form is thinking we can meet with God because of our good performance.

Do you remember a time when you sinned and afterward felt like you couldn't pray or worship God? Do you remember a time when you went for days obeying God's voice and resisting temptation? That is when you probably felt much more qualified to meet with God. But if either of those situations is true, you've experienced pride, simply because you depended on your own performance to be acceptable to God.

Here's a giant revelation: We aren't good enough. With that said once and for all, let us cling to Jesus and never stop trusting Him. It's as if we were in a hurricane on an old wooden ship. All we could do to keep from being thrown into the deep would be to cling to the mast with all our might. With tears swimming in our eyes, we would endure the violently deafening storm at the strength of the mast. There would be no other option for safety because letting go of the mast to find another stronghold would mean doom. That's the fervor with which we must cling to Jesus. A man with a soft heart realizes his hopelessness without Christ. He enters God's presence on that merit alone, where God always meets with him.

DAILY CONFESSION
Without wavering, I cling to hope in Christ,
and I am never moved.

"I SURRENDER" IS THE ONLY RESPONSE
THAT IS REQUIRED OF THOSE WHO HEAR GOD'S VOICE

"He must increase, but I must decrease."
John 3:30 (NKJV)

✤

As the crowd felt the Son's words pierce their hearts, words about heaven, giving, fasting, and forgiveness, astonished at His teachings, many began to voluntarily surrender their lives to Him. Christ, our prime example, completely surrendered control of His life to God. He willingly offered His spirit into the Father's hands, fulfilling the Father's will. To realize the immensity of His sacrifice, a great work must be done among the churches throughout the nations of this world. The last instruction of our Lord was, "Go therefore…"

But have we truly surrendered our lives to Heaven's desire? God wants all of mankind to know Him. We must realize that this work is the objective of every Christian. We are called to take them the good news and make true disciples. This commission must be the passion of our lives.

Throughout America, churches have reduced Christianity to a statement rather than a lifestyle. With no corresponding actions, our words are meaningless. We must demand of ourselves and of those with whom we associate an absolute and immediate surrender to the Word of God. **We cannot approach the throne room of Heaven requesting our personal assignment without first embracing the call to preach the Gospel to the entire world.**

God promises to lovingly mold us, skillfully teach us, tenderly guide us, and powerfully use us, but we must surrender completely before He can have His way.

DAILY CONFESSION
Father, I thank You that as I continually surrender my life to Your will,
You increase and I decrease.

THE DOOR OF CONSEQUENCES SWINGS OPEN WIDE
THE MOMENT YOU NEGLECT THE WORD OF GOD

"Why have you despised the commandment of the Lord, to do evil in His sight?
Now therefore, the sword shall never depart from your house. Thus says the Lord:
'Behold, I will raise up adversity against you from your own house;
and I will take your wives before your eyes and give them to your neighbor,
and he shall lie with your wives in the sight of this sun.'"
2 Samuel 12:9-11 (NKJV)

Originating with Adam and continuing until today, men and women reject God's Word. Too often we want to do what we want to do, whether or not it accurately aligns with God's Word. This factor causes multitudes of believers to suffer needlessly, and it gives the devil an open door to consume them as brutally as a lion on the plains of Africa viciously devouring his prey. Remember, Satan comes to steal, kill, and destroy, but Jesus came that we may have an abundant life.

Having been taught with authority from Heaven, not as the pious, stony-hearted scribes, those who heard the "Sermon on the Mount" realized there would be consequences for sin. Jesus clearly exhorts us by telling us that the path of His will is narrow and often difficult. Along that path, however, we find a life that is overflowing with the goodness of God, but not without great struggle.

No one desires to struggle, but **God's best doesn't come without cost,** just as Jesus' sacrifice did not come without great cost. In order to experience the blessings of God, we must first be willing to conform our will to the will of our Father.

DAILY CONFESSION
Father, I thank You that I am willing and obedient, and I eat the best of the land.
I keep Your commandment and pursue Your will for my life.

THE VIEW OF LIFE IS ALWAYS BEAUTIFUL WHEN LOOKED AT THROUGH THE WINDOW OF GOD'S WORD

"He did not waver at the promise of God through unbelief, but
was strengthened in faith, giving glory to God, and being fully convinced
that what He had promised He was also able to perform."
Romans 4:20-22 (NKJV)

✦

She didn't know if she could do it, but by putting faith in God she would really try. Carefully listening to the Teacher's words, the part about "loving your enemies, even those who hate you" stayed like a rock inside her mind. Her brother-in-law cursed her, falsely accused her, and humiliated her in the marketplace. But looking at things the way God sees them, through the window of His Word, she quickly made the decision: I will no longer hate, but love. I love him because of Your love for me. Likewise, the apostle Paul tells us in 1 Corinthians 2:9, "Eye has not seen, nor ear heard, nor has entered into the heart of man the things which God has prepared for those who love Him." According to this passage, we can only see into our future through the window of God's Word.

We cannot see Heaven's plan for our lives until we look through God's eyes. God called us to walk by faith and not by what we see. As many of us already know, faith is the substance of the things we cannot perceive with our senses. Just as the woman who heard Jesus' Words decided to love her brother-in-law, seeing things as God views them, when we begin to meditate upon the Word of God and view life through His eyes, then we see clearly what Heaven prepared for us.

We can never experience what our spirit man cannot see. Let us focus upon God's Word to paint a picture that will one day become a masterpiece. Begin to view life through the window of God's Word and see how beautiful life truly is.

DAILY CONFESSION
Father, I thank You that I am built up through Your grace.
I am raised with Christ. I set my mind on Heaven's riches and the things
above where Christ is seated.

PATIENCE IS THE OVEN
WHICH COOKS UP THE SIZE OF MY HARVEST

"For you have need of endurance, so that after
you have done the will of God, you may receive the promise."
Hebrews 10:36 (NKJV)

✦

"You're taller," the petite woman said to her six-foot husband. Stretching his toes to peek at the lines, scanning like an eagle over his territory, he motioned his wife. "This one's the shortest by far." Since neither of them had much patience when it came to waiting, wouldn't you know it, it just had to happen. The line they rushed into had some sort of mishap, a breakdown with the computer, a huge malfunction. Now this couples' patience would genuinely be tried! But patience is not the ability to wait in line without getting frustrated. Patience is the ability to withstand the pressure, lies, and temptation to shortcut God's system to obtain that for which we believe God.

Many Christians buckle under pressure and never experience true fulfillment. The enemy attempts to wear us down. If he causes us to grow weary, he limits the size of the harvest we receive. The more we sow, and the longer we are willing to hold off the harvest, the greater the reward. We live in a society that feeds off the desire for instant gratification. Desiring something before we are able to handle it or before our harvest is mature hinders us from walking in abundant life. I see many young men with high aspirations in life refuse to hold on for the long haul. It is a rarity to find an individual who decides to sow and refuses a harvest today, knowing it will be greater tomorrow.

We must learn to wait and prepare, knowing that God is never late to promote. Never forget, the more we sow and the longer we hold off our harvest, the greater our future.

DAILY CONFESSION
Father, I thank You that I endure patiently and obtain Your promise.
I need endurance so that after I do Your will, I receive the promised harvest.

OUR EMOTIONS ARE PRISONERS
OF OUR PRESENT FOCUS

"While we do not look at the things which are seen, but at the things
which are not seen. For the things which are seen are temporary,
but the things which are not seen are eternal."
2 Corinthians 4:18 (NKJV)

When Jesus came down off the mountain following His powerful sermon, great throngs began to follow Him. Their attention was focused upon the Man who spoke, produced thoughts and expounded wisdom like none other. And that clearly was the purpose of His sermon—to capture their focus so it would eventually alter their lives. **If something captures your focus, it eventually alters your life.** The emotions you feel, whether good or bad, reveal what snares your attention. God gave us all the power to control our focus.

You don't have to live discouraged, sad, or depressed! You can, through choosing your focus, live a happy, joyful, and peaceful life.

Please remember:

- *Harboring negativity prevents you from achievement.*

- *Negative thoughts keep you from pursuing what you want.*

- *If you think you can't, you won't, and you will never walk in the destiny God has for your life.*

Anything you want requires you to passionately pursue it, otherwise you fall short every time. Focus on God's Word, go after everything He promises you, and experience Heaven's blessings. Today, practice thinking upon that which is good and pure. You're destined to win!

DAILY CONFESSION
Father, I thank You that I do not look at the things which are seen,
but at the things which are not seen. For the things which are seen are temporary
and subject to change, but the things which are not seen are eternal.

FAITHFULNESS IS PROVEN THE MOMENT DISLOYALTY REARS ITS UGLY HEAD

"And may you, His people, always be faithful to the Lord our God.
May you always obey His laws and commands, just as you are doing today."
1 Kings 8:61 (NLT)

After expending Himself in the ministry, Jesus and His disciples boarded a ship for well-deserved solitude and rest. But the Sea of Galilee is often unpredictable, and while the waves lifted and shuddered, Jesus slept. Awakening Him from a sound sleep, the wide-eyed men pleaded with Jesus to save them. Astonished, Jesus could not understand how they could so quickly abandon their faith. Where was their faithfulness? Becoming our supreme example, Jesus was faithful to the brutality of the cross, showing complete faithfulness to the very end.

Faithfulness is a virtue that is only proven at the end of one's life. For example: a husband tells the counselor, "I have been faithful to my wife six days this week. I was with another woman just for one night." Was he faithful? Of course not! Neither are we, unless our faithfulness endures until our last day.

When we get to Heaven, every one of us wants to hear, "Enter in, good and faithful servant." Even God, the One who knows our hearts, does not judge another's faithfulness until they live their full life. Why is that? Because of this principle: **He who ceases to remain faithful proves he never was.** We must make the decision to live a life of faithfulness.

DAILY CONFESSION
Father, I thank You that I am always faithful to You.
I always obey Your Word and the laws of Heaven. And when I go home
to be with You, You will say to me, "Well done, good and faithful servant."

EXPECTATION IS THE DIFFERENCE BETWEEN AN ABUNDANT HARVEST AND A BARREN FIELD

"…it shall be done for you as you have believed."
Matthew 8:13 (AMP)

"Please God, help me find them." Searching everywhere, she continued to pray. When her brother called, he prayed too. Suddenly she thought: I was wearing that red coat…It must be… Extending her fingers inside the left pocket, there they were—the keys to her mailbox! The moment she realized those keys were missing was the moment she began to pray. And why did she bother to pray? She prayed because she rightly expected something in return—God's favor and assistance, the bountiful difference between harvest and a barren field.

You may have been taught it is wrong to expect something in return when you give to God, thinking it is a form of greed. Well, let's examine that teaching. Did you expect forgiveness when you confessed your sins to Christ? Of course you did! Was that greed? No, it was simply trusting God's character, exactly as the woman who lost her keys. In the same way, neglecting to expect a harvest from your seed steals the pleasure God enjoys from blessing you. God's greatest pleasure is to be believed. **Expectation is the key ingredient that makes the seed work for us.**

Whenever we come across a promise of God, we must expect that it will happen in our lives. God is not a respecter of persons. If He did it in the past for His children, He will certainly do it for you. Our faith moves the hand of God. Our obedience to His Word, wrapped in expectation, is what allows Him to move as He desires in our lives. As we sow a seed to meet a need we face, let us expect the promise of God to come to pass for us.

DAILY CONFESSION
Father, I thank You that You do not lie. What You speak comes to pass in my life. I place an expectation upon the promises in Your Word, knowing that it is done unto me as I believe.

THE MOST BLARING DIFFERENCE BETWEEN MEDIOCRITY AND EXCELLENCE IS FINISHING

"Finishing is better than starting. Patience is better than price."
Ecclesiastes 7:8 (NLT)

How many times have you come up to the final moments of a project and been tempted to take a break? In any endeavor, most people are great starters. They get in the middle of the project and start losing steam. Then, as they are about to round the last corner, the one that would take them to the finish line, they spin out of control! The last 10% of the project takes just as long as the first 90%! Are you guilty of this?

As Jesus' fame spread, blind eyes were opened and every sickness and every disease was totally healed. Peering down upon the multitude, the Master inwardly shook—scattered abroad without a shepherd (their bodies, spirits, and minds flowing with the wind), people began to faint, their eyes, hearts, and souls growing weary of diligence, excellence, and completion.

Yet, looking on the bright side, if you turn that last corner without losing your focus, there is a great boost of energy that drives you like a racecar, straight to the finish. **You can save yourself a lot of pain and lost time if you discipline yourself to take projects all the way through to completion.** This, by itself, is able to welcome you into a whole new level of excellence.

DAILY CONFESSION
Father, I thank You that You began a good work in me
and You will carry it through to completion. Likewise, I thank You
that I complete every work I begin with excellence and diligence!

DILIGENCE IS THE QUALITY
THAT SETS ONE APART FROM ALL OTHERS

"The hand of the diligent will rule, but the lazy man will be put to forced labor."
Proverbs 12:24 (NKJV)

Diligence is defined as the determined pursuit of a worthy goal.
We do not accomplish anything in life without diligence. It is the fuel
that propels us above the rest. It refuses to quit or give up. Diligence
stays active until completion or attainment of a desired goal.

Diligence says:

- *We must continually press toward God's will for our lives.*
- *We cannot settle for second best.*
- *We must refuse the temptation to quit or stop trying.*

The enemy disguised as inaction, however, is not going to back
down without a fight. Whatever we desire, Satan attempts to stop us
from achieving it. Only those who remain diligent and persevere rule
in the end.

Jesus died so we could have an abundant life. That life is only
achieved by those who are unwilling to stop when the times get tough.
If we want to stand head and shoulders above the rest, we must refuse
any backward motion and continue to press in when all others quit.

DAILY CONFESSION
Father, I thank You that I do not cast away my confidence.
I choose to diligently do Your Word, and I endure until the end,
knowing that there is a great reward that lies ahead.

THE REFUSAL TO CONQUER NEGATIVITY IS THE GUARANTEE THAT SOMEDAY IT WILL BECOME YOUR MASTER

"Let all bitterness, wrath, anger, clamor,
and evil speaking be put away from you, with all malice."
Ephesians 4:31 (NKJV)

"NO! NO! NO!" Stomping her feet, then throwing herself down dramatically, banging her head against the supermarket floor, the two-year-old screamed, completely aware that by throwing such a tantrum, Mother would have no choice but yield to her desire for three new toys and a bag of chocolate candy. Calmly pulling the child up from the ground, escorting her speedily out the front doors, in the privacy of their automobile, that mother knew what to do—she knew how to conquer negativity in her child's life so that it would not ultimately master her thoughts—in fact, three or four swats would conquer it for sure! And if we, as grown adults, refuse to eliminate negative things from our lives, those negative things ultimately destroy us, and there is nothing we can do about it.

Negativity is like a virus to a computer. Once you allow it into your system, it slowly kills you. And as in the case of this mother who desired to rid her child of negativity once and for all, the quickest way to rid ourselves of negativity is to separate from those who are negative. Negativity, you see, is a spirit that transfers from person to person.

Make a practice to see things from a positive perspective. When you make the life-changing decision to see things through the window of God's Word, that negativity soon vanishes from your life, once and for all.

DAILY CONFESSION
Father, I thank You that I put away from me all bitterness, wrath, clamor, and evil speaking. I decide to see things through Your Word and I choose joy.

VICTORIOUS IS THE MAN
WHOSE FOCUS IS FIXED UPON HEAVEN

"David was now in serious trouble because his men were very bitter
about losing their wives and children, and they began to talk of stoning him.
But David found strength in the Lord his God."
1 Samuel 30:6 (NLT)

✦

Our response to the storms life thrusts our way is dependent upon the perspective through which we view them. There are many today who tell God how big their problems are. They unceasingly tell God how they are not going to make it. Then there are those who tell their problem just how big their God is, and they declare the words of their father until the problems cease to exist.

In 1 Samuel 30, we see that David faced many troubles. The Amalekites took captive David's family and the families of his soldiers, his army was bitter and wanted to stone him, and Saul continued in hot pursuit of him. Yet, David maintained his poise unlike any other. His response was one few are willing to make. He turned his attention to the one and only God and began to encourage himself in the Lord. The moment David began to focus on God, his perspective changed. He knew God would take care of him.

We must respond the same way when Satan attempts to knock us out of the ring of life. We need to fix our eyes on Jesus, the author and finisher of our faith.

IT IS ONLY THE STORMS OF LIFE THAT HAVE
THE POWER TO REVEAL YOUR TRUE CHARACTER

"'Now, O King, establish the decree and sign the writing, so that it cannot be changed, according to the law of the Medes and Persians, which does not alter.' Therefore King Darius signed the written decree. Now when Daniel knew that the writing was signed, he went home. And in his upper room, with his windows open toward Jerusalem, he knelt down on his knees three times that day, and prayed and gave thanks before his God, as was his custom since early days."
Daniel 6:8-10 (NKJV)

We can never know the true character of an individual until we see them tested and tried. Daniel exemplifies this principle so perfectly. Although the decree went out stating that everyone who prayed to another besides the king would be killed, Daniel responded as though it were just another day. He went before the window in his room, facing Jerusalem as established by the Hebrew law, knelt down, and gave thanks to God, as was his custom.

Daniel's decision revealed he was truly a man of God. He trusted God and proved it by his response to the pressure life placed on him. Although life offers many rainy days, our response reveals our true character. Just as Jesus tested His disciples when the storm stirred upon the Sea of Galilee, life brings about storms. Who we truly are is ultimately revealed.

We must cultivate the character of God within our lives and stand ready for the rainy days to come. How will you respond when the storms hit your life? I believe we will all respond as Daniel did...trusting God.

DAILY CONFESSION
*Father, I thank You for the peace that surpasses all understanding.
I am an overcomer and walk above the pressures of this life
because I possess Your character.*

THE QUALITY OF CHARACTER
YOU DISPLAY BEFORE MEN IS A REFLECTION OF
THE INFLUENCE GOD HAS IN YOUR LIFE

*"Daniel soon proved himself more capable than all the other administrators
and princes. Because of his great ability, the king made plans to place him over
the entire empire. Then the other administrators and princes began searching for
some fault in the way Daniel was handling his affairs, but they couldn't find
anything to criticize. He was faithful and honest and always responsible."*
Daniel 6:3-4 (NLT)

His heart eagerly anticipating the precious moments alone,
although others trembled in fear at the detestable law, Daniel was a
man who spent quality time with God, bowing three times daily
before his window and offering thanks to God. His outward life was a
direct reflection of the time he diligently spent in the presence of
God. So it is with us. The quality of our character grows in proportion
to the time we spend in God's presence and in His Word.

**It is impossible to spend quality time with God and not be
changed.** Jesus exemplified this for us. He was a man of prayer who
continually spent hours alone with God. Whether trudging into the
wilderness at dawn or speedily boarding a ship, Jesus knew that apart
from His Father He could do nothing. Accordingly, if we desire to live
the life Christ has for us then we must do the same. As we continue
to spend time in His Word, we cultivate the very character of Christ.

Jesus said it like this, "If you abide in Me, and my words abide in
you...you shall bear much fruit." My desire is to grow progressively in
the likeness of Jesus. His presence and His Word are the only two
ingredients that cause us to live as He did. The more influence we
allow, the greater our character. Let His presence and His Word be our
greatest priority in this life.

DAILY CONFESSION
*Father, I thank You that I abide in Your presence.
I abide in You and Your Word abides in me, causing me to bear much fruit.
Apart from You I can do nothing.*

TO WALK THROUGH LIFE ACCORDING TO PRINCIPLE
OFTEN MEANS YOU MUST WALK ALONE

*"Blessed is the man who walks not in the counsel of the ungodly, nor stands
in the path of sinners, nor sits in the seat of the scornful…"*
Psalm 1:1 (NKJV)

Having come across less than a handful of other Christians in her
high school, the sixteen-year-old girl had few friends. Though always
friendly, many of the other kids just did not covet her as a close friend.
As in all schools, there were the different groupings—the honor roll
students, athletes, most popular, and average. But as she walked the
noisy hallways day after day, she noticed one thing—other kids
respected her because of the principles she held. They may not say it
out loud, but she sensed their respect. However, not everyone is interested in taking the proverbial "straight and narrow." **To walk through
life according to principle often means you must walk alone.**
Integrity requires you to walk in truth, thus affirming your faithfulness
to God and to those with whom you associate.

Integrity also means as you build relationships, both parties must be
willing to speak the truth in love, even at the expense of offending
each other. Solomon gives us some insight into this idea, "Faithful are
the wounds of a friend, but the kisses of the an enemy are deceitful."
Because we have a desire to be valued and affirmed, we tend to
gravitate towards those who tell us what we want to hear. We subcon-
sciously surround ourselves with individuals who put on a façade of
commitment because it feels good at the time.

This only leads to one place—a place of loneliness, with no bankable
relationships. Refuse to allow anyone into the intimacies of your life if
they are unwilling to agree and comply with the proven principles of
truth and integrity.

DAILY CONFESSION
*Father, I thank You that I refuse to walk in the counsel of the ungodly,
stand in the path of sinners, or sit in the seat of the scornful.*

THE FOG OF CONFUSION SURROUNDS THE MAN WHO IS UNWILLING TO SUBMIT TO AUTHORITY

"How I hated discipline! If only I had not demanded my own way!
Oh, why didn't I listen to my teachers? Why didn't I pay attention to those
who gave me instruction? I have come to the brink of utter ruin,
and now I must face public disgrace."
Proverbs 5:11-14 (NLT)

Utilizing the beauty and intrigue of nature, combined with illustrative truths presented from life, Jesus' usage of the parable surpassed much of His other teaching. While exercising this form of instruction, Jesus clearly explained the principle above when teaching the parable of the man who planted a vineyard in Luke 20. The entire parable focuses on the authority God established in the Body of Christ. Notice, Jesus did not say God came personally to gather the harvest.

Instead, God sent His servants three times, and the fourth time, He sent His Son. This is the authority God sent, and He continues today to send authority into our lives. He waits to see if we will subject ourselves to them or respond as the tenants who disregarded their responsibilities.

In God's eyes, if we reject His delegated authority, we reject Him. This rebellion prevents God from blessing our lives. Authority is established to lead and guide us down the joyous path of God's will for our lives.

If we are obediently subject to authority, then, and only then, can God use us for His glory; submission, therefore, is bowing our knee to God through a man. We do not submit to man, but to God. Unless we set aside our flesh, we are not able to receive instruction and submit to those called to lead us into the promises God has for us.

DAILY CONFESSION
Father, I thank You that I am obedient and submissive to those placed above me.
I have a beneficial future because I give them reason to lead and guide me joyfully.

THE OBEDIENT ARE THE ONLY ONES INVITED TO ATTEND THE BANQUET OF REWARD

*"Now listen! Today I am giving you a choice
between prosperity and disaster, between life and death."
Deuteronomy 30:15-18 (NLT)*

Choices:

- A **movie** *or a* **move** *of God through sacrificial prayer?*
- *Support of a new missionary* **outreach** *or the purchase of another new* **outfit**?

One of the greatest gifts anyone could ever receive is the power of choice. God gave us the ability to create our future. Whether it is prosperous or disastrous, the choice is ours. The apostle Paul encourages us with these words, "For God is working in you, giving you the desire to obey Him and the power to do what pleases Him." God doesn't just leave us as orphans to fend for ourselves. He knows there is an enemy out there whose sole purpose is to lure us into making wrong choices. If Satan causes us to make just one mistake, it may result in a lifetime of negative consequences.

We can see throughout the Scriptures that God did not predestine our choices. He did, however, predestine our consequences. We are to surrender our lives to the Spirit of God and trust in Him to help us make right choices.

The Holy Spirit is our helper; He guides us in the right direction. As all of us know for certain—**the rewards of obedience far outweigh the consequences of disobedience.** In the above passage God lays it out, "Now listen! Today I give you a choice between prosperity and disaster, between life and death. Choose to love the Lord your God and to obey Him and commit yourself to Him, for He is your life."

DAILY CONFESSION
*Father, I thank You for working in me, giving me the desire to obey
You and the power to do what pleases You. I choose life and not death.
I live a long, good life because I love You and obey Your commands.*

SUCCESS IS SUMMONED TO WALK ALONGSIDE ANYONE WILLING TO TRAVERSE THE ROAD OF LOVE

"We know how much God loves us, and we have put our trust in Him.
God is love, and all who live in love live in God, and God lives in them."
1 John 4:16 (NLT)

"Love never fails…"
1 Corinthians 13:8 (NKJV)

❧

God is love, and those who claim to be His children must express genuine love for others. God desires to richly bless us, but He can only do so in accordance with the measure we walk in love. Love is more than an emotion we feel towards another or a kind act we perform. Love is a state of being.

To love is to have God work through our lives:

- *God is patient.*
- *He is kind.*
- *He does not boast.*
- *He is long suffering.*
- *He believes all things.*
- *He hopes all things.*
- *He does not fail.*

As we allow Him to work in us, we begin to see the very same characteristics manifest in our daily lives. **The abundant life Jesus offers us is not necessarily a reward for our love to others; it is, however, a marvelous by-product of a life of love.** As we imitate the love God shows humanity we soon see the character of God manifest within our lives – the true life of success.

DAILY CONFESSION
Father, I thank You that I know how much You love me.
I put my trust in You. I know You are love and as I live in love, You live in me.

IN ORDER TO TRANSFORM YOUR LIFE, YOU MUST BE WILLING TO CHANGE YOUR MIND

"Don't copy the behavior and customs of this world, but let God transform you into a new person by changing the way you think. Then you will know what God wants you to do, and you will know how good and pleasing and perfect His will really is."
Romans 12:2 (NLT)

The moment you accept Christ as your Savior is the moment you no longer have to wonder when God is going to set you free. You are already free! Jesus already did all He's ever going to do to deliver you from demonic bondage, bad habits, or mental strongholds. But how do you live in the freedom that is already yours? Jesus tells us in John 8:31-32, "...If you abide in My Word, you are My disciples indeed. And you shall know the truth, and the truth shall make you free."

Right now you stand on the launching pad of life. God's Word already dwells within you. But only as you continue in the Word do you walk into God's freedom. And it all begins as you apply Romans 12:2 to your life: "And do not be CONFORMED to this world, but be TRANSFORMED by the renewing of your mind...."

As you look into the Word of God for your answers to life:

- *It dramatically changes the way you think.*
- *It dramatically changes the way you live.*
- *It dramatically changes everything about you.*

There is no other way for an inner transformation to take place. It comes only by renewing your mind with God's Word.

DAILY CONFESSION
*Father, I thank You that I am free because I abide in Your Word.
I refuse to conform to this world but I am transformed because
I allow Your Word to change the way I think.*

WISDOM AND UNDERSTANDING ARE THE RESULT
OF EMBRACING GOD'S WORD

"…because you have asked for yourself understanding to recognize what is just and right, behold, I have done as you asked. I have given you a wise, discerning mind… I have also given you what you have not asked, both riches and honor…"
1 Kings 3:11-13 (AMP)

Bang! Whack! Bang! Dashing into the bedroom to see what all the banging was about, the husband looked curiously over at his wife. "Honey, what are you doing with my screwdriver?" Caught red-handed (and red-faced), she really didn't want to admit it. "Well, I guess I was trying to hammer this nail into the wall." Chuckling though irritated that his costly tool was being unnecessarily dented by his wife's hammering, "Trying to pound that nail with my screwdriver is useless because it's not meant to be used as a hammer! I'll be right back with the hammer, okay?"

We may have the right tool in our hands, but if we don't know how to effectively use it, the tool becomes useless. Likewise, the Word of God becomes ineffective to us if we do not fully understand why God sent it and the power it possesses. If we do not acknowledge that the Word of God is true and able to transform us, we see no change after we hear it.

Understanding unlocks the power of the Word of God to flow into the life of the believer. The more we give ourselves to the Word of God, the more understanding we possess for every area of our life. For example, you can only experience Godly prosperity when you understand God's thoughts concerning provision.

God desires for all of us to live an abundant life—a life that has all the resources necessary to fulfill His call. Solomon pursued wisdom and understanding, and in return, prosperity pursued him.

DAILY CONFESSION
Father, I thank You that I take Your Word to heart.
I accurately understand the Word of truth. I follow Your instructions and live.

TO BECOME WHAT GOD HAS CREATED
YOU TO BE, YOU MUST CHOOSE TO IMPRINT
GOD'S WISHES ON YOUR HEART

"Be diligent to present yourself approved to God, a worker who does not need to be ashamed, rightly dividing the word of truth." 2 Timothy 2:15 (NKJV)

No one knew for sure how old it was, but the silver and turquoise cross dangling around her neck caused the teenager to stand out in a crowd. Manufactured over a century earlier in the historic Mexican village where most of her family was born, the cross, of an intricate mosaic design, identified her great-grandmother as a Christian, a staunch student of the Bible, a believer among a family of superstitious natives who practiced divination in its highest form. A tale about the cross was faithfully passed down through her family, fervently explaining that as the villagers caught a glimpse of the cross and the woman who wore it, their souls began to seek the true God, searching for His Word and His Son, eventually creating the Christian village it is today.

Why is it so imperative to faithfully study the Word of God? Because others witness in our lives what we read in the Book. That is how the world identifies us as Christians—by the profile of the new man described in the Word of God. Peter calls this new man "the hidden man of the heart." Paul calls him the "new creature." Regardless of what the new man is called, his entire profile is contained inside the Book.

As we diligently study God's Word, taking it deep into our souls, we eventually are transformed into what we read. This is the way God designed for us to grow in the truth. We won't get anywhere in our walk with God if we pursue Him as if He were only an escape from consequences. We have to get serious about discovering who we are in Christ instead of continually talking about who we are not. We must pursue truth if we desire to draw near to God.

DAILY CONFESSION
*Father, I thank You that I am approved by You,
a worker who does not need to be ashamed.*

NEVER ALLOW THE GIFTS
THAT HAVE BEEN BESTOWED UPON YOU
TO EVER ECLIPSE THE ONE WHO BESTOWED THEM

"I will praise You, for I am fearfully and wonderfully made;
marvelous are Your works, and that my soul knows very well."
Psalm 139:14 (NKJV)

✦

"Cha-ching, Cha-ching," proclaimed the pretty suburban mother of two young boys, retaining a smug snicker. The aunts, uncles, nieces, and in-laws who gathered around the Thanksgiving table stared in disbelief. "When I saw him downtown that night, I knew I couldn't let that one get away." Rosy-cheeked with embarrassment, her mother-in-law smiled with a hollow grin, yet inwardly she seethed like a trounced alley cat. Now everyone knows—she only married my son for the money!

I'll never forget the day someone I once trusted sat across the desk from me and ominously declared, "The only reason I wanted a relationship with you was because I knew what it would do for me." That statement revealed to me that all along, I was in relationship with a taker and a user. Those words crushed me, causing me to understand how important it is to never allow the gifts that have been bestowed upon you to ever eclipse the one who bestowed them.

Celebrate the people who deposit goodness into your life and take you to a place of success and favor. Celebrate your mentors in huge fashion, since this "attitude of gratitude" and humility keeps you from proudly thinking about the particular gifting of your own life.

- *Consistently refuse the temptation to seek the gift more than the giver.*

- *Treasure those whom God brings into your life.*

- *Never let those people go.*

DAILY CONFESSION
Father, I thank You and praise You for I am fearfully and wonderfully made.
Marvelous are Your works; my soul knows them very well.

FAVOR IS THE REWARD GUARANTEED TO THOSE WHO HAVE CHOSEN THE LIFE OF RESPECT

"Happy is the man who is always reverent,
but he who hardens his heart will fall into calamity."
Proverbs 28:14 (NKJ)

Respect is a lost virtue in twenty-first century society. It is a noble character trait few come to understand. The power of this virtue is remarkable. Men are drawn toward it; God is pleased by it. What does it mean to respect, and how is it expressed? These are questions that must be answered before we can experience the true rewards of respect.

Respect contains within it the willingness to treat another even greater than we desire to be treated. Respect has the capability to bring out the best in others. It causes those who receive it to stand as proud and as tall as the most esteemed king.

All men desire to be respected. Every employer, government official, husband, wife, or friend vigilantly searches for someone who is eager to respect not only them but also their time.

Respect is the commitment we make to those in authority over us, and as we do such, God makes the commitment to shower His favor upon our lives. We must always remember that to love something is to find it desirable; to respect something is to find it valuable. Do those above you know that you value them, their time, and their money? If they do, rest assured, favor is soon to manifest in your life.

DAILY CONFESSION

Father, I thank You for giving me the opportunity to show those above me the respect they rightly deserve. I live a life of respect and I expect to abound with the blessings of favor. I understand favor is granted exclusively to those who choose the route of respect.

NEVER ATTEMPT TO TAKE AUTHORITY
OVER SOMETHING FOR WHICH YOU ARE NOT RESPONSIBLE

"Jesus replied, 'If I want him to remain alive until I return,
what is that to you? You follow Me.'"
John 21:22 (NLT)

✦

"He would not do it!" Jesus made the commitment as a youngster; He would not do anything apart from what His Father instructed Him to do. And He certainly would never attempt to take authority over something for which He was not responsible. Do you realize that the pathway to promotion is abruptly halted when this principle is violated? It shows a superior that the current responsibilities are not enough for the employee, and that the employee didn't choose to go above and beyond in his or her duties. **Never attempt to take authority over something for which you are not responsible.** Allow me give you an example.

As we see in the above passage, Jesus rebuked Peter the moment he stepped outside of his responsibility. We see how seriously the Lord takes this issue. It wasn't that Jesus tried to keep something good from Peter by not telling him about John. Jesus tried to lead Peter on a path that would be best for him—and getting involved in someone else's business would sabotage his life! Peter had to focus 100% on his responsibility, which means that he could put no thought into what another person had to do.

While the Son of God did not take authority for what did not belong to Him, He did consistently lean upon the instructive authority of His loving Father. Why not follow His example by obeying this principle today?

DAILY CONFESSION
Father, I thank You that I mind my own business and do the things
I am commanded to do. I refuse to compare myself with those around me,
knowing that I do everything as unto You.

RENEGADE THOUGHTS ARE NO MORE THAN FUGITIVES OF THE PAST LOOKING UP AN OLD FRIEND

"Casting down arguments and every high thing that exalts itself against the knowledge of God, bringing every thought into captivity to the obedience of Christ."
2 Corinthians 10:5 (NKJV)

The only way to get a handle on the "undertow" of your life is to actively discern the source of all the voices in your head. Many of us really have no idea what is happening when our thoughts seem to go awry. We think there is something wrong with us. We think that somehow we have suddenly become as carnal men and that our spiritual walk falls short of what it should be.

If you received Jesus Christ as the Lord of your life, any thoughts in your mind that are contrary to God's Word are not your thoughts. How do I know this? Proverbs 12:5 (KJV) says, "The thoughts of the righteous are right, but the counsels of the wicked are deceitful." God declared you righteous—not based upon what you do, but upon what Jesus did.

Therefore, if thoughts come into your mind, thoughts that are the not right, they are simply not your thoughts. Therefore you must fight them with sword of God's Word and protect yourself with the shield of faith.

Don't allow those wrong and negative thoughts to linger for any length of time. If you do, they will take root like a weed and ultimately ruin your life. As Solomon put it, "Keep your heart with all diligence, for out of it spring the issues of life" (Proverbs 4:23 NKJV).

DAILY CONFESSION
Father, I thank You that I cast down arguments and every high thing that exalts itself against knowledge of You and I bring every thought into captivity to the obedience of Christ.

RENEWING THE MIND
IS THE FIRST STEP OF LIFE TRANSFORMATION

"And do not be conformed to this world, but be transformed by the renewing of your mind, that you may prove what is that good and acceptable and perfect will of God."
Romans 12:2 (NKJV)

&

That term "conformed" refers to being molded or shaped as a cake to a baking pan. God does not want you and me to be molded to the image of this world. When we become pliable to God and His Word, the process of transformation begins. As we pattern our lives according to God's Word, we soon walk as Jesus walked, and thus do the things Jesus did. Conformation means making changes on the outside; transformation is something that can only happen from within.

As the Jews listened to Jesus' parables—powerfully poignant accounts of the foolish and the wise, the one who sowed and his seed, and the wheat and the tares—the hearers were being transformed, deep down inside. We cannot change our lives from the outside in; we must first change the inside.

As we continually seek God's Word for the answers to life, our way of thinking transitions into God's way of thinking. Controlling our thoughts changes everything about us. There is no other way for true, inner transformation than by exchanging our thoughts for His.

DAILY CONFESSION
Father, I thank You that I am not conformed to this world,
but I am transformed by the renewing of my mind. I prove Your perfect will
in my life. I speak, think, and do the Word, and have good success.

THE WORD OF GOD IS THE GREATEST MAP
IN THE JOURNEY OF SUCCESS

"All Scripture is inspired by God and is useful to teach us what is true
and to make us realize what is wrong in our lives. It straightens us out and
teaches us to do what is right. It is God's way of preparing us in every way,
fully equipped for every good thing God wants us to do."
2 Timothy 3:16-17 (NLT)

⚓

"I would like to say, 'Good Morning, everyone,'" the radio announcer chattered with a sigh, "but with the rate this snow is falling, I guess whether or not it is actually good is left to your own discretion. For all you skiers out there, it's probably a wonderful morning indeed!"

Each day we wake up, we specifically choose what kind of attitude with which we live. We may erroneously think that others have the power to decide our attitude, but when it boils down to it, we make the decision of how we respond. By continually grafting the Word of God into who we are, we see instant results in all areas of life. We see ourselves becoming more patient, making wiser decisions, and avoiding evil.

We must, however, rely on God's Word to lead the way toward His will for our lives. If God's Word does not direct our steps, our destination will not be pleasant. I meet many people who are unhappy with the way life seems to presently be for them. They desire a great future but refuse to follow the guidelines established in God's eternal Word to make it happen.

The Word of God transforms us when we begin to get our daily dosage of God's success plan. It is a process, one in which we must be patient but willing to do whatever it takes to stay on the right path.

DAILY CONFESSION
Father, I thank You that all scripture is inspired by You and is useful
to teach me what is true and to make me realize what is wrong in my life.
It straightens me out and teaches me to do what is right.

STUDYING GOD'S THOUGHTS
WILL GIVE YOU CONFIDENCE IN PRAYER

"Now this is the confidence that we have in Him, that if we ask anything
according to His will, He hears us. And if we know that He hears us, whatever
we ask, we know that we have the petitions that we have asked of Him."
1 John 5:14-15 (NKJV)

✦

Confidence is a crucial attribute in a believer's life. Isn't it interesting to see how much confidence we have in the natural things of life—fully convinced that the sun will set, the grass will grow, and the birds will sing, but when it comes to God, we often walk in doubt? Friends, it was never designed to be this way. Let me give you an example. Ask any American today if they will ever starve. With a quick, confident retort their response will be a resounding "no." They are absolutely convinced that when they are hungry, they can and will get food to satisfy their hunger. Not only are they confident that food will satisfy them, but they stop whatever they are doing to satisfy that hunger.

Quoting Scripture when tempted in the wilderness, Jesus continually used the Word of God as a ready defense throughout His earthly ministry, confident in its power and authenticity. With Jesus as our example, why are we also not confident in God's Word? We have God's exact thoughts scripted for us on paper, yet we continually doubt Him.

When we go to God in prayer, the Bible says we can be confident in this one thing; if we ask anything according to His will (His Word), we can confidently know that we HAVE what we prayed for. Notice it did not say "will have" but it said, "We have." Finances, health, wisdom, peace, whatever the situation may be, find out His will and pray in accordance to the Word of God. Subsequently, **stand confident, knowing God is faithful to perform what He promised.**

DAILY CONFESSION
Father, I thank You I am confident that I can pray in line with Your Word
and You hear me. I know that since You hear me, I have whatever I ask.

YOUR LIFE TODAY IS THE RESULT
OF THE THOUGHTS OF YESTERDAY

"Casting down arguments and every high thing that exalts itself against the knowledge
of God, bringing every thought into captivity to the obedience of Christ…"
2 Corinthians 10:5 (NKJV)

The life you experience tomorrow is the direct result of the thoughts you plant today.

"I wish I was dead." The hideous words were scrawled upon the dingy white wall of her closet; a shocking summary of the nagging, negative voices that attempted to overwhelm the teenager's muddled mind. But just as soon as they came—"Aren't you dressed yet?" totally unaware, her loving mother suddenly interrupted the girl's tormented mind. "You know it's almost time for church, honey." Dismissing the thoughts as hastily as they came, "I really do have a lot to live for. I don't know where those thoughts came from; I know there's something I am supposed to do."

When nagging, distracting, negative voices begin to torment your mind, you have to make the wise choice by saying:

- *No, I'm not listening to that!*
- *I'm going to believe the Word, no matter what.*
- *I'm not going to give up; I'm not going to yank God's Word out of my heart.*
- *God's Word is everything to me.*

No matter what you hear or from whom, search and discover what God has to say about it. Don't care what anybody else says; find out what God says, and that's what you should believe! That's what you should plant securely inside your heart!

DAILY CONFESSION
Father, I thank You that I cast down arguments and every high thing
that exalts itself against knowledge of You, bringing every thought into
captivity to the obedience of Christ.

LACK OF TIME CAN'T PRODUCE FAILURE; ONLY MISMANAGED TIME CAN

"There is a time for everything, a season for every activity under Heaven."
Ecclesiastes 3:1 (NLT)

⚜

The excuse of not having enough time is a safe haven for many who want to justify their lack of productivity. But let's be entirely honest as you consider these five crucial questions:

- *How much of your time goes to waste on a daily basis?*
- *How often do you have five, ten, or fifteen minutes without a clear focus?*
- *How much time do you spend lingering in thoughts and actions that are unnecessary and unfruitful?*
- *Do you keep track of your time?*
- *Do you know what you need to accomplish each day?*

Planning your hours is a difficult task initially, but once you get the hang of it, you'll see how much time you actually have! You can be successful, not just financially, but in every area of your life. One of the requirements, though, is that you **learn to make every moment of your day worthwhile.**

I'm sure you have a lot to accomplish, so make it happen, and refuse to make excuses. Doing so always leads you closer to your dreams than ever before.

YOUR RESPONSE TO TRIALS REVEALS
YOUR LEVEL OF MATURITY

*"But Joseph refused. 'Look,' he told her, 'my master trusts me with
everything in his entire household. No one here has more authority than I do!
He has held back nothing from me except you, because you are his wife.
How could I ever do such a wicked thing? It would be a great sin against God.'
She kept putting pressure on him day after day, but he refused to sleep with
her, and he kept out of her way as much as possible."*
Genesis 39:8-10 (NLT)

The sharp aroma of the freshly trodden concrete wafted through
the chilly November air; their new home's foundation was finally
complete. "Most important part," the builder declared. "If the foundation's not right, might as well start all over again." Undeniably, the
foundation of our lives (the most important part) is our integrity. The
Bible repeatedly speaks of how important it is for us to have integrity
as the foundation of our character. Satan understands that if he
damages a man's character, he destroys his life. The list of Godly men
who bowed to his temptations is countless.

Temptation is not exclusive to just one area of our lives; Satan
tempts us in many avenues. He is like a lion prowling and seeking
whom he may devour, viciously preying on those who diligently do
the Word of God and build the Kingdom of God. And he comes with
full force as he did with Jesus, hoping to knock us down completely.

When Satan tempted Jesus in the wilderness, Jesus responded as a
true man of integrity. He used his sharply-compacted foundation of
the Scriptures and spoke the truth of God's Word. Now we must do
the same. **Wherever you are tempted to doubt God's faithfulness,
speak aloud the promises of the Word of God, and continue to do
so until He delivers you.**

DAILY CONFESSION
*Father, I thank You that no temptation overtakes me.
You are faithful, and You do not allow me to be tempted beyond
what I am able to bear. You give me a way of escape.*

CONDUCT IS THE MIRROR
THAT REVEALS YOUR SELF-PORTRAIT

"We even saw giants there, the descendants of Anak.
We felt like grasshoppers next to them, and that's what we looked like to them!"
Numbers 13:33 (NLT)

✦

"I can never do anything right," moaned the newly-wed wife in despair, gazing at the darkened pizza crust. "Now that's not true and you know it," her husband of four weeks soothed, flaking off bits of crust with a knife. "This pizza will be just fine, and anyway, you've made some delicious meals—some even tastier than my own mother." Grateful for her husband's insight and encouragement, she replied, "You're right, sweetheart, I shouldn't think that way."

We always act according to our inner self-image. Eventually, everyone must openly acknowledge what they genuinely believe about themselves. We can only fool ourselves for so long. **Our conduct is the only proof of what we believe about ourselves.** Those with negative habits continue in those habits because they persistently see themselves at that stagnant place. Talk to any teenager who doesn't fit in and you will see why he acts the way he does. He believes himself to be an outcast, a reject, or a burden.

As believers, we must be sensitive to the actions of others. Many times people cry out, asking for someone to help them. They are bound by their own self-image. However, God desires for us to embrace the image He has of us. The moment we accepted Christ, we were crucified with Him, and He gave us a new identity. The only way we can ever truly live a life of obedience is by embracing the true image we have in Him. As we continue to meditate upon the truths of God's Word concerning our identity, we soon respond as Joshua and Caleb did—with confidence in their God.

DAILY CONFESSION
Father, I thank You that I am crucified with Christ.
I no longer live, but Christ lives through me.
I live by faith in the One who loved me and gave Himself for me.

CHARACTER IS DEVELOPED BY LEARNING
THE DELICATE ART OF RESPECTING AUTHORITY

*"And we urge you, brethren, to recognize those who labor among you,
and are over you in the Lord and admonish you, and to esteem them very highly
in love for their work's sake. Be at peace among yourselves."*
1 Thessalonians 5:12-13 (NKJV)

Respect is a very interesting word. Society spent the last forty years dismantling the meaning of the word respect. As a result, many people don't even know what this word means. They don't respect themselves, let alone someone else! Nonetheless, respect is a powerful force, absolutely essential to multiply your life investment.

Respect means giving attention to. Respect also carries the idea of holding others in high esteem or deeming others as distinguished and worthy. Think about it—

- *Who do you hold in high esteem?*
- *To whom do you give your attention?*
- *Who are the distinguished people in your life
  whom you consider worthy of honor?*

Respect is a quality that lives on the inside of a person; it's not just how a person acts on the outside.

Respect deals with one's motives, not just one's actions. Choose to respect others today, but before you do—

Respect yourself and know God thinks the world of you!

DAILY CONFESSION
*Father, I thank You that I recognize those who labor among me and are over me.
I esteem them very highly in love for their work's sake.*

EVERY DAY IS A GIFT
JUST WAITING TO BE UNWRAPPED

"This is the day the Lord has made. We will rejoice and be glad in it."
Psalm 118:24 (NKJV)

✠

After six days of preaching and ministering to the crowds, quite unexpectedly, Jesus took Peter, James, and his brother John aside. Charges like lightening bolts seemed to fill the air, and with every curious step up the rocky mountain, the towns beneath them decreasing in size, the three of them wondered: *What is going on? What is the Master going to do now?* Upon reaching the summit, they all realized this day would be like no other—the Master's face shined as the brightest sun, His clothes glowed with whitest of lights. Then suddenly, two others appeared; instinctively they recognized them: Moses and Elijah! Peter began to speak, but a bright cloud overshadowed them all; a Voice thundered, declaring how the Father was well pleased with His Son— yes, that day was like a gift, just waiting to be unwrapped!

And every day God gives to man is a gift just waiting to be unwrapped. But how appreciative are you of the gift God gave you? How excited are you to find out what His gift contains? Our answers reveal a great deal about who we are. David declared, "We will rejoice and be glad in it." There is no reason why the people of God should be discouraged and depressed. Jesus is on the throne, and God's Word is still true as it ever was.

Today is God's day. I know you may be going through some rough times, but God is there. He wants you to enjoy the gift He gave you. Today is a gift just for you. There is so much for which to be thankful; let us show God how much we appreciate His gift by rejoicing when times are rough and by being happy when we don't feel like it. When you think of all He does, is this too much to ask? Certainly not!

DAILY CONFESSION
Father, I thank You that You made this day; I rejoice and am glad.
I choose to make it the best day of my life.

YOU ARE DESTINED TO WIN, WHETHER OR NOT YOU DO IS UP TO YOU

"But thanks be to God, who gives us the victory through our Lord Jesus Christ."
1 Corinthians 15:57 (NKJV)

Jesus realized this compelling fact and so should you—it doesn't matter what the devil says or thinks about you, and it surely doesn't matter if the devil says you are at a disadvantage because you don't have the necessary background, education, training, or experience. You may have been surrounded by people who failed to realize their dreams, but that doesn't mean you have to fail.

I made the decision long ago that:

- *It does not matter how I was raised or from where I came.*
- *It does not matter who the devil thinks I am.*

I'm going to win! God gave me the victory! You may not be able to see the full manifestation of my victory right now, but stay by the sidelines and watch — because I am going to win!

Remember this: **It takes just as much effort to breathe and lose as it does to breathe and win.** I'm not destined to lose! Neither are you!

DAILY CONFESSION
Father, I thank You that You gave me the victory through Jesus Christ my Lord.

YOUR THOUGHTS ARE THE RUDDERS
WHICH GUIDE YOUR HEART THROUGH LIFE

"For as he thinks in his heart, so is he."
Proverbs 23:7 (NKJV)

"For the weapons of our warfare are not carnal but mighty in God for pulling down strongholds, casting down arguments and every high thing that exalts itself against the knowledge of God, bringing every thought into captivity to the obedience of Christ."
2 Corinthians 10:4-5 (NKJV)

⚓

"I'll never make it;" "There's no way;" "I know I can't." Never, No, Can't—the thoughts we harbor in our mind are seeds that produce after their own kind. All self-limiting thoughts of weakness, failure, unhappiness, or poverty are harmful and self-destructing. Those thoughts are enemies attempting to hinder our future progress. The key is to strategically counterattack those thoughts whenever they try to take ground in our minds. They are the most devious of thieves, stealing your very ability to succeed. Also among their ranks are:

- *Bitterness*
- *Resentment*
- *Hatred*
- *Suspicion*

Even so, the apostle Paul tells us, "I see another law in my members, warring against the laws of my mind, and bringing me into captivity to the law of sin which is in my members." We are in a battle that is fought on the battlefield of our minds. However, Godly thinking is the elite stratagem, guaranteeing our victory. **God gave us a secret weapon with which to fight—His Word spoken from our lips and carried out in our actions.** We can use these weapons to bring every negative thought into obedience to Christ, replacing those thoughts with words like: Will, Yes, Can. If God did not say it, then we are not authorized to think it.

DAILY CONFESSION
Father, I thank You that I hold the thoughts,
attitudes, and purposes of Your heart.

WHAT YOU RECEIVE FROM THE HAND OF GOD
IS DEPENDENT UPON WHAT YOU BELIEVE
FROM THE WORD OF GOD

"For she thought to herself,
'If I can just touch His clothing, I will be healed.'"
Mark 5:28 (NLT)

❧

No eye has seen, no ear has heard, no mind can imagine what God so freely gives to His children. "Where is it?" you may ask. All of us must come to a point in our lives, especially when we experience circumstances contrary to the promises of God, when we truly wonder whether God's Word is true. We feel as though we are missing it but not sure where to pinpoint the problem.

I have chosen to believe God and His Word regardless of what happens in my life. God is not a man that He should lie. If God said it, we must believe it. Jesus tells us, "Be it done according as You have believed."

My present life is a by-product of the Word I believed yesterday. If we do not enjoy our present circumstances, we must examine what we truly believe. Is it God or is it what we see? The woman with the issue of blood received what she believed; I believe the same is true about you. Believe...your promise is on its way!

DAILY CONFESSION
I have the faith of God and I use that faith to manifest the promises of God in my life. I believe God and I refuse to walk by what I see. God is not a man that will lie, but He is almighty God. If he said it, then I believe it. I receive what I believe.

REALITY IS NEVER BASED ON WHAT YOU SEE, BUT BY WHAT YOU CHOOSE TO BELIEVE

"So we don't look at the troubles we can see right now; rather, we look forward to what we have not yet seen. For the troubles we see will soon be over, but the joys to come will last forever."
2 Corinthians 4:18 (NLT)

✦

What looks bigger in your life – your circumstance or God's Word? God's Word was true yesterday, it is true today, and it will be true tomorrow. Regardless of the struggles we face, God's Word does not change. I thank God that He does not lie; I know that I can stand on His Word and watch Him set me free. He is faithful, and He desires to show Himself strong on our behalf.

During your trying times, remember that God never said when He would deliver you; all He promised was that He would! The trials you go through are to refine your faith, creating gold from nothing but wobbly iron ore. The sooner you start trusting God, the sooner you'll come through the fire!

So, are you going to view God's Word through the magnifying glass of faith or the blindfold of sight? We must choose which perspective has its way in our heart, and our choice determines our destiny.

DAILY CONFESSION
Father, I thank You that I refuse to look at the troubles that I can see. I look at what I cannot see through the eyes of faith. I understand that Your Word does not change. I walk by faith and not by sight.

THE CHARACTER YOU POSSESS TOMORROW
IS LINKED TO THE CHOICES YOU MAKE TODAY

"Those who say they live in God should live their lives as Christ did."
1 John 2:6 (NLT)

"Follow God's example in everything you do, because you are His dear children.
Live a life filled with love for others, following the example of Christ,
who loved you and gave Himself as a sacrifice to take away your sins.
And God was pleased, because that sacrifice was like sweet perfume to Him."
Ephesians 5:1-2 (NLT)

❧

Our character is fashioned by every decision we make. Every choice, however insignificant, contains within it a series of consequences. **There are times when we may make mistakes, stumble, and experience temporary defeat. Nevertheless, we must choose to rise above those disappointments, get up, and brush ourselves off.**

Our example must be Jesus, whose character cannot be formed within us except by effort and daily practice. Teaching about such emotional issues as family, humility, and the workplace, Jesus realized that, however difficult, we need to exercise self-discipline and self-control by responding according to principle, not according to emotions. Circumstances themselves do not determine who we are, nor do they alter our character; it is how we respond that reveals who we really are.

Our lives are a result of the paths we choose to take. Life is a series of choices, not a series of chances. We can only sculpt our character into that of Christ by embracing Godly principles above human emotions.

DAILY CONFESSION
Father, I thank You that I live my life as Christ did. I follow Your example
in everything I do, loving others and following the example of Christ.

YOUR CHARACTER IS THE ANCHOR
WHICH GIVE YOUR RELATIONSHIPS SUBSTANCE

"Do not be deceived: 'Bad company corrupts good morals.'"
1 Corinthians 15:33 (NASB)

✦

"This thing's not going anywhere!" Spinning the pedals around and around, faster and faster, the bicycle would not move an inch. "Of course it's not moving, Son," the young dad laughed, "both tires are flat!" And the same holds true concerning relationship without character—it's like a ship without water or a bike without tires. You cannot sustain a relationship unless both parties are committed to the Word of God.

I like to say it like this: Integrity is the foundation upon which your life's work is built. **Always prize principle above relationship, otherwise, you soon compromise when others around you pressure you to do so.**

We notice throughout the Scriptures men of God who refused to compromise their character. We also see the importance of surrounding yourself with people who are just as committed to God as you. The Bible tells us, "Bad company corrupts good character." Your good character most often won't change the bad character of another, but bad character will most often stain your commitment to God.

Be serious about your commitment to God and surround your life with those who are serious as well.

DAILY CONFESSION
Father, I thank You that I am not deceived
for I know that bad company corrupts good morals,
so I choose to surround myself with those who are committed to You.

YOUR OUTWARD ACTIONS ARE LITTLE MORE THAN A PICTURE OF YOUR INNER CONVICTIONS

"So don't get tired of doing what is good. Don't get discouraged and give up,
for we will reap a harvest of blessing at the appropriate time."
Galatians 6:9 (NLT)

⚜

The future we desire is connected to the seed we hold in our hands. Many times people tell me, "I don't have any seed to sow." If that is true, then God appears to be a liar. In 2 Corinthians 9:10, the Scripture tells us God gives seed to the one who sows. **One of the reasons we may not have seed today is because we were unwilling to sow what we had yesterday.** God does not hand out seed to just anyone; He gives seed to those who sow. Without sowing, our future looks no brighter than our present circumstances. Why is that? We cannot create a better tomorrow if we don't sow better seed.

Over the years I observed how few people really understand this principle. All of us know it, but only a few apply it. **There is no greater revelation than the power of the seed.** Jesus placed more emphasis on His parable of the seed and soil that on any other parable. Our future lies within the seeds we plant today. We must not limit seed to money. Seed is anything you do that benefits another—

- *Your smile*
- *An encouraging word*
- *Praying for another*
- *Showing hospitality*

As we apply this principle, we see an increased opportunity to put it into practice. So don't get tired of doing what is good, as the Scripture tells us, for we have a bright and bountiful future when sowing becomes our daily focus.

DAILY CONFESSION
Father, I thank You that I don't get tired of doing what is good.
I reap a harvest of blessing at the appropriate time because I refuse to give up.

BEHAVIOR TOLERATED
BECOMES BEHAVIOR CELEBRATED

"People who cover over their sins will not prosper.
But if they confess and forsake them, they will receive mercy."
Proverbs 28:13 (NLT)

⋏

"I'll help you, Daddy," the little girl kindly offered, tugging at the dandelions with both hands. "That's good, Sweetheart, but you have to use this tool to get them out, see?" showing his young daughter the forked tool used for pulling weeds, "If you don't go way, way down deep into the dirt, those old dandelions will just shoot right back up again."

It's a well known fact—every one of us faces problems. But how many of us are willing to deal with the roots of these problems? As in the illustration above, a weed must be pulled up by its root, or else that weed has no choice but to return. The same is true with the problems we face.

There is a specific root to every problem. The enemy, however, wants us to pull the weed without attacking the root, and doing so only exacerbates the problem. Any problem allowed to mature forces us to live with it indefinitely—we become cozily accustomed to the lifestyle that problem creates.

We see in Proverbs 28:13 how it is impossible to prosper if we tolerate sin. **The very problems we tolerate become the giants that conquer us in the future.** We must ask God to help us understand what we must do in order to overcome the problems we face. Satan does not give up effortlessly, but he can be defeated by those who attack the root of their problems with the Word of God.

DAILY CONFESSION

Father, I thank You that I do not cover my sins. I confess and forsake them and I am shown mercy. I desire to walk in the abundance You have for me, and I know that tolerating any problem in my life hinders me from enjoying the abundant life.

WHEN SECRETLY YOU CHOOSE TO BENEFIT OTHERS, HEAVEN WILL CHOOSE TO CELEBRATE YOU OPENLY

*"And now about prayer. When you pray, don't be like the hypocrites who love to
pray publicly on street corners and in the synagogues where everyone can see them.
I assure you, that is all the reward they will ever get. But when you pray,
go away by yourself, shut the door behind you, and pray to your Father secretly.
Then your Father, who knows all secrets, will reward you."*
Matthew 6:5-6 (NLT)

"Shhhh—she didn't hear the cookie jar clang, did she?" Shaking
her head, the youngster and her sister munched on chocolate cookies,
never believing that they would be caught, that is, not until they
heard the footsteps coming closer and closer...

What you do in secret always finds a way into the open. For some,
that is a frightening thought. But as a believer, your secret life should
only be filled with good things. In secret is when you have the opportunity to develop yourself. You can use that time to:

- *Pray*
- *Study the Word of God*
- *Learn new skills*
- *Become a person of Godly character*

God is faithful. He will not forget how hard you work for Him, nor
will He allow the law of sowing and reaping to evade you. The sacrifices
you make in secret will one day bring a reward to you and to others.
Make a point to focus your secret life into a fruitful activity. It may be
one of the areas listed above, or it may be something unique to you.
Whatever it is, don't allow your secret life to become purposeless or
scattered. Use it for the glory of God.

DAILY CONFESSION
*Father, I thank You that You cause me to be rewarded
as I seek You in my secret life. Show me how to use my time wisely
so that I may become all You plan for me.*

WHEN HEAVEN'S OPPORTUNITIES KNOCK, YOUR DESTINY IS REVEALED BY ANSWERING THE DOOR

"A wise youth works hard all summer;
a youth who sleeps away the hour of opportunity brings shame."
Proverbs 10:5 (NLT)

Opportunity comes to all of us, but very few people are able to recognize it and take advantage of it when it arrives. Opportunity is defined as a good chance for advancement or progress. All of us desire to advance in life, but we must make the necessary preparations before we can go to that next level.

Let me illustrate my point. Suppose an elementary school encouraged its students to take the entrance exam into an Ivy League university. The results would be shameful, because elementary students are not prepared for collegiate exams. God deals with us in the same way. He withholds opportunities from our lives until we are adequately prepared to experience them. **We are only able to enter the doors of opportunity when we prepare for the responsibility of the opportunity.**

Jesus used every opportunity He could to demonstrate the Kingdom of God. Whether through miracles, forgiveness, parables, or compassion, Christ opened the doors of opportunity for those who prepared, bringing the transformation of God's kingdom directly into their lives.

God sends certain people, specific ideas, and particular instructions our way for our preparation. If we make the most of them, when the doors of opportunity open, we can run through them to achieve the plan God has for us.

DAILY CONFESSION
Father, I thank You that I do not sleep away
the hour of opportunity in my life. You give me wisdom,
and I work hard to seize every opportunity You have in store.

THE VALUE YOU PLACE UPON GOD'S WORD
IS IMMEDIATELY REVEALED BY YOUR WILLINGNESS
TO ACT UPON IT

"The law of the Lord …more precious than gold…sweeter than honey
…there is great reward for those who obey them."
Psalm 19:7–11 (NLT)

⚔

"Who wants this old junk?" Pushing aside all her old clothes from the '70's, she continued cleaning out boxes stored way back in her closet. The woman's daughter came in with eyes as big as saucers. "Wow, Mom, where'd you get all the great clothes?" "What great clothes? You mean all these old rags?" Fingering the silver belts, bell-bottomed pants, and flowery headbands, "Wow, Mom, I can't wait to try these on." "Well, honey," the woman shook her head, "they're all yours!"

All of us possess things that are valuable. What we consider valuable, however, may not necessarily be valuable to someone else. In this portion of scripture, we clearly see what is valuable and priceless to David, and what he considered to be the most treasured possession of his life. We must be willing to gaze upon what we consider valuable and compare ourselves to David. What do we consider to be sweeter than honey? What is more valuable to us than gold? We know the blessings David had throughout his life, and in this passage, we see how and why they came. Even though we may not be at the level David was with his love for God, we can create an appetite for it just as we do for paintings, artifacts, and great artwork.

We must secure His Word the same way. We cannot afford to allow the enemy to steal the Word from our hearts or steal our time from the Word. It is imperative that we are diligent to secure and protect the Word that is richly sown within our hearts. As we place a high value on God's Word and protect it, we see God's Word transform our lives more rapidly than ever before.

DAILY CONFESSION
Father, I thank You that my delight and desire
are in Your Word day and night.

YOUR FAITH IS PURIFIED THE MOMENT
YOU REFUSE TO BUCKLE UNDER PRESSURE

"These trials are only to test your faith, to show that it is strong and pure.
It is being tested as fire tests and purifies gold…"
1 Peter 1:7 (NLT)

"Anyone who listens to My teaching and obeys Me is wise, like a person
who builds a house on solid rock. Though the rain comes in torrents and the
floodwaters rise and the winds beat against the house, it won't collapse, because
it is built on rock. But anyone who hears My teaching and ignores it is foolish,
like a person who builds a house on sand. When the rains and floods come and
the winds beat against that house, it will fall with a mighty crash."
Matthew 7:24–27 (NLT)

In the above scripture, Jesus speaks to His disciples about life's challenges. Notice that Jesus did not say "if" the storms of life come, He said "when" the storms of life come. We are going to encounter some storms in life!

Storms, tests, and life's pressures are going to come knocking and we must choose who is going to answer. Pressure proves who we truly are. As you squeeze a tube of toothpaste (in the same way life applies pressure to us) what comes out is what lies hidden within. **Begin to prepare, begin to build your house on character, integrity, and righteousness; the storms of life are coming, the question is…will you be ready?**

THE VALUE YOU PLACE UPON WISDOM WILL DETERMINE THE LIFE THAT IT CAN PRODUCE FOR YOU

"Getting wisdom is the most important thing you can do!"
Proverbs 4:7 (NLT)

As we see in this Scripture, wisdom is the most important thing to obtain in this life—more important than any material possession. When we value wisdom, the material things that are necessary for our life make their way to us. All of us have moments in life when we wish we knew the right answer or knew exactly what to do in a certain situation. By obtaining wisdom, we have the answer in those situations, and are rewarded for it.

At the time of Christ, most Jews ceased to travel through the region of Samaria. The Samaritans were a people of mixed blood—half Israelite, half heathen—and great wisdom was needed in order to appropriately deal with the people. How would one show them God's love? Without condemnation, Jesus drew upon not only the Samaritan woman's physical thirst, but her spiritual thirst as well, demonstrating to her His love and priceless wisdom. And it was only through this wisdom that the Samaritan woman was won.

To love something is to find it desirable, but to value something is to find it essential. Wisdom is essential to the outcome of our lives. Therefore,

- *Do we just want wisdom, or do we truly value it?*
  Our pursuit proves the answer.

- *How much time do we spend in God's Word?*

- *How much of an effort do we make to hear the wisdom of men and God?*

Be honest with yourself as you consider these questions, then think of a way to pursue the wisdom of God today.

DAILY CONFESSION
Father, I pursue Your Word with all my heart.
I love Your wisdom, and as I pursue wisdom, I gain understanding as well.

THE CONTROL OF ONE'S DESIRES
IS THE TRUEST MEASURE OF CHARACTER

"Until the time came to fulfill His Word, the Lord tested Joseph's character."
Psalm 105:19 (NLT)

Tucking her Bible into the very bottom of her purse, she dare not take it out until after work when the office was completely empty, with no one around to make jokes about her "strict" lifestyle, causing her heart to beat rapidly and her eye make-up to run. And furthermore, how could she show up at choir practice that night if her emotions were all out of whack, incited by some crazy incident that happened at work? That sure wouldn't look good, would it?

Did you know that the proof of a man's character is found in his daily actions? Our actions reveal who we truly are. As we travel through life, we encounter many people who appear to be one way, but when they are alone, they are completely different people.

We must clearly understand that **true character is who we are when no one is looking.** Never forget that God sees us at all times. He sees us at home, when we are traveling, when we are alone—He steadfastly records every one of our actions. **We cannot fool God. We may fool others, but God knows the things we hide.**

Satan attempts to fuel the desires of our flesh and bring them out into the open. He is on a constant pursuit of baiting our flesh to embrace sin. As we choose to surrender our lives to the Holy Spirit, we are empowered to deny what our flesh demands of us. We then have the ability to live a life that is pleasing to God.

DAILY CONFESSION
Father, I thank You that I refuse to bow my knew to the desires of my flesh. Instead, I surrender my life to Your Spirit, disciplining my body and causing it to come into line with Your Word. I am a person of noble character.

THE INTAKE OF BIBLE DOCTRINE
IS THE MOST VITAL INGREDIENT TO PURSUING
AND EXPERIENCING TRUTH

"If you abide in My Word, you are My disciples indeed."
John 8:31 (NKJV)

How can we learn the truth? First, we must understand this about ourselves: Our flesh and our mind are not who we are. We need to grasp that simple fact because our flesh and our mind tell us that they are who we are.

You and I have a flaw within us that was given to us at the fall – an inclination toward deception. Our natural tendency is to accept false ideas. In fact, according to Proverbs 14:12, the ways of death actually appeal to our human reasoning: "There is a way that seems right to a man, but its end is the way of death." The bottom line is that the father of lies easily deceives us. That is why **the intake of Bible doctrine is the most important habit in our pursuit of excellent character.**

Jesus knew the importance of studying the Word of God; that is why He was consistently found at the temple discussing the Scriptures. And in today's world, the consistent intake of the Word of God on a daily basis is the only thing that takes us to the point of truth in our lives. Any growth or increase in life occurs only through soul prosperity.

When we fill our minds with His Word, our souls begin to prosper. This is where many individuals miss it. Divine prosperity can never happen in the external realm before it happens foremost in our minds.

Right now, we must begin to infiltrate our minds with His Word; only then do we truly pursue truth.

DAILY CONFESSION
Father, I continue in Your Word. I am a doer and not a hearer only.
I know the truth and the truth makes me free.

IT IS IMPOSSIBLE FOR GOD
TO PROVIDE YOU A FUTURE UNLESS YOU WILLINGLY
MAKE THINGS RIGHT IN THE PRESENT

*"Therefore do not worry about tomorrow, for tomorrow will worry
about its own things. Sufficient for the day is its own trouble."*
Matthew 6:34 (NKJV)

⚓

"I know you have promised us a house, God," the young woman
prayed tearfully, "but when is it coming? And where is it going to be?
And how is it all going to come about? And..."

People who live by their emotions often want to know what God is
going to do with them in the future. However, they haven't come to
terms with this basic principle of character stated above. There is
no bright future for us if we refuse to confront the weaknesses in our
character; for as soon as we arrive at tomorrow, it is renamed today—
complete with the same problems that limited us yesterday. That is
why we must thoroughly fix where we are right now.

Therefore, **it is essential to ask the needed questions and find out
what must be fixed in our lives before we can be promoted to the
next level.** After making the necessary changes, we must then ask
more of the right questions so we can move further along the road
toward excellence.

We must examine our present beliefs and actions, discover what
hinders our walk with God, and then take the necessary steps to deal
with those weaknesses. As we make things right in the present, God
promotes us.

DAILY CONFESSION
*Father, I thank You that I examine myself daily and deal with any weakness
or flaw in my life. I look forward to my future as I take care of my present.
I do not worry about tomorrow, for tomorrow worries about itself.*

YOUR PROMOTION FROM GOD IS GREATLY DEPENDENT ON YOUR SUBMISSION TOWARDS MEN

"Therefore I exhort first of all that supplications, prayers, intercessions, and giving of thanks be made for all men, for kings and all who are in authority, that we may lead a quiet and peaceable life in all Godliness and reverence."
1 Timothy 2:1-2 (NKJV)

One of the most damaging things we can ever do to ourselves is disregard a person in authority over us. In doing so, we actually show a disregard for God's authority in our lives. We forget that **every one of our thoughts, words, and actions is a seed we plant in the field God gave us.**

A disobedient individual is someone who continually shows disregard for the instructions that are required of him. He might even be a nice person; however, when an authority asks him to do something, he just doesn't seem to find the time to do it. We cannot operate that way in the Kingdom of God if we expect to be used by Him. With God, everything is very precise.

- *Does He forgive us? Yes.*
- *Does He love us? Absolutely.*
- *Does He think we are wonderful? We are tops in His eyes!*
- *But are we going to be used by Him? No!*

Why not? Because Proverbs 25:19 says, "Putting confidence in an unreliable person is like chewing with a toothache or walking on a broken foot."

God does not put His confidence in an unreliable person because He doesn't want to put Himself through that kind of pain. Let's be reliable and prove our love for Him by respecting those in authority over us.

DAILY CONFESSION
Father, I thank You that I pray and intercede on behalf of my authorities and I give You thanks for placing them in my life.

EXPERIENCE IS THE TEACHER
THAT NEVER PASSED HER TEST

"Caleb quieted the people before Moses, and said, 'Let us go up at once and possess it; we are well able to conquer it.' But his fellow scouts said, 'We are not able to go up against the people [of Canaan], for they are stronger than we are.'"
Numbers 13:30-31 (AMP)

You can say what you have or you can have what you say.

Since the fall, man filters God's Word through his experience. We erroneously tell God:

- *How big our situation is.*
- *What is happening to us.*
- *Why we may not make it.*

However, we should instead tell our situation just how big our God is. Is God's Word true or are circumstances true?

God calls that which does not exist as though it does exist. Let us do the very same thing and begin to declare what God speaks in His Word. We must refuse the temptation to believe our circumstances over His Word. **Believing and acting on God's Word is the key to receiving anything promised from the Lord.**

God responds to our faith, and our circumstances respond to our actions. What we say and do determine the outcome of our lives. Let us be willing and obedient to believe only what our Heavenly Father says about our situations.

DAILY CONFESSION
Father, I thank You that I keep a watch over my tongue.
My tongue has the power of life and death. I choose to speak Your Word only,
holding fast to my confession of faith. I am satisfied from the harvest of my lips.

THE HEART OF THE SERVANT DETERMINES THE HARMONY OF THE TEAM

"…whoever desires to be great among you must be your servant."
Mark 10:43 (AMP)

⚜

Sitting with tax collectors and thieves; lingering around town with the mentally ill and infirmed; preaching to prostitutes and to those the Jews despised; it was Jesus' true desire to demonstrate the qualities of a servant's heart. A true servant isn't one who just serves others. There is a difference between being a servant and serving. Becoming a servant begins with one's heart. **Our attitude determines the level of fulfillment we receive from serving others—**

- *What is our motive for serving others? (That is a question we must ask before we bow our knee to serve.)*
- *Why do we do what we do?*
- *Is it to get something in return, or because we want to bless someone? (We must always remember God looks at the heart and judges the motives behind our actions.)*
- *Do we attempt to bring harmony through our serving or simply try to get brownie points?*

David cried out to God, "Lord, search me, and know my heart! Try me and know my thoughts! See if there is any wicked or hurtful way in me, and lead me in the way of everlasting life." Serving people must be done out of a pure desire to honor God.

Today is the day we must decide to be joyful, love-motivated servants of the living God. This brings true harmony to any team environment.

IN LIFE WHEN THERE IS MORE THAN
ONE PATH TO FOLLOW, ALWAYS CHOOSE THE DIVINE

"Make me walk along the path of Your commands,
for that is where my happiness is found."
Psalm 119:35 (NLT)

✦

The high road is the road God desires for us to take in every situation we encounter. We may think that the devil is our greatest enemy, but the truth is, mediocrity – settling for something less than God's best – is a greater enemy. That is why we have to determine that we will always pursue the divine in every area of our lives.

One of the problems I have discovered in the body of Christ today is that so many individuals live in mediocrity; yet God called us to take the people for whom we are responsible to a higher level. We must be the ones to take a stand and show others how to live a life full of God.

We have been given a divine mandate to help people eliminate the "just good enough" attitude – the attitude that says, "What I do with my life is good enough. Everything is just fine; I don't need to change." We must, however, continue to press for a better life every day.

The excellence we live today is not good enough for tomorrow. Jesus gave His excellence in everything He did—therefore, we must in turn, desire to give Jesus more tomorrow than what we gave Him today.

DAILY CONFESSION
Father, I thank You that I walk along the path of Your holy Word,
for that is where my happiness is found. I always choose the high road
for that is where I find You.

NEVER GIVE LIFE TO SOMETHING
GOD HAS CONDEMNED TO DEATH

"Knowing this, that our old man was crucified with Him, that the body of sin might be done away with, that we should no longer be slaves of sin."
Romans 6:6 (NKJV)

He just didn't want to do it anymore. He had no desire for those old friends, held no interest in their tawdry amusements, and possessed no longing for their lurid jokes. Although they still called (hoping he'd forget all that "church" nonsense and come to his senses), he was finished, done, crucified with the One who was crucified for him. The above passage powerfully declares that we have been crucified with Christ. I can tell you from personal experience that this particular verse, when acted upon, is of inestimable value to us in our pursuit of God.

So many Christians still struggle with their past – with sins and habits that held them captive before they were born again. Many of these same people try to justify where they are in their spiritual walk because deep down inside, they are unwilling to repent and forsake their sin.

Notice that the Scripture says "our old self" was crucified with Jesus in the new birth. Our old sinful nature is dead. That is very good news for us because death is our only escape from those generational curses that attempt to attach themselves to our lives.

When we count our old man as dead and begin to walk in the newness of life that Jesus purchased for us, we fiercely break the power of those strongholds that controlled our lives for so long. So don't give life to something God put to death. Instead, feed your spirit and walk in the fullness of all God has for you.

DAILY CONFESSION
Father, I thank You that my old self was crucified with Christ.
Everything from my old life was crucified with Him. I escape curses
that attempt to attach themselves to my life.

WORKS ARE NEVER PROOF OF SALVATION, BUT A LACK OF THEM IS PROOF OF THE ABSENCE OF IT

*"So also faith, if it does not have works (deeds and actions of obedience
to back it up), by itself is destitute of power (inoperative, dead)."*
James 2:17 (AMP)

There are people today who wear the title of "Christian" but don't live a life representative of Christ. Our pursuit of God is rock solid proof that we are truly Christ's disciples. Jesus told us that we are to judge ourselves according to the fruit we produce. We are to believe what we do, not what we say. The same is true with others. We can't allow ourselves to believe the best of someone when facts prove otherwise.

Jesus even warned others of the Pharisees. As Israelites, the Pharisees avoided all contact with the heathen as much as possible, even shunning the non-Pharisee as well, thinking him as unclean before God. Holding such harmful, legalistic attitudes, why didn't Jesus just believe the best about these men? You must understand, Jesus had to protect others from being falsely led away, and therefore had to tell the truth. Jesus also understands that we always succumb to the level of pursuit of God as those with whom we associate. James tells us, "Faith without works is dead." **God did not call us to judge another person's destiny; we must simply examine their actions according to the Word of God.** All of us must ask ourselves two vital questions:

- *Am I guilty of being a Christian?*
- *Is there enough evidence to convict me?*

Our actions must make that clear; what we do is the proof that God did a new work in our lives. As we live for Him, confident assurance continues to rise within us. Let us prove today that we are a part of Heaven's family.

DAILY CONFESSION
*Father, I thank You that I am saved, born again, and destined for Heaven.
I believe in my heart and confess with my mouth Your Lordship over my life.
I walk by the Spirit and not by the flesh.*

YOU CAN NEVER KNOW WHAT GOD DESIRES UNTIL
YOU FIRST FULFILL WHAT HE REQUIRES

"If you keep My commandments, you will abide in My love, just as I have kept
My Father's commandments and abide in His love."
John 15:10 (NKJV)

Noiseless as the center of a dark cave, she crept softly downstairs, a sole nightlight illuminating the hallway. The microwave clock read: 3:36, a flare of excitement blasted her heart, although her eyes could barely focus. He had summoned her once again—a rendezvous in the middle of the night, an uninterrupted appointment in which His heart would be revealed.

There is a protocol when it comes to knowing what God desires, and as we continue on this journey through life, **we must move beyond the place of contentment with what God merely requires, and move to the place of seeking what He truly yearns for and desires.**

God does not reveal His deepest desires to everyone. He does not share the desires of His heart until we do what He requires — the things He instructs in His Word. Psalm 25:14 tells us, "Friendship with the Lord is reserved for those who fear Him. With them He shares the secrets of His covenant." Let us not overlook that word "secrets." That word gives a picture of two people sitting together in close deliberation in an intense, intimate setting. Within this setting, God establishes His covenant with those who fear Him.

If we truly want to know our assignment from God, we must choose to do the written will He set before us. God labeled David, "A man after My own heart," not because God favored him, but because David lived a life of obedience to His Word. As we obey, we qualify to know the desires of God's heart.

DAILY CONFESSION
Father, I thank You that I keep Your commandments
and abide in Your love. I fear You, and You share
the intimate secrets of Your covenant with me.

PAIN AND STRUGGLE
LINE THE PATHWAY TO SUCCESS

"And not only that, but we also glory in tribulations,
knowing that tribulation produces perseverance; and perseverance, character;
and character, hope. Now hope does not disappoint…"
Romans 5:3-5 (NKJV)

I noticed that those who understand success and have achieved success view failure differently from those who don't succeed. The way we interpret failure determines how far we go with the hope of becoming all God desires for us to become.

Bricks of disappointment pave the road of progress. The greatest writers, most successful athletes, and most talented inventors convey their stories of how temporary setbacks played a crucial part in their success. Failure is never final, but quitting is! Those who endure the pain that comes with failing ultimately succeed in any endeavor.

Success does not mean avoiding making mistakes; it simply means the ability to press on when failure comes knocking on the door. The only people who avoid failure completely are those who never leave their home and try. Also remember that:

- *We must not fear the pain of failure.*
- *We must face it courageously as David did,*
  and use it as a means to accomplish our destiny.
- *We must have the right attitude, so that failure*
  is neither fatal nor final.

In Proverbs 24:16 the Bible tells us, "Though a righteous man fall seven times, he rises up again." We must rise up also if we desire to experience true and lasting success in our lives.

DAILY CONFESSION
Father, I thank You that I count it all joy when I fall into various trials
knowing that the testing of my faith produces patience, character, and hope,
and that hope will not disappoint me.

A HEART FILLED WITH INTEGRITY
WELCOMES THE EXAMINATION OF SCRUTINY

"Test all things; hold fast what is good."
1 Thessalonians 5:21 (NKJV)

⋏

"Keep the door SHUT!" Whatever was going on inside that apartment surely couldn't have been good. Crashes and bangs at all hours of the night, then loud music blaring, and piercing screams, then more bangs; the couple who lived inside kept to themselves, never making friends or even greeting any of the neighbors. But it really wasn't all that odd because everyone knew they had something to hide.

Men and women of integrity, however, have nothing to hide. They are willing to open themselves to personal examination. **Trust is the foundation of all leadership, and integrity is the foundation of trust.** Those around us and above us have a right to examine our lives. Why is that? Trust can then be built, and our influence increases.

In order for my relationships to trust me, I must continually walk a life of integrity. Since 1975 I have walked that path and have seen their trust grow stronger. **Although integrity creates a trust within those who follow your example, it also keeps you from ever walking in the wrong direction.**

Embrace examination as much as Jesus did! Personal examination causes us to measure our progress and it brings to light areas we need to confront and correct. As we grow in character, we influence a greater number of people, and our stock grows in the eyes of those above us.

Let us never forget that integrity is proven by the willingness to be examined.

DAILY CONFESSION
*Father, I thank You that I am willing to open myself
to personal examination. I test all things. I examine myself
and I hold fast to what is good.*

NEVER CRITICIZE SECRETLY
WHAT GOD IS EXALTING PUBLICLY

"Don't speak evil against each other, my dear brothers and sisters.
If you criticize each other and condemn each other, then you are criticizing
and condemning God's law. But you are not a judge who can decide whether
the law is right or wrong. Your job is to obey it."
James 4:11 (NLT)

✦

"And he calls himself a minister of the Gospel—with a family like that?" The moment his son was arrested was the exact moment criticism began—from the media, family members, and even the church. Have you realized yet that a critical spirit attempts to infiltrate the body of Christ? Well, I am certain of this: **Criticism keeps many people from receiving the promises of God. God simply does not permit us to speak against one another!** Speaking against your brother in Christ condemns God's law and brings us under judgment.

In Proverbs 18:2, Solomon tells us, "A fool has no delight in understanding, but in expressing his own heart." The apostle Paul exhorts us to, "Let no unwholesome word proceed out of your mouth, but what is good for the necessary edification that it may impart grace to the hearers."

Are we guilty? Many of us are. We must, however, be willing to change what we say and put a bit in our mouths in order to see God's hand rest upon our lives. We no longer can allow ourselves to believe that Heaven gives us the freedom to be critical and air our own opinions. This critical spirit separates the body of Christ. God abhors this because it brings discord among the brethren, according to Proverbs 6:19. No Godly fruit is ever produced from a critical heart. May the words we speak build up others and impart grace to the hearer.

DAILY CONFESSION
Father, I thank You that my job is to obey the law, and I do so
without criticizing or condemning. I let no unwholesome word proceed
from my mouth, but I only speak that which is edifying to the hearer.

THE SEEDS OF MEDITATION
PRODUCE THE HARVEST OF GOOD SUCCESS

"This Book of the Law shall not depart from your mouth, but you shall meditate in it day and night, that you may observe to do according to all that is written in it. For then you will make your way prosperous, and then you will have good success."
Joshua 1:8 (NKJV)

The vivid picture that we perceive in our mind's eye is clearly articulated in our daily lives, and this is evident in all areas of life. God desires that we prosper in every facet of our lives, not just our finances. Although the rich man may see himself wealthy, his marriage may be deteriorating. And the poor man sees himself lacking money, but his marriage may be doing well. However, neither man lives in God's perfect will.

God wants us to be blessed and prosperous in every endeavor and area of our lives. Why is that? We cannot accurately and confidently fulfill God's purpose without His prosperity. Through meditation, we begin to create the picture of who God says we are. This picture soon expresses itself into the man or woman God called us to become. **The moment the picture gets painted onto the canvas of our mind, our actions are internally guided.**

But we cannot rise above our inner self-portrait.

- *Our thoughts determine our actions.*
- *Our actions determine our character.*
- *Our character determines our destination.*

We must choose what we are going to meditate on because that choice holds within it the power to determine the outcome of our lives.

DAILY CONFESSION
Father, I thank You that I meditate on Your Word day and night in order to create the picture that governs my life in the direction of Your will.

PATIENCE IS THE INSTRUCTOR THAT MONITORS THE CLASSROOM OF ADVERSITY

"My brethren, count it all joy when you fall into various trials, knowing that the testing of your faith produces patience. But let patience have its perfect work, that you may be perfect and complete, lacking nothing."
James 1:2–4 (NKJV)

Whether awaiting the results of a recent medical test, anticipating closure on a new house, or believing for the deliverance and salvation of a family member, our faith has no hope of enduring without the instructor called patience. Patience is the ability to stay consistent upon God's Word during any contrary circumstances you may face.

It seems, however, that the promises of God never seem to manifest as quickly as we would desire. Therefore, we must continually rest in the fact that God knows what He is doing…His timing is always perfect.

Patience is the very thing that proves our trust to God, even during the times of overwhelming odds and extraordinary situations. We must lay hold to the promises of God and hold fast to our confession of faith, for He who promised is faithful. Never allow Satan to discourage you. Stand your ground and don't move! Your promise is on the way.

We must understand that our attitude towards the storms of life determines whether we succumb to the adverse pressures that it presents or triumphantly overcome them.

DAILY CONFESSION
Father, I thank You that when trials come my way, I count them all joy knowing that You have Your hand upon my life. Patience has its perfect work with me, that I may become complete, lacking nothing, for You are faithful.

THE INVESTMENT OF YOUR TIME
DECLARES THE LIFE YOU WILL ENJOY

"Make the very most of the time because the days are evil."
Ephesians 5:16 (AMP)

⚜

"Where did the time go?" Glancing at the kitchen clock, after making breakfast, showering, and tidying up the house, she couldn't believe it, but it was almost noon! Suddenly she remembered—the morning news program had a fashion show, and then her sister called about the family birthday party on Saturday. Before anyone realized it...

If we desire to improve any area of our life, we must be willing to consciously choose how and where we spend our time. Time is the essence that makes up our life. Ultimately, it is who we are and what we do. Think of time as a form of currency or exchange. Spending one's time unwisely surely brings unprofitable results. **One cannot change his or her life while neglecting to make a decision to think like God.**

As we make a committed decision to meditate upon God's Word and do what is written, we possess an inner knowing that our life is in line with His will. And when our time is invested wisely, we reap an abundant and beneficial harvest.

DAILY CONFESSION
Father, I thank You that I choose to spend my time wisely; no longer do I allow life to choose for me. No longer do I waste my time, but I continually use my time to produce the life You desire for me.

THE EXCELLENT REFUSE TO FEAR MEDIOCRITY; THEIR DESIRE IS TO DESTROY IT

"For the thing which I greatly fear comes upon me,
and that of which I am afraid befalls me."
Job 3:25 (AMP)

✦

Jesus' thoughts were constantly upon the people—what they were thinking, how they interpreted His teachings, how much faith was in their hearts, having compassion over them as mere flesh. Even so, it was necessary for Jesus to move precisely in the direction of His most dominant thought—that of bringing salvation to the world.

We always move in the direction of our most dominant thought. If those thoughts are fear driven, then that is what we experience. But if those thoughts are driven by the Word of God, we experience the fulfilled promises of God. We must build up a great resistance toward mediocre living.

The reason many resist growth is because they fear change. Satan attempts to sow fear into every aspect of our lives, but God's love casts out all fear. Embrace the fact that He loves you so much that He walks with you step by step until you see the changes in your life that you so deeply desire.

God called all of us to the pursuit of excellence; that seed already dwells within us. It would do well for us to commit to pursue it every day of our lives. When we do, we soon see change that lasts a lifetime.

DAILY CONFESSION
Father, I thank You for allowing me access to Your thoughts.
I refuse to allow myself to live in mediocrity any longer. I choose to exchange
my thoughts for Your thoughts. I desire transformation.

EXCELLENCE SHRINKS BACK FROM THOSE WHO CLOSE THEIR EYES TO EVEN THE SMALLEST OF DETAILS

"For truly I tell you, until the sky and earth pass away and perish, not one smallest letter nor one little hook will pass from the law until all things are accomplished."
Matthew 5:18 (AMP)

⚓

"Sweetheart, what are you doing with those scissors; you're not starting one of those big craft projects of yours again, are you?" Giving her husband a cheery glance, "No craft projects today, it's your shirt that I'm concerned about." Peering down towards his stomach, "What's wrong with my shirt?" Snipping the thread that had been hanging there through several washings, "That string needed to be cut for days; I can't believe you didn't see it." Shrugging his shoulders...I guess some things are just more important than others.

Detailed living is very important. So what does it mean to be a detailed individual? **To be detail orientated is to be one who sees what others do not; it is the one who is concerned about quality and not just finishing.** How do we become a detailed individual?

- *We become a detailed person through the power of choice.*

- *We must decide to be detailed.*

- *We must pay very close attention to the small things, because details pass by those who are unwilling to notice them.*

When you hear an instruction, follow it through precisely as it was communicated. As we place an importance on the seemingly non-important issues of life, we are prepared for the big things when they come our way.

YOU CAN SEARCH THE WORLD OVER
AND STILL DISCOVER THAT THERE IS NO SUBSTITUTE
FOR THE PRESENCE OF GOD

"Dwell in me and I will dwell in you. Just as no branch can bear fruit of itself without abiding in the vine, neither can you bear fruit unless you abide in me."
John 15:4 (AMP)

✦

Everything that was ever created has an intended environment. The environment for fish is water; the stars are to be held by the Heavens; the environment for seed is the soil; the Promised Land was prepared for the Hebrews; God's Word is to find its home in the heart of the believer. If it is true that everything has an intended environment in which it produces life, then what about you and me? Does man have an intended environment?

Remember:

- *Mankind is a spirit.*
- *He has a soul.*
- *He lives in a body.*

God is a Spirit. A believer thrives in the presence of God. In God's presence, life is produced in the heart of those who believe Him. Outside of His presence, spiritual death is imminent. As a fish cannot survive outside of water, neither can a believer survive outside of the presence of God.

Pursue His presence through prayer, reading the Word, and confession of His precious promises. Maintain His presence through obedience to what is written.

DAILY CONFESSION
Father, I thank You that as I dwell in You, You dwell in me. I understand that I cannot bear any fruit without a continual abiding in Your presence, therefore, I choose to make spending time with You a priority. I seek You and Your presence first because I love to spend time with You.

PROMOTION BELONGS TO THE BOSS'S PET — ASK ANY MEDIOCRE EMPLOYEE

"Do you see a man who excels in his work?
He will stand before kings; he will not stand before unknown men."
Proverbs 22:29 (NKJV)

As Jesus instructed His disciples to preach to the people of Israel, He realized that many would not listen to the disciples' words—they would, conversely, persecute, harass, and hate the very ones who brought the truth of God's Kingdom. Deceived by the enemy, Jesus reminded the disciples to simply "shake off the dust" from those cities that would not receive them. Yet, those cities did not realize that their chance for promotion exited along with the disciples.

If we hear the principles of the Word, but do not apply them to our daily life, we deceive ourselves. **We may dream of being promoted, in either our career or spiritual life, but we never see any type of promotion arrive until we apply God's principles to our life.** We must go from conversation to demonstration in every aspect of our living.

We must understand that **promotion is a reward, not a right.** God guarantees promotion to the person who is willing to apply the principles they learn from His Word. God's principles, when put into effect, work for you.

The moment you begin to embrace God's principles is the moment you are on your way to receiving the promotion you rightly deserve.

DAILY CONFESSION
Father, I thank You for the principles You established in Your Word.
I commit to walk in excellence knowing that promotion soon follows.
I do not only hear the Word, but I do it.

ONLY WHEN YOUR CRITICISM BECOMES COMPASSION DOES THE SPIRIT OF GOD BEGIN TO USE YOU TO DELIVER ANOTHER FROM BONDAGE

"When He saw the throngs, He was moved with pity and sympathy for them,
because they were bewildered like sheep without a shepherd."
Matthew 9:36 (AMP)

🔥

Savoring the final notes of the wonderful worship music that the Sunday evening church service usually offered, almost everyone thought the young, attractive children's worker was a superb Christian—always attending services, giving her tithe, serving with the kids, a smile on her face. But then he suddenly sat right smack dab next to her—the weirdest, most detestable teenager in the entire assembly. Laughing at inappropriate times, making strange, disturbing noises, and grinning a grin of what most certainly was of the devil. She couldn't stand that oddball, especially as he perched his feet nearly touching hers. Tapping his fingers on his backpack as the preacher spoke, "STOP IT," she shouted over to him (as if he were some nasty little boy, one without feelings to boot). Hunching down in his seat, did anyone wonder what Jesus thought?

As believers, we can never afford to criticize that which another lacks. **The moment we walk into the arena of criticism is the moment God can no longer use us to help another.** Criticism must become compassion before God uses us to help those in trouble. Love manifests itself persistently in the form of compassion. We are called to love one another.

So let us always remember that the only time we are to ever look down upon another is when we bend over to pick them up.

OBEDIENCE TO THE VOICE OF GOD IS DEPENDENT UPON GOD'S CHARACTER, NOT OUR CIRCUMSTANCES

"God is not a man, that He should tell a lie, neither the son of man,
that He should feel repentance. Has He said and shall He not do it?
Or has He spoken and shall He not make it good?"
Numbers 23:19 (AMP)

✦

"Pray for me, honey, I think this is it." "We thank You, God, through Jesus, that this job belongs to us. Amen." Cradling the phone against his shoulder, her husband nodded, eagerly listening to one of the company's managers. Smiling at his wife, he gently hung up the phone. "So," she anxiously said, holding her breath, "you got the job, didn't you? I know God doesn't lie; He said you were assured to get the job." "Yep," he replied, his face registering joy. "God doesn't lie; I start in two weeks."

We are distinctly called to walk by faith, not by what we mistakenly perceive with our senses. God speaks only truth because it is impossible for Him to lie. His Word is His bond. He doesn't say one thing and then do another. What He said must become the final word even in the midst of very challenging circumstances.

Oftentimes, we declare that God is a liar by our reaction to the circumstances in which we find ourselves. What we see is temporal, but what we don't see (the promises of God's Word) is eternal. Choosing to live by the unseen promises of God guarantees a life that is built on a solid foundation.

DAILY CONFESSION
Father, I thank You that You are not a man that You tell a lie.
I know that if You said it, You will do it.

EXCELLENCE REFUSES TO REMAIN
AT ANY DESTINATION FOR TOO LONG

"I press on toward the goal to win the prize to which
God in Christ Jesus is calling us upward."
Philippians 3:14 (AMP)

⚜

Always on the move, Jesus never stayed anywhere for very long—Judea, Galilee, Samaria, Jerusalem. Always traveling—three days here, two weeks there, a month north, and two months south, He pressed on toward the call that God placed upon His holy life.

In our lives, we must be the same way. **In our own journey of excellence we must continue to press forward without looking back.**

Do you realize that the moment we allow ourselves to be satisfied or get comfortable with our present position in life is the moment we no longer grow? God specifically uses those who desire more and who want to go further in life, and God has more for us than we think. He wants us to experience more of Him and what He has to offer.

I know in my own life there are times when I feel as though I've reached a plateau, but I refuse to stay there. I just keep pressing on like a soldier going into battle. Abundant life belongs to those who refuse to remain at any destination for too long.

Why not ask God to help you continue to press on in life?

DAILY CONFESSION
Father, I thank You that I press on toward the goal to win
the supreme and heavenly prize to which You call me upward.

Worship Begins The Moment You Place Your Life Upon The Altar Named Sacrifice

*"And so, dear brothers and sisters, I plead with you to give your bodies to God.
Let them be a living and holy sacrifice—the kind He will accept. When
you think of what He has done for you, is this too much to ask?"*
Romans 12:1 (NLT)

✦

Feeling His body shudder with agonizing pain, crucifixion was the Master's holy sacrifice. Jesus gives us a prime example of what it truly means to worship God—laying down His life in order to please His Father. Remember:

- *We owe God our lives.*
- *We owe love to man.*
- *We owe obedience to authority.*
- *We owe worship to God.*

God delights in the praises of His children, and if we refuse to worship the Lord, we rob Him of what is His due.

It is not enough that we obey God; it is not enough that we thank God. The apostle Paul pleads with us to give our bodies, our lives, everything to God, for this is our reasonable worship. All of us must ask ourselves: Have I begun to worship God? We can never say we worship our Father until we first lay our lives upon the altar of sacrifice. God asks all of us today, "Will you lay down your life and worship Me?" Is this too much to ask? Certainly it is not!

Daily Confession
*Father, I willingly lay down my life
as a living and holy sacrifice which is pleasing to You
for this is my reasonable worship.*

INDIGNATION IS THE VERY THING THAT WILL KEEP YOU FROM RECEIVING FROM THE MAN OF GOD WHO HAS BEEN SENT INTO YOUR LIFE TO DELIVER YOU

"But when the chief priests and scribes saw the wonderful things
that He did, and the children crying out in the temple and saying,
'Hosanna to the Son of David!' they were indignant."
Matthew 21:15 (NASB)

Resentment of those who are called to help you blockades the anointing on their life from setting you free.

Watching with suspicious eyes, whispering with accusing tongues, and listening with pious ears, the Pharisees were never able to experience the freeing power of Jesus because of their indignation. Their acrid resentment kept them from a relationship with God. Remember these four vital points:

- *Your resentment to the men and women*
  above you causes a separation from God.

- *You respect God through a man.*

- *Never attempt to resent a man of God,*
  but continue to respect God.

- *If you resent the man of God, you resent God.*

DAILY CONFESSION
Father, I thank You that I have respect for all people,
especially for those You call to help me.

YOU CAN NEVER TRANSCEND THE STANDARDS
SET BY YOUR CLOSEST ASSOCIATIONS

*"Blessed is the man who walks and lives not in the counsel of the ungodly nor stands
in the path where sinners walk, nor sits down where the disrespectful gather."*
Psalm 1:1 (AMP)

⸎

You become like those with whom you choose to associate. The
moment the pursuit of Heaven becomes the primary relationship you
desire, you begin to move up higher in life. Those who do not choose
to pursue the things of God with the same fervor as you soon no
longer walk with you.

Please remember, however, that you must always relate to God's
Word first and then to people, not vice versa. This is the critical mistake of even the most sincere believers.

We must always prize principle above relationship. Consequently,
when one chooses the same principles as you, they truly walk with you.

The disciples walked with Jesus because they followed His principles,
having disassociated with those who did not pursue God. So we also
must not allow ourselves to believe that we can supercede those with
whom we choose to associate.

We are only as strong as the weakest link.

DAILY CONFESSION
*Father, I thank You that I no longer walk and live in the counsel of the
ungodly, nor stand in the path where sinners walk, nor sit down where
the disrespectful gather. I choose to prize principle above relationship.*

SELF-DISCIPLINE IS A KEY INGREDIENT IN CREATING HABITS NEEDED FOR SUCCESS

"But (like a boxer) I buffet my body (handle it roughly, discipline it by hardships) and subdue it, for fear that after proclaiming to others the Gospel and things pertaining to it, I myself should become unfit."
1 Corinthians 9:27 (AMP)

✠

- *Discipline simply means to train or drill by instruction.*
- *Self-discipline is the bridge between your desires and their fulfillment.*
- *Self-discipline only has one purpose, and that is to form positive habits in our life.*

Withdrawing from the crowds at the right time was essential for Jesus—for His spiritual as well as physical well-being. Withdrawing from others is essential for every believer, but we must create it as a habit. We are not creatures of discipline but rather, creatures of habit. **Through resolute discipline, however, we can create the habits that we need in order to accomplish God's will for our lives.**

One of the reasons we may have difficulty creating the right habits is because we attempt to change too many areas of our life at one time. We must be patient with ourselves. I encourage you to take the time to focus on one area of your life that you would like to change, and then begin to apply the necessary discipline to that area. Forming positive habits requires time and diligence.

If we refuse to quit, we see positive habits formed in our lives—habits that bring success.

DAILY CONFESSION
Father, I thank You that I buffet my body. I handle it roughly and discipline it by instruction and training. I subdue it and make my body my slave. I am a soldier of Christ Jesus, and I refuse to entangle myself in any affair that causes my focus to be broken.

GOD REQUIRES OF US TO STRETCH OUR WITHERED HAND BEFORE HE WILL STRETCH HIS MIGHTY HAND

"Then He said to the man, reach out your hand.
And the man reached it out and it was restored, as sound as the other one."
Matthew 12:13 (AMP)

Never expect God to give what is in His hand before you give what is in yours. Therein lies the principle of faith. You reach first on the basis of the character of the One to whom you are reaching. **You must reach out to God first, and then He responds.**

As Jesus performed miracle after miracle, He demonstrated the power of God, but He also taught the Israelites faith. Faith that says: Nothing is impossible with God; God can do all things; I believe, although I have yet to see. And as the crowds observed and were astonished, people began to stretch out their hands toward Him in faith, and He responded to their trust.

Never allow yourself to believe you can't reach. Refuse to tell God what you believe you cannot do, but focus on what the Lord is going to do.

DAILY CONFESSION
Father, I thank You that You are willing to stretch Your hand toward my life.
I commit and choose to give You what is in my withered hand in expectation
to receive what is in Your mighty hand. I am full of faith.
Be it done unto me according to my faith.

CHANGE IS THE RESULT OF CHOICES
NOT CHANCES

"Dear brothers and sisters, I close my letter with these last words: Rejoice.
Change your ways. Encourage each other. Live in harmony and peace.
Then the God of love and peace will be with you."
2 Corinthians 13:11 (NLT)

Everything revolutionized when the Master approached. The blind grew hopeful, the sick grew optimistic, and the lame saw buoyancy where beforehand, only wretched dismay threaded their unusable limbs. There was a great desire for change, and as that exhilaration of change was in the offing, it was all due to the Master, the Teacher who created positive situations out of lifetimes of negativity.

Change—true, positive change is always a result of personal choice. We must choose to change, but before we can do that, we need to know what we want to change. For instance,

- *How do you go about making positive changes for your future?*
- *How do you know exactly what needs to change?*

Each of us has a certain degree of insight into our own flaws and shortcomings; those we can, and must, change by ourselves. But each of us also has blind spots that are detrimental to our future success if we don't eventually address them. For these, we need the help of those closest to us.

I encourage you to make a practice of asking your closest friends and family members what they would change about you. You may be surprised, or even upset by their answers, but therein rests the key to success. Change. As you open yourself to the suggestions of these individuals who love you, you start taking steps closer to becoming the person you must become.

DAILY CONFESSION
Father, I thank You that I have the power to change.
Create inside of me all that is pleasing to You!

CHARACTER IS REFINED
BY LEARNING HOW TO USE PRINCIPLE
WHILE REFUSING TO USE PEOPLE

"…just as the Son of Man did not come to be served, but to serve,
and to give His life a ransom for many."
Matthew 20:28 (NKJV)

⁂

Whether explaining salvation to Nicodemus, feeding a multitude with five loaves and a few fish, or declaring, "The truth shall make you free," Jesus was known for His art of serving, not serving "artfully" by stepping on others in order to get ahead.

Over the years, I have seen far too many people use other people in the name of God. We must never use other people for our own benefit. When two individuals enter a relationship with only the thought of giving, they both end up as receivers.

What I personally plan to bring to any relationship is give/give, not give/take. When the other person enters the relationship feeling the same duty and responsibility to give/give, the benefits for both of us are abundant!

This reciprocity, this interdependence and complementary exchange, becomes impossible if you enter relationship with someone who uses others. Regretfully, our society is filled with depraved individuals who make it their sole aim to merely use their relationships to feed their own greed and perverted lusts.

Your character is refined when you learn to use principle, not people.

DAILY CONFESSION
Father, I thank You that as the Son of Man came to serve,
I posture as a servant in all my relationships.

EVERYTHING IN LIFE WILL REMAIN A SEED
UNTIL YOU CHOOSE TO SOW IT

"I tell you the truth, unless a kernel of wheat falls to the ground and dies,
it remains only a single seed. But if it dies, it produces many seeds."
John 12:24 (NIV)

⚜

Evening gowns, spring dresses, designer jackets, cashmere sweaters;
they were stored idly on the shelves of her closet, useless since she lost
twenty-nine unsightly pounds. Tugging the boxes down the hall stair-
case, the surest way to a new wardrobe was giving the old one away to
those who truly needed it. She handed the last of the huge cartons to
the driver for the women's shelter. Now that the seed was planted,
whatever time it took for the harvest was just fine with her.

We can see that our seed is entirely dormant until we place it in the
proper soil. While seeds are in storage, like the clothes stored in the
woman's closet, they are only seeds. But once they are planted, the
seeds "die," and new plants grow in their place. Jesus told us that this
would happen. The seeds of our lives remain just that until we strategically plant them in fertile soil. What seeds do you hold in your hand?
What have you been unwilling to let go?

Take a good look around your life. Everything you have is a potential
seed, but the only way to receive a harvest is to sow. Be aware, though,
that the Scriptures speak of seed, time, and harvest. Your harvest will
take time, and you have to be prepared to wait. Rest assured that just as
crops spring up without the farmer's knowledge or assistance, your seed
also grows up and brings you a harvest at the appointed time.

DAILY CONFESSION
Father, I thank You that You give seed to the sower
and that You cause my harvest to come so I can sow again.

YOUR LIFE CANNOT BE ALTERED
UNTIL YOUR THOUGHTS HAVE BEEN FILTERED

*"Casting down arguments and every high thing that exalts itself against the
knowledge of God, bringing every thought into captivity to the obedience of Christ."*
2 Corinthians 10:5 (NKJV)

⚓

"Middle-East Crisis Worsens!" "24-hour Gambling Boat—Next Exit" "Don't Be Left Out—Attend Downtown's Biggest Sale Of The Year!" "Enjoy Hollywood's Newest Blockbuster Film—'The Bloodiest Murder Of The Century'"

We live in a day and age where we are constantly bombarded with negative thoughts coming at us from every direction. Whether it is the news programs of television, the seduction of expressway billboards, the luring advertisements of radio, the violence of movies, or the explicit lyrics of pop music, Satan attempts to infiltrate our minds. The apostle Paul tells us about a war between the spirit and the flesh that takes place in the battlefield of our minds. Satan understands if he can control our thoughts, he ultimately controls our lives. That is why it is imperative that God's Word be the avenue through which we filter our thoughts.

We are to bring our thoughts into subjection to the Word of God. Thoughts that are contrary to the Word of God come our way. We must, however, filter those thoughts through the knowledge of what God writes to us, about us, and for us. Only then do we see transformation in our lives.

Remember, transformation begins in the mind. When we filter our thoughts, we alter our lives. That is why God tells us to not be conformed to this world but be transformed by changing the way that we think.

DAILY CONFESSION
Father, I thank You that I have the mind of Christ
and I am changed into Your likeness. I embrace Your thoughts
as my own and I choose to filter every thought through Your Word.

GENUINE OBEDIENCE BEGINS IN YOUR HEART BEFORE IT EVER FINDS ITS WAY INTO YOUR ACTIONS

"And I will give you a new heart with new and right desires,
and I will put a new spirit in you. I will take out your stony
heart of sin and give you a new, obedient heart."
Ezekiel 36:26 (NLT)

Jesus told the story of two boys who were given an instruction. One said he would do it, and never did. The other say he wouldn't do what he was asked, but shortly afterwards, he felt conviction in his heart and completed the instruction. Even though this boy denied the instruction with his lips, his sense of obedience permeated all the way to his heart. From there, he went to work, and no doubt afterwards, he returned to his father to inform him that he had indeed obeyed.

I believe very strongly in voicing our desire to obey, but I believe even more strongly in putting our obedience into action. If you are a believer, God gave you a new heart that really desires to obey. But sometimes, heartfelt obedience is imprisoned by a trio of fatal enemies:

- *Pride*
- *Bitterness*
- *Offense*

We must, at all costs, go to battle against this trio of pride, bitterness, and offense to rescue the obedient heart God gave us. Then, we can get to work with our instructions, both from men and from Heaven. And last, we can say, "I obeyed."

DAILY CONFESSION
Father, I thank You that You take out my old, stony heart of sin
and give me a new, obedient heart in its place. Help me to follow through
with every instruction I'm given, both from You and from men.

IT IS A LONELY JOURNEY ACROSS
THE NARROW BRIDGE OF TRUTH

"Enter by the narrow gate; for wide is the gate and broad is the way that leads to destruction, and there are many who go in by it. Because narrow is the gate and difficult is the way which leads to life, and there are few who find it."
Matthew 7:13–14 (NKJV)

"From that time many of His disciples went back and walked with Him no more. Then Jesus said to the twelve, 'Do you also want to go away?' But Simon Peter answered Him, 'Lord, to whom shall we go? You have the words of eternal life.'"
John 6:66–68 (NKJV)

Truth is one thing everyone needs, but few are willing to embrace it. The master of all teachers, the Most High God in human flesh, was not even able to convince men of the truth. Jesus told us, "…narrow is the gate and difficult is the way which leads to life…" Truth is not always the easy route because truth rightly exposes people, and then righteously sets people free.

We must embrace the truth of God's Word concerning all areas of our lives if we ever desire to enjoy the rewards that come as a result of eternal life. We must not be of those who turned their backs on the truth that Jesus spoke. As Jesus said to the disciples, so He says to us, "Do you also want to go away?"

I am confident we will all reply as Peter did, "Lord, to whom shall we go? You have the words of eternal life." Crossing the narrow bridge of truth determines how much freedom you will one day come to enjoy.

DAILY CONFESSION
Father, I thank You that You have the words of eternal life and I enter by the narrow gate to find life. I embrace truth though it may not be the easy route, for I desire the reward of eternal life. My heart retains Your Word.

ALL FAILURE IS UNDENIABLY LINKED
TO A DISREGARDED INSTRUCTION

"My child, listen to me and do as I say, and you will have a long, good life.
I will teach you wisdom's ways and lead you in straight paths. If you live a life guided
by wisdom, you won't limp or stumble as you run. Carry out my instructions;
don't forsake them. Guard them, for they will lead you to a fulfilled life."
Proverbs 4:10–13 (NLT)

Cicero, Illinois – (c. 1925) While mercilessly teased at the electric plant where she worked, the immigrant teenager did not relent; she read her Bible at lunch, no matter what. It didn't matter that they dubbed her, "Holy Helen;" "Here comes Holy Helen," they taunted. "She's reading her Bible all the day long." But beginning in her teenage years, all the way until her death in 1980, Helen's life was successful—spiritually, emotionally, socially, and personally.

The Word of God constantly points us in the direction of success in all areas of life. We have the blueprint of success achieved by the men and women of God who, like Helen, faithfully ran this race before us. This blueprint shows us the reward of a life filled with wisdom.

The only time we have breakdowns in our lives is simply because we miss, disobey, or disregard an instruction. We basically miss an ingredient in the recipe of life and our cookies burn. However, when we follow the instructions of the Master and do what He says, we can only expect a life of fulfillment and peace with others.

Remember, failure comes only to those who choose the narrow pathway that leads to success. Today, let us strive for the application of the wisdom of God and watch how our lives are transformed and blessed.

DAILY CONFESSION
Father, I listen to Your Word and I do what You say. I live a life guided
by wisdom; I won't limp or stumble as I run. I carry out my instructions
and guard them for they lead me to a fulfilled life.

THE PLANNING OF TODAY DETERMINES YOUR PERFORMANCE OF TOMORROW

"Good planning and hard work lead to prosperity,
but hasty shortcuts lead to poverty."
Proverbs 21:5 (NLT)

⚜

The college student began thinking about his thesis that morning, though its due date was six months away. A twenty-five-year-old teacher surveyed his retirement possibilities, carefully noting the options. Scampering around the yard as if being hunted, the russet-tailed squirrel buried black walnuts deep into the ground, even though winter was several weeks in the making.

Good planning and our futures—understanding this principle is vital to the imminent progress of our lives. There are many, however, who are unhappy in life because they're not where they would like to be. There are others who experience great joy because they reap the rewards of the life they planned. And there are far too many believers who reject the interval of time when God attempts to lay the groundwork and develop their character. **This season of planning is necessary to qualify them for what God desires for them to accomplish.**

We cannot afford to neglect to plan for our future. What type of builder would attempt to build a skyscraper without first consulting a blueprint? Why is it any different when building a life? God wants to bring all of us a great future, but only those who specifically plan ever experience it. Although opportunity comes to all, only those who ready themselves recognize the opportunity when it comes.

Develop a plan to attain the future you desire. It is time to get ready for the future for which you planned.

DAILY CONFESSION
I am patient in my season of preparation and I look forward to the future God desires for me. I do not grow weary in well doing, for in due time, I reap the harvest of a better tomorrow.

THE PRIZE OF CHARACTER IS ALWAYS GREATER
THAN THE PRICE OF ADVERSITY

*"These trials are only to test your faith, to show that it is
strong and pure. It is being tested as fire tests and purifies gold—and
your faith is far more precious to God than mere gold. So if your faith remains
strong after being tried by fiery trials, it will bring you much praise and glory
and honor on the day when Jesus Christ is revealed to the whole world."*
1 Peter 1:7 (NLT)

"Why do they hate me so much? I've never done anything to them."
Feeling the silent barbs of her husband's family, even though they
smiled to her face, their snide remarks, subtle stares, and hushed whispers
spoke volumes. "They're just convicted, honey," the husband
tried to reassure his tearful wife. "Every time we come around they see
Jesus, and they also see their sin. Things probably won't change until
they change and follow God."

I admit, in this world you could suffer for choosing Godly character.
The Scriptures warn us that this could happen as we follow Christ.
One thing is for sure, though, when this life is over and we step into
eternity, there will no longer be any injustice. Whatever price you
have to pay for Godly character pales in comparison to the rewards
that await you. You will have difficulty here on earth, but if you
choose God's righteousness, you never regret the adversity it may
include.

God is very interested in rewarding you. He is gracious and loving
beyond comprehension, but we must step up to the plate to receive
what we deserve. God's goodness can only be released by our commitment
to walk in His ways.

The only way we accomplish our task and are rewarded for it is if we
choose the prize of character, despite the price of adversity.

DAILY CONFESSION
*Father, I thank You for Your grace that enables me to represent You.
I choose to do what is just in Your sight.*

FREEDOM IS YOURS THE MOMENT
YOU TRUST HEAVEN'S OPINION

"I will walk in freedom, for I have devoted myself to Your commandments."
Psalm 119:45 (NLT)

⚜

"As the scriptures hath said." It was a customary phrase for Jesus—quoting the scriptures, bringing knowledge and freedom to the children of Israel. So always remember, there is no freedom outside of the Word of God. The Scripture tells us we are all born slaves to sin. Through our acceptance of what Jesus Christ did on the cross, we are set free from the bondage of sin.

Even though we have been set free, we still wonder how to walk in that freedom. It is one thing to be free, but walking in the fullness of that freedom is something completely different. I am convinced that **the most miserable man in the universe is the one who has been set free, yet has no idea how to walk it out.**

God gave us the knowledge we need in order to walk in the fullness of our redemption. We know David discovered it because of the words he penned, "I will walk in freedom, for I have devoted myself to Your Word." So many see that as information they already know, but to David, it was revelation that utterly transformed his life. David's decision to devote himself to the Word of God enabled him to walk in the liberty that was rightfully his…and the same holds true for us. It is of necessity that we commit ourselves to meditate on the Word of God every day.

In whatever area you may struggle, the freedom you desire lies within the pages of God's holy Word.

DAILY CONFESSION
Father, I thank You that my freedom lies within the pages of Your Word.
I embrace what You say and exchange what I think for what You think.
I am free and I reign over the sin that had me bound.

WHILE PEOPLE OF THE WORLD CHOOSE CONFORMATION, THOSE WHO BELIEVE IN GOD CHOOSE TRANSFORMATION

"And do not be conformed to this world,
but be transformed by the renewing of your mind, that you may prove
what is that good and acceptable and perfect will of God."
Romans 12:2 (NKJV)

✦

Your mind can only hold one thought at a time. Therefore, the easiest way to get rid of negative thoughts is to replace them with positive thoughts. The most effective way to do this is with your spoken words. Your mind has to entertain what your mouth says.

The mind is never empty; it is always occupied with a thought. Spoken words override unspoken thoughts. By substituting your thoughts, you can replace troubling thoughts with a God-thought that has the power to transform your life.

You can't be filled with nagging fear, relentless doubt, and abject worry when you constantly meditate upon God's Word.

As long as you don't allow negative thoughts to be planted into your mind, growing like weeds in your flower garden, you discover peace, joy, and happiness. But **the transformation of your life is linked to your commitment to change the way you think.**

DAILY CONFESSION
Father, I thank You that I am not conformed to this world but I am transformed
by the renewing of my mind. My mind is renewed by Your Word.

A MAN WHO IGNORES THE TRUTH
IS ON THE PATHWAY OF DESTRUCTION

"My people are destroyed from lack of knowledge…"
Hosea 4:6 (NIV)

⚹

Jesus proclaimed that His Word is truth and those who know the truth shall be set free. Regardless of what we plainly see, distinctively hear, or clearly perceive with our natural senses, God's Word still holds true. It amazes me that God's people perish from a lack of knowledge because of the simple fact that God gave us His Word so that ignorance would be eradicated in our lives.

The truth of God's Word brings light to any dead and dark situation. As we begin to meditate upon the pages of God's written Word, freedom begins to manifest itself in our lives.

- *His Word brings understanding where there was no understanding.*
- *His Word brings hope where there was no hope.*
- *His Word brings freedom where once there was once only bondage.*

God desires for all of His people to be free and live long, healthy, and abundant lives. But until we embrace the truth of God's Word, it is impossible to walk in the freedom that God provided for us or to become victorious in that truth.

DAILY CONFESSION
Father, I thank You that You gave me Your written Word.
I meditate upon Your Word and apply it to every situation bringing light into all areas of my life. I know the truth of Your Word and the truth makes me free.

WHAT YOU EXPERIENCE TODAY ARE
LITTLE MORE THAN THOUGHTS YESTERDAY

"Keep your heart with all diligence,
for out of it spring the issues of life."
Proverbs 4:23 (NKJV)

The range of voices and the gallery of thoughts that enter your mind are seeds. You have a choice over which seeds get planted, and which get rejected. Your heart becomes the fertile soil where those seeds are planted. When planted, those seeds mature and produce fruit in your life.

There is no way to avoid this process of "heart germination," for the Bible tells us in Proverbs 4:23 that this is how God designed the human heart to function. "Keep [manage, tend, protect, safeguard, watch over, preserve, chaperon, care for, be a good steward over] your heart with all diligence, for out of it spring the issues of life." The only way to assure good outcomes in your life is to plant good seeds in your heart.

When I was going through a difficult time in my life, it was because early in my childhood, bad seeds were planted in my heart, grew up, and produced bad fruit. Destructive thought-seeds take root and begin to grow because you choose to believe them. Erroneously, you begin to believe that what they say is the truth. You begin to believe evil about yourself. **However, it is important to realize that any thought left unchallenged is established as fact.**

Why not deposit an abundant crop of good seeds into your heart today, so that you too create a bountiful future?

DAILY CONFESSION
Father, I thank You that my heart is the soil where
my thoughts become seeds that create my future.

YOUR MIND IS THE CANVAS UPON WHICH THOUGHTS PAINT THE PICTURE OF TOMORROW

"For as he thinks in his heart, so is he."
Proverbs 23:7 (NKJV)

✦

What you think today becomes a reality tomorrow. You must, however, stay long enough under the Word of God for it to transform you in order to create a better tomorrow. Stooping down upon the ground, all eyes were locked on the Teacher. *What's He doing now?* Trembling in fear, the woman who had been caught with another man held her breath—would He condemn her also? But NO! Something was happening; an utter impossibility.

One by one, from the oldest to the youngest, the scribes and the Pharisees slipped away with their countenances covered, all having departed until only Jesus and the woman were alone. As He told the woman to, "Go, and sin no more," Jesus painted a picture of tomorrow for all Israel, brushing strokes of salvation upon the canvas of their minds, potently replacing the negative thoughts of yesterday into their lives.

When you understand the truth behind the origin of negative thoughts, you have the know-how to take control over them. As you take control, you are then able to worship the Lord your God with your entire mind and be free from guilt over wrong and negative thoughts that Satan brings your way.

All of God's power and promises are at our disposal, but only those who pay the price and saturate their mind with the Word of God experience the blessings of God.

DAILY CONFESSION
Father, I thank You that I keep Your Word in my heart and on my mind,
for as I think in my heart, I am.

A MAN'S CHARACTER
IS A PROPHECY OF HIS DESTINY

"He who walks with integrity walks securely,
But he who perverts his ways will become known."
Proverbs 10:9 (NKJV)

If you want to know the outcome of your life, closely examine your character. You cannot separate yourself from your character. Character is who a person is. The good thing is, character can be developed. You are not born a good person; in fact, you are programmed to fail the moment you are born. The Bible says we are all born slaves to sin. But God sent His Son to die and rise again so we can walk as He walked. Jesus' destiny was predicted long ago by His unwillingness to compromise. When tempted in the wilderness, He refused to negotiate His integrity for momentary pleasure. When tempted to forsake suffering and death on the cross, He walked in the veracity of His Father.

Your character is a prophecy of your destiny.

It is up to you. You can, through God's Word, cultivate the character of Christ. Heaven and Hell are destinies of a chosen path. Walk according to God's Word, and Heaven is your final destination. Choose to live according to the desires of your flesh, and Hell awaits you. Today, cross-examine yourself with God's Word. Ask God to help you live like Christ and pay whatever price you must to ensure you never lower your standard of living.

DAILY CONFESSION
Father, I thank You that my character is a prophecy of my destiny,
therefore I choose to live a life of integrity and honesty before You.

AN ABUSED LIFE IS LITTLE MORE
THAN A LIFE WITHOUT PURPOSE

*"Store your treasures in heaven, where they will never become moth-eaten
or rusty and where they will be safe from thieves. Wherever your treasure is,
there your heart and thoughts will also be."*
Matthew 6:20-21 (NLT)

✦

"Do you think anyone can actually use some of this junk?" Sifting
through broken tools, worn filters, flattened tires, and empty cans of
oil, their deceased grandfather's garage was filled to the brim with
stuff. "This is where he spent the majority of his time," one of his
grieving grandsons reminisced. Tossing the debris into a heavy-duty
garbage bag, "It's too bad he didn't start a mentorship program or
something, you know, for guys in trouble. They sure could have prof-
ited from our grandpa's experience, the best auto mechanic this town
has ever seen. Now, I guess it's just too late."

And the person to whom Jesus refers in Matthew 6 is also one who
lives without a purpose. People like these have lives filled with great
temporary things, but they do nothing that brings them an eternal
return. Since everything around us is going to disappear one day, how
foolish it is to live just for the here-and-now. We could call that "life
abuse."

We have a choice to make every morning. Either we use the day to
make something out of the life God so graciously gave us, or we
squander our hours on fleeting pleasures and aimlessness. **God's grace
is available to all who come to Him, unequivocally offering themselves as living sacrifices.** That must be the first step. God has the
final authority in our life, and we should do whatever we must to
make sure our life is used to the fullest, both for our good and for the
good of the people around us. Live your life on purpose!

DAILY CONFESSION
*Father, I thank You for giving me the gift of life. I thank You
for giving me the grace I need to make each day worthwhile and full of purpose.*

THE WORD OF GOD IS THE GREATEST MAP
IN YOUR DAILY JOURNEY OF SUCCESS

*"All Scripture is inspired by God and is useful to teach us what is true and
to make us realize what is wrong in our lives… It is God's way of preparing us
in every way, fully equipped for every good thing God wants us to do."*
2 Timothy 3:16-17 (NLT)

Groping to the window to open the blinds, the young executive glared at the barren tree. *Oh how I despise these cold dark months, trees without leaves, the smell of death everywhere.* On the opposite side of the vastly wide yard, a middle-aged accountant peered at the same tree. He had never noticed it before, but the tree was formulated into the letter "V", two sturdy trunks reaching high into the air. *Ah, yes. "V" is for victory. That's what is coming at me today.* The same tree—but two dramatically disparate attitudes! Each day we wake up and explicitly choose with what kind of attitude we are going to.

We may erroneously think that others have the power to decide our attitude, but when it comes down to it, we make the decision of how we respond. By continually grafting the Word of God into who we are, we see instant results in all areas of life.

We must rely on God's Word to lead the way toward the success we desire. If God's Word does not direct our steps, our destination is not pleasant. I have come across many people who are unhappy with the way life seems to presently be for them. They desire a great future but refuse to follow the guidelines established in God's eternal Word to make it happen.

We must take His Word and lay it down before our lives and live in accordance to the instructions given to us if we ever desire to see great things happen. The Word of God transforms us when we begin to get our daily dosage of God's success plan.

DAILY CONFESSION
*Father, I thank You that Your Word fully equips me
for every good work You have for me to do.*

TIME IS THE TOOL GIVEN TO YOU
BY GOD WITH WHICH HE EXPECTS YOU
TO CHANGE THE WORLD

"So be careful how you live, not as fools but as those who are wise.
Make the most of every opportunity for doing good in these evil days.
Don't act thoughtlessly, but try to understand what the Lord wants you to do."
Ephesians 5:15-17 (NLT)

Twisting the keys into the door, the twenty-eight-year-old banker stuffed them back into his pocket, the tangled keys cushioned by some sort of paper. Oh yeah—that's the tract I was going to give to that new teller with all the problems. I'll have plenty of time to give it to him tomorrow, won't I, Lord?

God gave all of us a commission to reach the ends of the earth with the Gospel of Jesus Christ. This will not only take our resources, but it will also require of us our time. All of us have been given twenty-four hours in a day with which we are to change the world around us. Whether it is in the workplace, social arena, home, or church, we must look at each hour as an opportunity to solve problems and add value to those with whom we associate.

The next time we go to work, we must see those eight hours as a gift from Heaven giving us the ability to influence and impact those for whom we work, and those with whom we live. The day we begin to use our time as a tool to change our world is the day the body of Christ begins to touch the entire world.

DAILY CONFESSION
Father, I thank You for giving to me the gift of time. I choose to use
my time wisely so I can impact my world for You. I refuse to act thoughtlessly,
but I will understand what You want and what I am to do.

GOD'S WORD IS THE PLACE
WHERE FAITH IS PRODUCED

"The thorny ground represents those who hear and accept the good news,
but all too quickly the message is crowded out by the cares of this life
and the lure of wealth, so no crop is produced."
Matthew 13:22 (NLT)

The Bible tells us that worry chokes the Word of God and makes it of no effect. Can you imagine that worry can actually stop the powerful Word of God from working in your life? We must understand, however, that worry is not something to be played with or to be taken lightly. Jesus exhorted us to look at the delicate lilies of the field; exotically beautiful, they grow but never work to adorn themselves. Do they worry? Never; these gorgeous flowers are dressed to the hilt, yet never, ever worry.

Worry is the proof that faith is absent!

You cannot worry and walk in faith simultaneously. The moment faith enters is the moment worry must exit. It is interesting to note that when we worry, we document that we don't believe what God said. Remember, God's greatest pleasure is to be believed and His greatest disappointment is to be doubted. What does our worry say about our faith in God?

Although we may get excited about the principles taught to us on Sunday, it takes refusing worry on Monday to see God's Word manifest in our lives. Never forget, when worry knocks at your door, let the Word of God answer! Worry will flee in terror!

DAILY CONFESSION
Father, I walk by faith and not by sight. I refuse to look at my circumstances
knowing that whatever I focus on multiplies. I stand on Your Word
and refuse to allow worry to enter my home.

WHATEVER CONTROLS YOUR MIND CONTROLS YOUR LIFE

"For as a man thinketh in his heart, so he is…"
Proverbs 23:7a (KJV)

⚶

Whatever controls your mind controls your life. The starting point of the journey to regain control of your mind begins with one basic truth—Nothing, can take the place of your commitment to continually feed on God's Word.

What I share here is not a theoretical understanding of renewing the mind. I have applied these principles in my own life. If they worked for me, they can certainly work for you! God already gave you everything you could ever need to achieve victory in your mind. Yet, here are two crucial questions:

- *How are you going to bring that victory into a real experience?*
- *How do you accomplish mind renovation where and when it really counts?*

This is a subject that is very real to me. I came to Christ in 1975 while being treated in a mental institution. Psychologists told me there was nothing that they could do to help me. They assisted and guided me through the toughest part of what they called a "deep character disorder" and then informed me I would be that way for the rest of my life.

But the power of God's Word delivered me! One hundred percent of the deliverance I enjoy is through the application of the principles outlined in God's Word. And I believe the same can be true for you!

DAILY CONFESSION
Father, I thank You that whatever controls my mind controls my life, therefore, I consistently feed upon Your Word. The consistent intake of Bible doctrine is the most important thing in my life as a believer.

THE PROOF YOU HAVE MASTERED YOUR FLESH
IS IN YOUR ABILITY TO SAY "NO" TO NEGATIVE PASSIONS

"Until the time came to fulfill his word, the Lord tested Joseph's character."
Psalm 105:19 (NLT)

✦

Just two or three presses of the buttons and poof! He could be on the website in no time, and who would ever be the wiser? But the young husband and father of two, through intense prayer and reading of the Bible, consistent help from his church and a local Christian outreach program, had the ability to say "no" because he surrendered to God and mastered his flesh. There is no greater way to prove a man's character than to observe his daily actions. Our actions reveal who we truly are.

As we go through life, we encounter many people who appear to be one way, but when they are alone, they are a completely different person. **We must understand true character is who we are when no one is looking.**

Never forget…God sees all. He sees us when we go home, He sees us when we travel in the car, and He sees us when we are all alone. He looks upon every one of our actions. We cannot fool God! Although our outer, improved character may fool others, God knows the things we hide on the inside. Satan attempts to lure the desires of our flesh and bring them out into the open. He is on a constant pursuit to bait our flesh in the direction of sin.

As we choose to surrender our lives to the Holy Spirit, we are empowered to deny what our flesh demands of us. We then have the ability to live a life that is pleasing to God.

DAILY CONFESSION
Father, I thank You that I refuse to bow my knew to the desires of my flesh.
Instead, I surrender my life to Your Spirit, disciplining my body
and causing it to come into line with Your Word.

THE GREATEST SEED OF MAN
IS THE SEED OF OBEDIENCE TO GOD

"But he who looks carefully into the faultless law,
the [law] of liberty, and is faithful to it and perseveres in looking into it,
being not a heedless listener who forgets but an active doer [who obeys],
he shall be blessed in his doing (his life of obedience)."
James 1:25 (AMP)

Realizing that He was the standard, not only for Israel but for the world, Jesus knew that without daily obedience (even in the little things), there is no life of reward. God searches the earth, looking for someone He can shower His blessings upon. God is a good God and desires to bless His children. We must understand, however, that God does not reward disobedience. We can see throughout all of Scripture how God resists those who choose the route of disobedience and rebellion.

The greatest pleasure Heaven ever receives is to be believed. **There is no greater proof that we believe the Word of God than obedience to it.** If we want to please God and receive the rewards He has for us, we must choose to obey.

The greatest seed one can ever sow is the seed of obedience…it harvests an abundant crop of reward. James exhorts us with these words, "…being not a heedless listener who forgets but an active doer [who obeys], he shall be blessed in his doing (his life of obedience). The life we desire lies within the seed of our obedience.

DAILY CONFESSION
Father, I thank You that I commit to look into the faultless law, the law of liberty, and I am faithful to Your written Word. I am an active doer; I look forward to a life of reward because I am obedient to Your Word.

IT IS A LONELY JOURNEY
ACROSS THE NARROW BRIDGE OF TRUTH

"Enter by the narrow gate; for wide is the gate and broad is the way that leads to destruction, and there are many who go in by it. Because narrow is the gate and difficult is the way which leads to life, and there are few who find it."
Matthew 7:13–14 (NKJV)

"It's just a little lie; no one will ever care!"

But Jesus does care, and truth is one thing everyone needs; but few are willing to embrace it. The Master of all teachers, the Most High God in human flesh, was not even able to convince men of the truth. Jesus told us, "…narrow is the gate and difficult is the way which leads to life…" truth is not always the easy route because truth exposes people and then sets people free. And indeed it had been a lonely journey for Jesus, a lonely trial, a lonely beating, a lonely suffering on those wooden beams. YET—that lonely journey led somewhere, to the narrow bridge of truth, which the world was soon to discover.

We must embrace the truth of God's Word concerning all areas of our lives if we ever desire to enjoy the rewards that come as a result of eternal life. We must not be of those who turned their backs on the truth that Jesus spoke. As Jesus said to the disciples, so He says to us, "Do you also want to go away?"

I am confident we will all reply as Peter did, "Lord, to whom shall we go? You have the words of eternal life." Crossing the narrow bridge of truth determines how much freedom you one day come to enjoy.

THE BIRTH OF YOUR FUTURE IS
SOLELY DEPENDENT UPON THE DEATH OF YOUR PAST

"I have been crucified with Christ; it is no longer I who live,
but Christ lives in me; and the life which I now live in the flesh I live by faith
in the Son of God, who loved me and gave Himself for me."
Galatians 2:20 (NKJV)

The music suddenly sounded detestable; the old friends no longer enjoyable; and the jokes, the addictions, all of it was no longer palatable. She hadn't discovered it until recently, but her old self was gone, vanished like smoke into thin air.

Knowing that your old self no longer exists is the foundational truth that gives you not only the understanding, but also the confidence, that your future is going to be better than your past. **Understanding who you are in Christ is the foundation of your Christian life.** It helps you better identify which thoughts are God's, and which thoughts are not. Understanding and embracing this new identity protects you from past issues that hinder your progress. Your new identification is the master key to your future success.

People constantly say to me, "You know, I read the Bible, I pray, I go to church, and I witness to people about the Lord. So why does it seem like whenever and the pressure is on, I resort to my old ways?"

The answer to that question is simple. You haven't yet come to realize who Jesus made you, and what He did for you through His death, burial, and resurrection. In order to successfully withstand the pressures of this world and renovate your mind according to the new life that is yours in Christ, you must understand righteousness—the ability to live continually in right standing with God.

DAILY CONFESSION
Father, I thank You that I am crucified with Christ.
It is no longer I who live, but Christ lives in me. And now I live
by faith in the Son of God who gave up His life for me.

HUMILITY CONTAINS WITHIN IT THE WILLINGNESS TO ACKNOWLEDGE PAST MISTAKES

"For I recognize my shameful deeds – they haunt me day and night.
Against You, and You alone, have I sinned; I have done what is evil in Your sight."
Psalm 51:3–4 (NLT)

✦

It is impossible to make continual progress in life while holding sin in our hearts. God is not a respecter of persons. What He says…He does! God tells us that any man who chooses to hide sin in his heart soon comes to ruin. He also tells us the man who is humble soon comes to wisdom.

Humility is the access key into the presence of God. God resists the proud. We must continually examine ourselves and ask God if there is pride within our hearts. One of the ways we can continue to walk with a humble heart is to willingly acknowledge our past faults. Pride refuses to reveal itself in the form of repentance. However, we must repent if we ever sincerely desire to experience true progress once again.

DAILY CONFESSION
Father, I thank You that You give me the divine example of a life of humility.
I humble myself under Your mighty hand, and in Your good time, You will honor
me. I give all my worries and cares to You for I know You tenderly care for me.

CHOICES ARE THE ONLY WITNESSES SUMMONED
TO APPEAR IN THE COURTROOM OF CONSEQUENCE

"If you do this, you will live and become a great nation, and the lord your god will bless you and the land you are about to enter and occupy. But if your heart turns away and you refuse to listen, and if you are drawn away to serve and worship other gods, then I warn you now that you will certainly be destroyed. You will not live a long, good life in the land you are crossing the Jordan to occupy."
Deuteronomy 30:15–18 (NLT)

- *Should I go to church tonight in this pouring rain, or just stay home and relax?*

- *Although this book has a lot of curse words, should I read it anyway?*

- *Even though God's Spirit is prompting me to turn off the television, another thirty minutes or so wouldn't hurt, would it?*

One of the greatest gifts anyone could ever receive is the power to choose. God graciously granted us the power of choice. Whether it is prosperous or disastrous, the choice is ours. The apostle Paul encourages us with these words, "For God is working in you, giving you the desire to obey Him and the power to do what pleases Him."

God doesn't just leave us as orphans to fend for ourselves. He knows there is a devil out there whose desire is to lure us into wrong choices. Satan knows that if he can convince us to make just one mistake, it may cause a lifetime of consequences. We can see throughout the scriptures that God did not predestine our choices. He did, however, predestine our consequences. We are to surrender our lives to the Spirit of God and trust in Him to help us make right choices.

The Holy Spirit is our helper. In the above passage God lays it out, "Now listen! Today I am giving you a choice between prosperity and disaster, between life and death…" It is our choice.

DAILY CONFESSION
Father, I thank You that You work in me giving me the desire to obey You and the power to do what pleases You. I choose life and not death.

YOUR FUTURE IS ONLY AS BRIGHT
AS THE PRINCIPLES YOU EMBRACE

*"Now it shall come to pass, if you diligently obey the voice
of the Lord your God, to observe carefully all His commandments
which I command you today, that the Lord your God will set you high
above all nations of the earth. And all these blessings shall come upon you and
overtake you, because you obey the voice of the Lord your God...*
Deuteronomy 28:1-2 (NKJV)

Unwilling to join in the criticism, jokes, and complaints about their bosses during lunch hours and breaks, the newlywed woman stayed to herself, remaining loyal to the company's lawyers inwardly, as well as when she approached them face to face. When it was time for reviews, she consistently received the highest marks, and even when she could no longer work for the firm, citing family duties, the firm's founding father did everything he could to keep the conscientious employee from leaving since whenever she received an instruction, it was instantly carried out.

Christianity today embraces the person of Christ, but woefully neglects His principles. The person of Jesus creates your peace; His principles create your productivity. Both, however, are necessary! People want to prosper, but very few are willing to accurately apply God's principles to their lives. **Our willingness to do what God says is the key to experience what God promises.**

God never promised you something without first giving you an instruction. God rewards obedience. He does not hand out promises and rewards to just anyone. He is selective in whom He blesses. You are the one who determines whether or not God blesses your life.

DAILY CONFESSION
*Father, I thank You that I diligently obey Your Word
and I observe Your commandments. Blessings come upon me
and overtake me because I choose to obey You.*

FUTURE SUCCESS IS UNDENIABLY LINKED TO UNDERSTANDING YOUR NEW IDENTITY IN CHRIST

"I have been crucified with Christ; it is no longer I who live,
but Christ lives in me; and the life which I now live in the flesh I live by faith
in the Son of God, who loved me and gave Himself for me."
Galatians 2:20 (NKJV)

God sees you in Christ— He sees greatness in you. He has a destiny for you. When He looks at you, He sees success and a winner. He sees Jesus, His Son!

You are not destined to lose, because He made you victorious through Christ. Second Corinthians 2:14 says, "Thanks be to God who always leads us into triumph in Christ Jesus."

If God made you a winner, then what are you waiting for? If God already gave you the victory and sees you as a winner, then what keeps you from success? God waits for you to believe it about yourself. Truly, it doesn't even matter what God believes about you; what really matters is what you believe about you. Which are you going to believe, your past or what God says?

Whatever you meditate on and think about soon manifests into action reflecting the thoughts you harbor, good or bad. Your life is an outer image reflecting your inner projection. Every thought God has concerning you is written on the pages of His Word. He tells you who you are, what you have, and all you can do through Jesus Christ. You are born into the family of God through the incorruptible seed of the Word of God.

DAILY CONFESSION
Father, I thank You that I am crucified with Christ.
It is no longer I who live but Christ who lives in me and through me.

SCRIPTURE WAS NOT WRITTEN
TO INCREASE YOUR KNOWLEDGE
BUT TO TRANSFORM YOUR LIFE

"Your Word is a lamp to my feet and a light to my path."
Psalm 119:105 (NKJV)

✦

David said it so perfectly—God's Word is a lamp unto our feet and a light unto our path. Every time we go to the Word of God, we must go with a willingness to surrender to the Word of God. We must look to do whatever we read. When we surrender our lives to the Word of God, heaven is able to guide our footsteps.

Many people see God's Word as a history book or some informational book about God. We cannot degrade the Holy Scriptures by taking it to the same level as just another ordinary book. God's Word is not written to increase our knowledge, but to direct and transform our lives. His Word contains the answer to every problem and question that could ever arise.

As we open our hearts to the Holy Spirit, He begins to teach us the meaning of what we read. We can go to the Word and expect to hear God speak to us. The words on those pages are God's voice to His people. He desires to speak to us and guide us in the path of righteousness. His Word is the lamp we are to shine upon the path we are called to take.

As we continue to use the Word of God as our roadmap for life, we experience true and abundant blessings along the way.

DAILY CONFESSION

Father, I thank You that I use Your Word as a guide for my life.
Your Word is a lamp unto my feet and a light unto my path. I understand
scripture was not written to increase my knowledge, but to direct my life.

SELF-CONTROL BEGINS BY EXPOSING EVERY THOUGHT TO THE LIGHT OF GOD'S WORD

"But if we walk in the light as He is in the light, we have fellowship with one another, and the blood of Jesus Christ His Son cleanses us from all sin."
1 John 1:7 (NKJV)

It was through self-control that Jesus endured death upon a cross, a death which ultimately led to resurrection, manifestation of the light. Self-control begins when we decide to expose our thoughts and feelings to the Word of God before we ever put them in front of others. If we walk in the light as God is in the light, we have fellowship with Him. But that means I must continually expose my thoughts and feelings to the light of the Word of God. Once God's Word reveals the true nature of my thoughts and emotions, I have to decide whether or not I want to unload them on people. It becomes so much easier to exert self-control after spending time in the light.

Therefore,

- *When we are full of the Word, why would we want to put our brothers and sisters in the Lord on red alert just so we can spend a few hours, days, or weeks in the flesh?*

- *Why wouldn't we expose our bad attitudes to the Word of God and let the Word correct them before we ever unload those bad attitudes on other people?*

It is important for us to be changed in God's presence. We must allow God to continually transform us by His Word, each and every day!

DAILY CONFESSION
Father, I walk in the light as You are in the light. I fellowship with You and with those who love You. I am cleansed and washed by the blood of Jesus Christ.

A GREAT FUTURE REQUIRES A DETAILED MAP

"For which of you, intending to build a tower, does not sit down first and count the cost, whether he has enough to finish it — lest, after he has laid the foundation, and is not able to finish, all who see it begin to mock him, saying, 'This man began to build and was not able to finish.' Or what king, going to make war against another king, does not sit down first and consider whether he is able with ten thousand to meet him who comes against him with twenty thousand?"
Luke 14:28-31 (NKJV)

The Father created a meticulous plan for salvation: The miraculous Birth, an outstanding Life, an excruciating Death, and the glorious Resurrection of His Son, Jesus Christ. There is nothing God does without first laying out a detailed plan. Solomon tells us, "A man's heart plans his way, but the Lord directs his steps." God is into details. When we are committed to our dream and express it with a detailed plan of carrying it out, we provide ourselves with a visual reminder of where we are going, and how believe we will arrive there.

The journey of life always starts with a vision, but too many individuals stop right there, parking as if permanently stationed in the lot of a supermarket. They go no further than the vision. **We must understand that every journey has great costs associated with it.** These costs may be in terms of time, energy, finances, choices, sacrifices, and a number of other factors.

We must begin to take the vision we have for our lives and carefully write it out, making it plain before our eyes. As we do, God begins to birth within us a roadmap that will give us the necessary directions to fulfill what He assigned us to do. Without a detailed plan of action, our destinies are never reached; but with it, our lives become a dream come true.

DAILY CONFESSION
Father, I thank You that I have a vision for my life.
I consider the cost and carefully write out a detailed plan of action
to bring it to fulfillment.

GOD CANNOT REWRITE YOUR PAST
SO HE PROVIDED YOU A NEW ONE

"Therefore, if anyone is in Christ, he is a new creation;
old things have passed away; behold, all things have become new."
2 Corinthians 5:17 (NKJV)

An abusive father; an argumentative sibling; bad grades in school; destructive relationships; embarrassing addictions; getting fired from a job—God cannot rewrite our pasts, so He provided us a new one. Friends, it won't do us any good to hold on to the past. I come from a past that is worthy to forget. I could sit here and think, "Boy I sure hope that someday old things pass away. I sure hope that someday all things become new for me. Oh, God, please do something for me. Please free me from my past." But I don't do that; I always find out what the scriptures say.

God said, "If anyone is in Christ…" I know I am in Christ. The scripture above says that if I am a believer, old things have passed away, and if something has passed away, then it is dead. Our pasts are dead. That old sinful creature that dwelled within is dead. Our old lives can only live if we resurrect them from the dead. The devil cannot resurrect the past. He can scream all day long, but that doesn't change the fact that God says our pasts are dead.

When the old self gives us problems, attempting to direct us toward a carnal lifestyle, then that is the time to remind ourselves of what we already know—our old self was crucified with Christ. And if our old self was crucified with Him, then our old self cannot make us do anything! We must decide today that we are going to embrace the new future God provided, and then we will experience the true freedom for which we have been searching.

DAILY CONFESSION
Father, I thank You that I am in Christ. I am a new creation.
Old things have passed away, and everything has become new.

GOD MUST GET FINANCES THROUGH YOU BEFORE HE CAN EVER GET FINANCES TO YOU

*"For God is the one who gives seed to the farmer and then bread to eat.
In the same way, He will give you many opportunities to do good, and
He will produce a great harvest of generosity in you."*
2 Corinthians 9:10 (NLT)

⚜

We must be conduits for God's blessings. Solomon tells us, "…those who withhold what is justly due, come to want." Everyone has within them the desire to hoard, the desire to keep, the desire to save. But God tells us that prosperity belongs to those who freely give. The world undoubtedly understands this more than the body of Christ does.

The principle of giving is taught in self-help seminars all across the nation, yet Christians still hoard. **Sowing is proof that greed has been conquered. The moment we prove to God that we have conquered greed is the moment God begins to release what He intended for us to have.** He is just waiting for those who will allow Him to distribute His finances freely throughout the earth. Will you be that conduit? I believe you will!

DAILY CONFESSION
*Father, I am a giver and not a taker; I give freely, yet I continue to gain.
I choose to be a conduit through which You can distribute
Your blessings to Your people.*

THE EXCELLENT VIEW LIFE
THROUGH THE EYES OF UNBROKEN FOCUS

"My son, give attention to my words; incline your ear to my sayings.
Do not let them depart from your eyes; keep them in the midst of your heart..."
Proverbs 4:20–21 (NKJV)

⚜

Involved in an intense conversation with her teenage daughter about boys, sex, and God, suddenly, the doorbell rings. Now who's that at the door? I've already broken my train of thought!

One of our greatest enemies in life is broken focus. The Bible tells us, "Where there is no vision, the people perish." People of excellence refuse to break focus, because they realize doing so results in their demise. **The mediocre always focus on what they go through...the excellent focus on what they go to.**

How many times have we decided to rise earlier in the morning to have more prayer time? Then, the distractions begin. Perhaps an untidy area catches your attention and you want to straighten it; your child calls and you tend to them; and then a phone call which eats away your time. All the while, in your mind, you tell God, "I'll be back in a minute." One thing leads to another and before you know it, the day is half gone. This type of situation is not uncommon, and days lead to weeks, which lead to months, until one day we look back at our lives and ask, "How did I get here and how do I change my life?"

During His lifetime on earth, Jesus' focus was constantly upon the cross, His assignment for mankind. Now, Jesus' focus is on our future— preparing Heaven, interceding, looking straight ahead, being ready to perform the Father's will at any given moment. And so must we continue to look straight ahead and not allow ourselves to be distracted.

DAILY CONFESSION
Father, I thank You that I attend to Your Words, and incline my ears to Your sayings. I keep Your principles before my eyes; I keep them in the midst of my heart, for they bring life and health to all my flesh.

EXCELLENCE DESCENDS INTO MEDIOCRITY
THE MOMENT IT IS UNWILLING TO CHANGE

"For if anyone is a hearer of the Word and not a doer, he is like a man
observing his natural face in a mirror; for he observes himself, goes away,
and immediately forgets what kind of man he was."
James 1:21–24 (NKJV)

A sharp flurry danced in the air—transformation occurred everywhere. People who were blind since birth could suddenly see, the deaf had the joy of listening to parables of the Master, the disturbed were vibrantly whole, and thieves became as honourable as the temple rabbi. Yes, there were some who were unwilling to change. Many thought the Teacher, the Messiah, was merely another man, but because they were unwilling to embrace change, the miraculous for them was as distant as the Mediterranean Sea.

Ultimately, excellence can be devoured through our unwillingness to change. **Life passes us by and causes us to live in regret over the lack of productivity from our past. The moment we become unwilling to embrace change is the moment we no longer achieve or reach the high standards to which Christ calls us.**

Inherently, humanity has within itself the desire to settle, to hit a plateau and go no further. However, as men and women of excellence, we must refuse the cosy invitation to settle. We must be resilient and continue to climb the ladder of excellence. It is a daily pursuit requiring focus and persistence. When we are dedicated to this call, we walk victoriously over the enemy of mediocrity. Mediocrity can be beaten…we can overcome! We must, nevertheless, pursue excellence every day of our lives. The only question is this: Will we or won't we pursue?

DAILY CONFESSION
Father, I thank You that I am a doer of Your Word.
I look into the perfect law of liberty and continue in it. I am not a
forgetful hearer but I am an effectual doer and I am blessed in all I do.

PROGRESS IS GUARANTEED
TO THOSE WHO PURSUE IMPROVEMENT

"Therefore, if anyone is in Christ, he is a new creation;
old things have passed away; behold, all things have become new."
2 Corinthians 5:17 (NKJV)

To evolve means to gradually acquire new traits or characteristics. In order to improve in any endeavor, we must be willing to acquire new traits and skills. These new acquisitions cause us to excel above the rest. Always remember: **The excellent get ahead during the times the mediocre waste.**

We must spend any spare moment to improve our relationship with God, marriage, friendships, or our personal character. Our time is precious, and time is the price we must pay in order to see our lives continually improve.

- *Why are people unwilling to evolve?*
- *Why don't people want to change?*

There are two reasons that I have discovered over the course of many years of ministry. The first reason is that people have a *fear of failure*. Ask the person who tried to overcome a negative habit in the last few years why they gave up. It is because they continually failed and don't want to go through the pain of acknowledging their unwillingness to overcome that way of life. The second reason people don't want to change is because *they don't know how*. The desire is there, but the teacher to instruct them is not.

I am focused on one thing…change. When people come around me, they have the desire to change things in their lives. Why is that? Because that is how it is with God. The moment we got saved, He has been changing us and He has not stopped since.

DAILY CONFESSION
Father, I thank You that I am a new creature.
Old things are passed away; behold, everything has become new.
I am righteous because I am in Christ and Christ is in me.

THE MOMENT YOU FULFILL
HEAVEN'S INSTRUCTIONS IS THE MOMENT
YOU BECOME SUCCESSFUL IN GOD'S EYES

*"Now it shall come to pass, if you diligently obey the voice of the
Lord your God, to observe carefully all His commandments which I command
you today, that the Lord your God will set you high above all nations of the earth.
And all these blessings shall come upon you and overtake you,
because you obey the voice of the Lord your God."*
Deuteronomy 28:1–2 (NKJV)

⚜

I'm not sure about you, but I want the blessings of God to come upon me and overtake me. Jesus talked about producing a more abundant life for His followers, and all of us certainly desire for God to shower His diverse blessings upon our lives. However, success doesn't come to just anyone. It isn't something that just shows up in your life, like an unexpected package in the mail; it is something one accomplishes.

So how does Heaven define success? **Success is the ability to walk in the freedom Jesus purchased on the cross.** Freedom is the ability to walk above the onslaught of hell that daily attempts to derail our lives. David said it like this, "I have hidden Your Word in my heart that I might not sin against You." There is no success outside of the Word of God. One can attain the world's money, enjoy its prestige, bask in its power, and benefit from assorted relationships, and still not be successful in the eyes of God. Walking a life victorious and in control is true success.

We must always remember: Success comes only to those who are willing to comply with the counsel of Heaven. And, as we obey, the blessings of God soon overtake us and freedom is truly ours.

DAILY CONFESSION
Father, I thank You that I hide Your Word in my heart.
I diligently obey Your voice and observe carefully to do all You command me.

TIME WILL ALWAYS REVEAL
ANY TRUTH THAT PRESENTLY SEEMS HIDDEN

"For there is nothing hidden which will not be revealed,
nor has anything been kept secret but that it should come to light."
Mark 4:22 (NKJV)

⚜

Finally alone, the handsome young couple sits inside the car, staring at one another, talking in hushed tones. "Will you marry me?" Surprised by his nervous tone but not that taken aback, the ponytailed blonde studies the young man's unmistakably serious eyes. "It's a little too soon, don't you think?" Clutching her hand, he wasn't sure if he could wait—not even one more minute! "You think it's too soon? We've been going together now for five weeks; isn't that enough time?" "Of course not, silly," replied the pretty blonde. "I have to get to know you more—we need a little more time."

Whether it is the character of another, a particular hidden lie that seemingly slips by, or talents that lie dormant within one's heart, none go on without one day being revealed. "Proving time" is something with which we struggle in society today. We have been brainwashed into thinking that everything has to be right now, whether it be as simple as a meal, a desired relationship, a business decision, or ministry opportunity.

We probably have all come to notice that many of the mistakes people make are simply because they didn't allow time to reveal the truth of their situation. Through our unwillingness to wait and allow time to prove the truth, we have made some bad choices. If we desire to see a new and bright future, we must allow time to reveal any truth that now seems to be hidden.

DAILY CONFESSION
Father, I thank You that You are not slack concerning Your promises.
If You said it, I have confidence knowing You will do it.
I know You will bring all things to light concerning decisions I need to make.

GRATITUDE IS THE ONLY GIFT
THAT MUST BE GIVEN TO THE ONE
WHOM YOU CAN NEVER REPAY

"When I learn Your righteous laws, I will thank You by living as I should!"
Psalm 119:7 (NLT)

Taking the bread, His disciples' eyes were locked upon the Master. Before parting the bread, distributing the symbol to each one, Jesus stopped; He needed first to give thanks to God.

And David understood thanksgiving as much, if not more, than any other man in all of scripture. David said this when writing Psalm 119, "…I will thank You by living as I should."

We cannot repay God for what He does for us in our lives. There is nothing we can do to fully return all God bestows upon us. Our gratitude is not a repayment; it is a declaration and recognition that we owe God our very lives. Please consider these two questions concerning gratitude:

- *Is gratitude too much for God to ask of us?*
- *How are we going to properly return our gratitude?*

Just as David did, we must also thank the Lord by living as we should. There is no greater pleasure Heaven can receive when one has a heart of gratitude.

DAILY CONFESSION
Father, I am thankful for all that You do for me. I know I cannot repay You, but I choose to show my gratitude through living as I should. I desire to prove to all of Heaven that I am grateful for the sacrifice of Christ Jesus my Lord.

THE ENVELOPE OF LOVE
IS STAMPED WITH "KINDNESS" AND "TRUTH"

"Do not let kindness and truth leave you; bind them around your neck,
write them on the tablet of your heart."
Proverbs 3:3 (NAS)

"My little children, let us not love in word or in tongue, but in deed and in truth."
1 John 3:18 (NKJV)

⚜

Love is the evidence separating those who believe on the Lord Jesus Christ, from those who don't believe. In 1 John 3, the apostle John writes, "We know that we have passed from death to life because we love the brethren." Love is demonstrated in many forms, but no more than that of kindness and truth. Jesus exemplified this more than any other man in all of history. He was a Man of hard truth, speaking the realities of life to the Pharisees, but He always spoke with extreme kindness, narrating the parables with a storyteller's tenderness, capturing the attention of the young and old.

In today's church, love seems to no longer include truth. The body of Christ has come to embrace unconditional love as an action that is all-inclusive and does not offend. No one can find that portrayed in the life of Christ. Although Jesus was the kindest man to ever live, He offended many (particularly the legalistic Pharisees and the intellectual scribes) because He passionately cared more about the truth being manifested than someone continuing to settle for a life of sin.

We must choose to love those around us, and embrace those who are willing to tell us the truth. Remember, the truth sets you free.

DAILY CONFESSION
Father, I thank You that I can know love and walk in love because
Jesus laid down His life for me. I never allow kindness and truth to leave me;
I lay down my life for others.

THE PREPARATIONS OF TODAY DETERMINE
YOUR QUALIFICATIONS FOR TOMORROW

"But David said to Saul, 'Your servant used to keep his father's sheep,
and when a lion or a bear came and took a lamb out of the flock, I went out
after it and struck it, and delivered the lamb from its mouth; and when it
arose against me, I caught it by its beard, and struck and killed it.'
And Saul said to David, 'Go, and the Lord be with you!'"
1 Samuel 17:34–37 (NKJV)

As you pursue personal happiness, preparation is essential. What would happen to the athlete who neglected to train before the season began? He would lose his race. It is no different when it comes to you. If you don't prepare, you'll grow weary before you reach your life's destiny.

The process of preparation determines if you move toward or away from your destiny. Preparation is your ticket to success. Just as you can't get on a plane without a ticket, you can't succeed without first preparing. Simply arriving at the gate on time doesn't earn you a ticket for the flight.

I encourage myself with these words: **Learn to wait and prepare because God is never late to promote.** There is always a required time period of preparation prior to any season. An athlete who does not put himself through a physical training program will not be able to endure the season ahead. The same is true for you and I. **Neglecting to prepare for success is actually preparation for failure.**

DAILY CONFESSION
Father, I thank You that I am patient in my season of preparation
and I look forward to the future You desire for me. I do not grow weary
in well doing, for in due time, I reap the harvest of a better tomorrow.

SUCCESS IN LIFE IS IN DIRECT
PROPORTION TO THE COMMITMENT OF CONQUERING
THE GIANT NAMED "MAINTENANCE"

"The path of lazy people is overgrown with briers;
the diligent walk down a smooth road."
Proverbs 15:19 (Message)

🔦

"Where are you going?" the wife curiously asks, noticing his hurried steps crunching the basement stairs. With varied clangs and sharp bangs, the husband yells upstairs, "I have to get my tools; the lawn-mower's handle is so loose it's about ready to fall off, and the mailbox post is leaning, so that needs some quick hammering. And by the way, as long as I'm out there, can you think of anything else that needs maintenance?"

Human bodies; homes; businesses; relationships; vehicles; land; our inner spirits; our souls—just about everything needs maintenance! But have you yet realized that maintenance is the key to a prolonged life of victory? **The vast chasm between the excellent and the average is the willingness to maintain.** All of us must come to recognize that life is won or lost in the details. When details are neglected, they become too overwhelming for any one individual to face. The more the tasks of life are neglected, the larger they become.

Solomon depicts this very cleverly in the above passage when he observes a lazy man who choses to neglect the maintenance of life. He paints us a picture to illustrate this principle very clearly, "…all overgrown with thorns; its surface was covered with nettles; its stone wall was broken down…" As you can see, the destination of those who neglect to fight the giant named "maintenance" means ultimate ruin in every area of life. Let us allow God to help us as we seek to maintain the details in life that cause us to become one who overcomes in every situation.

DAILY CONFESSION
Father, I thank You that I am one who walks in excellence in my life.
I painstakingly maintain all of life's details…all of which You give me.

Peace Is Not The Absence Of Enemies,
It Is The Acknowledgement Of God's Presence

"Have I not commanded you? Be strong and of good courage; do not be afraid,
nor be dismayed, for the Lord your God is with you wherever you go."
Joshua 1:9 (NKJV)

⬥

Let's see—hair's looking good, make-up's not smudged, clothes stylish (no hanging strings), my coat has all the buttons, and my Bible has no old bulletins sticking out of it. Yep, I guess I'm all set for church, right Lord? For some reason, no answer emits from Heaven; in fact, it's as quiet as a church parking lot on Monday morning!

And it is a sad fact that far too many individuals attempt to change their life from the outside in. Society infiltrates the church with the warped thinking that our circumstances determine our inner peace. That is the farthest thing from the truth! The life of a believer can only be lived from the inside out.

Our peace is not dependent upon outward circumstances; it is dependent upon the God who dwells within us. Peace can be defined as the inner state of one's heart causing one to be neither moved nor shaken by present circumstances. The more we come to understand the presence of God among us, the more Heaven's peace continues to increase in our hearts. All of mankind in the world today longs for peace.

True peace...the peace that Christ gives us, comes through the acknowledgement of God's presence in the lives of His children.

Daily Confession
Father, I thank You that You never leave me or forsake me.
I am strong and courageous...I do not fear; You are on my side.

THE POWER OF GRATITUDE
RESTS IN ITS WILLINGNESS TO REMAIN VULNERABLE

"Thank (God) in everything [no matter what the circumstances may be, be thankful and give thanks], for this is the will of God for you [who are] in Christ Jesus…"
1 Thessalonians 5:18 (AMP)

⚓

"You didn't have to," the snowy-haired woman gaped at the beautifully-wrapped package, a tiny tear starting in the corner of her eye. "Grandma, it's not that I had to, I want to. You've done so much for me—helping with my tuition, chipping in on the car. This gift is just a small token of my gratitude." Bending down to hug the wheelchair bound woman, there was nothing in the world that could have stopped him from showing his thanks. And there is nothing in the entire world that can conceal the heart of a thankful individual.

Gratitude is the one attribute that carries with it the ability to live open before all of Heaven and earth. It has the power to protect an individual from the temptation of pride and discouragement. Those who truly possess a thankful heart are granted access to both the power and presence of God.

In Luke 17:15, Jesus curiously questioned the lone leper who returned to offer his thanks, "Were there not nine others who were made well? Where are they?" Remember, Heaven searches for men and women who are eager to proclaim their praise for the things God does.

As we cultivate a heart of gratitude and live a life of thanksgiving, we soon experience a favorable response from Heaven.

DAILY CONFESSION
*I bless the Lord at all times and thank Him for all He does in my life.
The Lord is good; I do not forget all His benefits. I have a favorable response
from Heaven because I possess a heart of thanksgiving.*

OBEDIENCE IS THE ONLY EVIDENCE
NECESSARY IN THE COURTROOM OF HEAVEN
TO PROVE YOUR LOVE FOR GOD

"He who has My commandments and keeps them, it is he
who loves Me. And he who loves Me will be loved by My Father,
and I will love him and manifest Myself to him."
John 14:21 (NKJV)

⚜

As the worship time came to a close, her thoughts were on every-thing—everything but God!

"Oh, what is tomorrow going be like at work?—hope no one calls in sick—those lazy, lying good-for-nothings. I better stop by the store after this; is there any milk left or did the boys gulp it all down? If I give that amount God told me, will I still be able to go shopping on Saturday?"

How can we say we love God, but deliberately neglect the things He instructs us to do—like love one another and completely forsake care and worry? We must understand, however, God is the One who adequately determines whether or not we truly love Him. God made it clear to us that He wants us to show His love to others, not only through the words that we speak but also through the actions we perform.

It is when we leave the futile realm of insincere words and move into the mode of obedience that Heaven and earth know we love God. Obedience was foremost in Jesus' mind at the final Passover before His death. It was the only evidence necessary for God's plan of redemption to continue, and Jesus Himself confirmed it saying, "So that the world may know that I love the Father, I do as He commanded." As we begin to do what God commanded, we soon have enough evidence to bring before the courtroom of Heaven to prove we truly love God.

DAILY CONFESSION
Father, I thank You for giving me the opportunity to prove my love to You.
Not only do I declare my love with the words I speak, but I prove
my love through my daily obedience.

THE REWARDS OF LIFE
ARE DELIVERED ONLY UPON THE DOORSTEPS
OF THE OVERCOMERS

"To him who overcomes I will grant to sit with Me on My throne,
as I also overcame and sat down with My Father on His throne."
Revelation 3:21 (NKJV)

✦

Being a believer does not necessarily qualify us to receive the abundant life Jesus desires for us to wonderfully achieve and blissfully enjoy. Diplomas are not passed out on registration day for your freshman year in college. God calls for those who truly put their trust in Him to reign in this life. It is our God-given right and responsibility to reign over our flesh and the enemy that comes against us.

So why is it that so many Christians do not walk in a life of abundant rewards? We must not kid ourselves when answering this question. We can clearly see in scripture that rewards come only to those who overcome. Nobody gets rewarded for participation—divine rewards come only to those who win the contest.

We are in a battle and Satan is not going to surrender or lose effortlessly. He will, however, bow his knee and fall to defeat if we continue to retaliate with the spiritual weapons that we possess. As we resist his onslaught and become people who conquer, we soon experience the abundant and rewarding life God desires for us.

DAILY CONFESSION
Father, I thank You that Jesus came to give me abundant life.
I am victorious over my flesh and the enemy that continues to pursue my life.
I reign forevermore and enjoy the rewarding abundant life You desire for me.

FREEDOM IS YOURS THE MOMENT
YOU TRUST IN HEAVEN'S OPINION

"I will walk in freedom, for I have devoted myself to Your commandments."
Psalm 119:45 (NLT)

✦

No more hangovers; no more obnoxious blackouts; no more embarrassing D.U.I. convictions. Although a believer, the thirty-year-old accountant hadn't been able to break the bondage of alcohol that had virtually devastated his life, leaving him near death about a year earlier. But now that he was genuinely liberated, he was determined to walk in that freedom, becoming accountable to the small group of recovering alcoholics with whom he had voluntarily joined. The group, devoted to the teachings and commandments of the Word of God, brought him to trust completely in heaven's opinion instead of his own.

There is absolutely no freedom outside of the Word of God. The scripture tells us we are all born slaves to sin. Through our acceptance of what Jesus Christ did on the cross, we are set free from the bondage of sin. Even though we have been set free, we still wonder how to walk in that freedom. It is one thing to be free, but walking in the fullness of that freedom, like the recovering alcoholic believer, is something completely different. I am convinced that the most miserable man in the universe is the one who has been set free, yet has no idea how to walk it out.

Yet, God gave us the knowledge we need to walk in the fullness of our redemption. We know David discovered it because of the words he penned, "I will walk in freedom, for I have devoted myself to Your Word." So many see that as information they already know, but to David, it was revelation that transformed his life. David's decision to devote himself to the Word of God enabled him to walk in the liberty that was rightfully his. It is of necessity that we commit ourselves to meditate on the Word of God every day.

DAILY CONFESSION
Father, I thank You that my freedom lies within the pages of Your Word.
I embrace what You say and exchange what I think for what You think.

THE PRESENCE OF FEAR IS PROOF
THAT ONE IS FOCUSING ON THE LIES OF
THE DEVIL RATHER THAN THE PROMISES OF GOD

"Yea, though I walk through the valley of the shadow of death,
I will fear no evil; for You are with me; Your rod and Your staff, they comfort me."
Psalm 23:4 (NKJV)

⚜

- *What have you been focusing on lately?*
- *Is it God's Word, or is it the problems you face?*

Accurate focus is the most vital ingredient to the success of any believer. If we learn how to focus on what God said concerning all facets of our situation, everything falls right into place. But if we fail to focus on His Word, we see our situation turn out to be insurmountable for us to overcome. We must understand—whatever we focus upon enlarges, expanding as large as the Red Sea. But this doesn't happen in the physical realm as much as it occurs in the strategic battlefield of our minds.

The more we focus on what God said, the smaller our problems seem. Remember, every person believes they are the one with the biggest problem. An adult may be consumed with forty-five thousand dollars of credit card debt, while a seven-year-old boy may owe the classroom bully forty-five cents. Both problems are great to each individual because the magnitude of any problem lies within the mind. If we want to see fear depart from our lives, we must simply begin to focus on what is written. What God said is *the* truth not *a* truth. As we embrace the truths of Heaven, the infection of fear is soon cured.

DAILY CONFESSION
Father, I thank You that You did not given me a spirit of fear but of love and of a sound mind. Though I walk through the valley of the shadow of death, I fear no evil for Your are with me, Your rod and Your staff are a comfort to me.

EVERY MAN WANTS MORE FAITH;
BUT FEW PEOPLE WANT MORE OF THE WORD OF GOD

"So then faith comes by hearing, and hearing by the Word of God."
Romans 10:17 (NKJV)

✦

As believers in Jesus Christ, we are called to walk by faith and not by sight. Our obedience brings Heaven no pleasure until it is first mixed with faith. Faith is not a magical powder Heaven showers upon those who ask for it. Faith is not something for which one can pray, nor does it come because we go through a negative experience.

We only find two ways in all of Scripture that indicate how we can increase our faith:

- *Hearing the Word of God.*
- *The confession of our mouths.*

Before we can understand why that is, we must understand that faith is the substance of things hoped for, the evidence of things not seen. God's Word is full of truths that many of us have yet to experience in our lives. The more we meditate upon the truths of God's Word and confess them throughout our day, the more faith begins to rise up within our hearts. We then possess the necessary power to overcome the assorted array of giants in our life.

Once faith is released through our mouth and ignited by our actions, we soon see the manifestation God's promises in our lives.

DAILY CONFESSION
Father, I thank You that I walk by faith and not by sight. I continually incline my ear to hear Your Word and I meditate upon it day and night. I know that Your promises are manifest in my life.

STAY FOCUSED ON WHAT YOU ARE GOING "TO"
NEVER STARE AT WHAT YOU ARE GOING "THROUGH"

"...who for the joy that was set before Him endured the cross, despising the shame,
and has sat down at the right hand of the throne of God."
Hebrews 12:2 (NKJV)

At Jerusalem's annual Passover celebration, meeting together in an upper room, the Master ominously warned the disciples of His betrayal. Afterward, He prayed in such agony that sweat drops and blood dotted the ground. The chief priests, captains, and elders of the temple, along with Judas, arrived with swords, preparing to arrest Jesus and put Him on trial.

Ever before God's Son was the cross. And Jesus, our greatest example, demonstrates the supreme power of accurate focus, even in the chaos of His trial and crucifixion. James 1:2 tells us that life brings many storms and tests our way. Only those who focus on the grapes of Canaan survive. We can have the determination to press on if we prepare by asking ourselves:

- *Where am I headed in life?*

- *What do I want to accomplish, possess, and become?*

It is a reality that those who have nowhere to go usually have no internal fortitude to advance. We must always remember—**our lives move in the direction of our focus.** Although what we go through may seem too difficult to overcome, it is imperative we focus on the victory that awaits us. For Christ, that focus was the cross. And just as an athlete focuses on running the race to win the prize, so we also must have a clear, distinct image of the victory, and not the storm. As we focus on what we are going to, Heaven gives us the strength to make it through.

DAILY CONFESSION
Father, I am thankful for the promises of Canaan in my life.
I declare that I will go up and take possession of what is rightfully mine.
I look to Jesus who is the author and finisher of my faith.

YOUR RIGHTEOUSNESS IS DEPENDENT UPON WHAT JESUS CHRIST PURCHASED WHEN HE WENT TO THE CROSS

*"That I may be found in Him, not having any righteousness that can be called
my own, based on my obedience to the law's demands (my personal performance)
but possessing a right standing with God, which comes from God."*
Philippians 3:9 (AMP)

❧

Trim since a young girl, her long, silky blond hair caught the attention of onlookers of all ages. Playing the piano with confident expertise, her father owned a large moving company so fashionable clothes, the latest cars, and frequent trips came without thought. Hovering about her as she dropped into church on Sunday morning to fill in for the regular pianist, her performance went without a hitch—every note played to perfection, not a sour note in any of the seven hymns. Yet, no one had ever heard her testimony. Had she truly followed Christ? Was she in right standing with Him after all?

Our right standing with God lies within the act of Jesus on the cross two thousand years ago. Don't believe that you can achieve righteousness of your own merit. If that is true, Jesus died in vain. Never diminish the power of the cross by attempting to stand before God righteously based upon your good performance.

Remember, in the eyes of God, all of our righteousness is as filthy rags.

DAILY CONFESSION
*Father, I thank You that I have right standing with You.
You declare that I am the righteousness. I live in obedience to Your Word,
and I enjoy the rewards of being righteous.*

THERE IS NO SUCH THING AS A SHORTCUT TO A BETTER LIFE

"Wealth from get-rich-quick schemes quickly disappears;
wealth from hard work grows."
Proverbs 13:11 (NLT)

The wisest man who ever lived wrote, "Wealth from hard work grows." Isn't it interesting, though, that men sometimes believe that there is a shortcut to wealth? Notice that Solomon didn't say you couldn't get wealth in a get-rich-quick scheme. Actually, he said just the opposite; he said that you can get rich quick! The catch is that as quickly as it comes, it disappears.

The reason get-rich-quick schemes don't work out for long is because they bypass the stages of growth and maturity that are necessary for a person to be able to handle wealth. It is like giving a teenager his license without any training behind the wheel. Sure, he could legally drive, but he would doubtlessly have an accident in no time.

God's ways, however, are always best. His instruction to us is that we, once and for all, do away with shortcuts to a better life. But we must embrace prosperity God's way—

- *Hard work*
- *Diligence*
- *Refusal to give up*

Then we find a better life is ours in no time.

DAILY CONFESSION
Father, I thank You that You know all my needs, and You always
provide for me. I ask you to give me strength to work hard
and see Your prosperity come into my life.

MEDITATION UPON GOD'S WORD IS THE KEY THAT UNLOCKS THE DOORS TO GOD'S PURPOSE IN LIFE

Don't copy the behavior and customs of this world, but let God transform you into a new person by changing the way you think. Then you will know what God wants you to do, and you will know how good and pleasing and perfect his will really is.
Romans 12:2 (NLT)

It has become a celebrated fact that we live in a civilization of head-throbbing commotion and nerve-shattering anxiety. Lifetimes frantically begin and end in a whirlwind of superficial activity and nonstop bustling, all this simply to "make a living." Yet, at the core of every person is a passionate desire to discover something deeper. The heart of every man possesses profound longings for life's meaning and purpose.

Have you ever met an individual who appears to have it all together but remains dissatisfied? Although he has achieved some degree of success, the lack of fulfillment gnaws at his soul like a semi taking a chunk from his rear bumper. He is not happy, though he has every reason to be, and there's no explanation in the world for it. Continually he asks the question, What does this all mean? His void of purpose stretches as far as the longest superhighway across three states.

So when the streetlights are illuminated and we are alone with our thoughts, the questions begin to emerge: Why am I here? Is there a purpose for my life? Is there a specific assignment that I am supposed to fulfill? How do I discover that assignment? And once I do, how do I bring it to pass?

DAILY CONFESSION
Father I thank you that I do not conform myself to this world,
but I allow you to transform my life by changing the way I think.
I embrace your Word, therefore I will discover my purpose in life.

PROGRESS IS GUARANTEED
TO THOSE WHO PURSUE IMPROVEMENT

"Therefore, if anyone is in Christ, he is a new creation;
old things have passed away; behold, all things have become new."
2 Corinthians 5:17 (NKJV)

⚜

To evolve means: to gradually acquire new traits or characteristics. In order to improve in any endeavor, we must be willing to acquire new traits and skills. These new acquisitions cause us to excel above the rest. Always remember: **The excellent get ahead during the times that the mediocre waste.**

We must spend any spare moment to improve our relationship with God, marriages, friendships, or our personal character. Our time is precious, and time is the price we must pay in order to see our lives continually improve.

DAILY CONFESSION
Father I thank you that I am a new creature.
Old things are passed away, behold everything has become new.
I am righteous because I am in Christ and Christ is in me.

GOD'S COMMANDS REVEAL TO MAN HIS PERFECTION; THE CROSS REVEALS TO MAN GOD'S FORGIVENESS

"Therefore by the deeds of the law no flesh will be justified in His sight,
for by the law is the knowledge of sin. But now the righteousness of God apart
from the law is revealed, being witnessed by the Law and the Prophets…"
Romans 3:20-21 (NKJV)

Sadly, most Christians don't understand righteousness. Instead, they live in the New Covenant with an Old Covenant mind. What do I mean by that? Well, under the Old Covenant, God wrote His commandments in stone with His finger. He told His people, "Don't commit adultery. Don't bear false witness. Don't have any other gods before Me. Don't covet your neighbor's wife. Don't do this, and don't do that."

A Christian who doesn't understand his own righteousness before God eventually begins to live like a robot, consumed with his efforts to fulfill all the do's and avoid all the don'ts. On the inside, though, his mind rips him apart as he struggles with old, carnal desires to do wrong things.

God made a new covenant with man through the blood of His Son, and now He sees no fault in humanity. That's not to say that humanity has no fault—it does. Rather, it's to say that what Jesus did was enough to eradicate the resulting spiritual separation.

DAILY CONFESSION
Father, I thank You that by the deeds of the law, no flesh
is justified in Your sight. But now Your righteousness apart
from the law is revealed to me and in me.

BIBLE IN A YEAR

JANUARY

1	Gen. 1-3
2	Gen. 4-6
3	Gen. 7-9
4	Gen. 10-12
5	Gen. 13-15
6	Gen. 16-18
7	Gen. 19-21
8	Gen. 22-24
9	Gen. 25-27
10	Gen. 28-30
11	Gen. 31-33
12	Gen. 34-36
13	Gen. 37-39
14	Gen. 40-42
15	Gen. 43-45
16	Gen. 46-48
17	Gen. 49-Ex. 1
18	Ex. 2-4
19	Ex. 5-7
20	Ex. 8-10
21	Ex. 11-13
22	Ex. 14-16
23	Ex. 17-19
24	Ex. 20-22
25	Ex. 23-25
26	Ex. 26-28
27	Ex. 29-31
28	Ex. 32-34
29	Ex. 35-37
30	Ex. 38-39
31	Ex. 40

FEBRUARY

1	Lev. 1-3
2	Lev. 4-6
3	Lev. 7-8
4	Lev. 9-10
5	Lev. 11-13
6	Lev. 14-15
7	Lev. 16-18
8	Lev. 19-21
9	Lev. 22-23
10	Lev. 24-25
11	Lev. 26-27
12	Num. 1-2
13	Num. 3-4
14	Num. 5-6
15	Num. 7
16	Num. 8-9
17	Num. 10-11
18	Num. 12-13
19	Num. 14-15
20	Num. 16-18
21	Num. 19-20
22	Num. 21-22
23	Num. 23-25
24	Num. 26-27
25	Num. 28-29
26	Num. 30-31
27	Num. 32-33
28	Num. 34-36

MARCH 2015

1	Deut. 1-4
2	Deut. 5-7
3	Deut. 8-10
4	Deut. 11-13
5	Deut. 14-16
6	Deut. 17-20
7	Deut. 21-23
8	Deut. 24-27
9	Deut. 28
10	Deut. 29-31
11	Deut. 32-34
12	Josh. 1-3
13	Josh. 4-6
14	Josh. 7-8
15	Josh. 9-10
16	Josh. 11-13
17	Josh. 14-16
18	Josh. 17-19
19	Josh. 20-21
20	Judg. 22-24
21	Judg. 1-2
22	Judg. 3-5
23	Judg. 6-7
24	Judg. 8-9
25	Judg. 10-11
26	Judg. 12-14
27	Judg. 15-17
28	Judg. 18-19
29	Judg. 20-21
30	Ruth 1-4
31	1 Sam. 1-3

APRIL

1	1 Sam. 4-7
2	1 Sam. 8-11
3	1 Sam. 12-14
4	1 Sam. 15-16
5	1 Sam. 17-18
6	1 Sam. 19-21
7	1 Sam. 22-24
8	1 Sam. 25-27
9	1 Sam. 28-31
10	2 Sam. 1-2
11	2 Sam. 3-5
12	2 Sam. 6-9
13	2 Sam. 10-12
14	2 Sam. 13-14

15	2 Sam. 15-16
16	2 Sam. 17-18
17	2 Sam. 19-20
18	2 Sam. 21-22
19	2 Sam. 23-24
20	1 Ki. 1-2
21	1 Ki. 3-4
22	1 Ki. 5-7
23	1 Ki. 8
24	1 Ki. 9-11
25	1 Ki. 12-13
26	1 Ki. 14-15
27	1 Ki. 16-18
28	1 Ki. 19-20
29	1 Ki. 21-22
30	2 Ki. 1-3

MAY

1	2 Ki. 4-5
2	2 Ki. 6-8
3	2 Ki. 9-10
4	2 Ki. 11-13
5	2 Ki. 14-15
6	2 Ki. 16-17
7	2 Ki. 18-20
8	2 Ki. 21-23
9	2 Ki. 24-25
10	1 Chr. 1-2
11	1 Chr. 3-5
12	1 Chr. 6-7
13	1 Chr. 8-10
14	1 Chr. 11-13
15	1 Chr. 14-16
16	1 Chr. 17-20
17	1 Chr. 21-23
18	1 Chr. 24-26
19	1 Chr. 27-29
20	2 Chr. 1-3
21	2 Chr. 4-6
22	2 Chr. 7-9
23	2 Chr. 10-13

24	2 Chr. 14-17
25	2 Chr. 18-20
26	2 Chr. 21-24
27	2 Chr. 25-27
28	2 Chr. 28-30
29	2 Chr. 31-33
30	2 Chr. 34-36
31	Ezra 1-2

JUNE

1	Ezra 3-5
2	Ezra 6-7
3	Ezra 8-9
4	Ezra 10
5	Neh. 1-3
6	Neh. 4-6
7	Neh. 7-8
8	Neh. 9-10
9	Neh. 11-12
10	Neh. 13
11	Esth. 1-3
12	Esth. 4-7
13	Esth. 8-10
14	Job 1-4
15	Job 5-8
16	Job 9-12
17	Job 13-16
18	Job 17-20
19	Job 21-24
20	Job 25-29
21	Job 30-33
22	Job 34-37
23	Job 38-40
24	Job 41-42
25	Psa. 1-9
26	Psa. 10-17
27	Psa. 18-22
28	Psa. 23-30
29	Psa. 31-35
30	Psa. 36-39

JULY

1	Psa. 40-45
2	Psa. 46-51
3	Psa. 52-59
4	Psa. 60-66
5	Psa. 67-71
6	Psa. 72-77
7	Psa. 78-80
8	Psa. 81-87
9	Psa. 88-91
10	Psa. 92-100
11	Psa. 101-105
12	Psa. 106-107
13	Psa. 108-118
14	Psa. 119
15	Psa. 120-131
16	Psa. 132-138
17	Psa. 139-143
18	Psa. 144-150
19	Prov. 1-3
20	Prov. 4-7
21	Prov. 8-11
22	Prov. 12-15
23	Prov. 16-19
24	Prov. 20-22
25	Prov. 23-26
26	Prov. 27-31
27	Eccl. 1-4
28	Eccl. 5-8
29	Eccl. 9-12
30	Song 1-8
31	Isa. 1-4

AUGUST

1	Isa. 5-9
2	Isa. 10-14
3	Isa. 15-21
4	Isa. 22-26
5	Isa. 27-31
6	Isa. 32-37

7	Isa. 38-42	14	Dan. 4-6	22	Lk. 2-3
8	Isa. 43-46	15	Dan. 7-9	23	Lk. 4-5
9	Isa. 47-51	16	Dan. 10-12	24	Lk. 6-7
10	Isa. 52-57	17	Hos. 1-6	25	Lk. 8-9
11	Isa. 58-63	18	Hos. 7-14	26	Lk. 10-11
12	Isa. 64-66	19	Joel 1-3	27	Lk. 12-13
13	Jer. 1-3	20	Amos 1-5	28	Lk. 14-16
14	Jer. 4-6	21	Amos 6-9	29	Lk. 17-18
15	Jer. 7-10	22	Obad. 1	30	Lk. 19-20
16	Jer. 11-14	23	Jon. 1-4	31	Lk. 21-22
17	Jer. 15-18	24	Mic. 1-7		
18	Jer. 19-22	25	Nah. 1-3	**NOVEMBER**	
19	Jer. 23-25	26	Hab. 1-3	1	Lk. 23-24
20	Jer. 26-28	27	Zeph. 1-3	2	Jn. 1-3
21	Jer. 29-31	28	Hag. 1-2	3	Jn. 4-5
22	Jer. 32-33	29	Zech. 1-7	4	Jn. 6-8
23	Jer. 34-36	30	Zech. 8-14	5	Jn. 9-10
24	Jer. 37-40			6	Jn. 11-12
25	Jer. 41-44	**OCTOBER**		7	Jn. 13-16
26	Jer. 45-48	1	Mal. 1-4	8	Jn. 17-18
27	Jer. 49-50	2	Matt. 1-4	9	Jn. 19-21
28	Jer. 51-52	3	Matt. 5-6	10	Acts 1-2
29	Lam. 1-2	4	Matt. 7-9	11	Acts 3-4
30	Lam. 3-5	5	Matt. 10-11	12	Acts 5-6
31	Ezek. 1-4	6	Matt. 12	13	Acts 7-8
		7	Matt. 13-14	14	Acts 9-10
SEPTEMBER		8	Matt. 15-17	15	Acts 11-13
1	Ezek. 5-9	9	Matt. 18-20	16	Acts 14-16
2	Ezek. 10-13	10	Matt. 21-22	17	Acts 17-19
3	Ezek. 14-17	11	Matt. 23-24	18	Acts 20-22
4	Ezek. 18-21	12	Matt. 25-26	19	Acts 23-25
5	Ezek. 22-24	13	Matt. 27-28	20	Acts 26-28
6	Ezek. 25-28	14	Mk. 1-3	21	Rom. 1-3
7	Ezek. 29-32	15	Mk. 4-5	22	Rom. 4-7
8	Ezek. 33-36	16	Mk. 6-7	23	Rom. 8-10
9	Ezek. 37-39	17	Mk. 8-9	24	Rom. 11-13
10	Ezek. 40-42	18	Mk. 10-11	25	Rom. 14-16
11	Ezek. 43-45	19	Mk. 12-13	26	1 Cor. 1-4
12	Ezek. 46-48	20	Mk. 14-16	27	1 Cor. 5-9
13	Dan. 1-3	21	Lk. 1	28	1 Cor. 10-13

**PLEASE STOP BY OUR NEW ONLINE STORE:
WWW.WINNERSEDGESTORE.NET**

**Robb Thompson's NEWEST Book!
Solitary Refinement:
The Hidden Power Of Being Alone**

The Great Exchange: Your Thoughts For God's Thoughts

Heaven's Design: Building Your Marriage From God's Perspective

Heaven's Design: The Husband's Role

Heaven's Design: The Wife's Role

Everyday Ways To Enjoy Success At Work

The Ten Critical Laws Of Relationship

Breaking Free: Change Your Life Forever

Your Passport To Promotion

Excellence In The Workplace

Excellence in Character

Excellence in Attitude

Excellence in Ministry

Shattered Dreams

Excellence in Seed, Time, and Harvest

Endless Pursuit of Excellence